Jewish Masochism
from Abraham the Patriarch to Woody Allen
and Other Essays

MANFRED GERSTENFELD

Jewish Masochism from Abraham the Patriarch to Woody Allen

and Other Essays

RVP Press
New York

RVP Publishers Inc., NY
info@rvpp.com

RVP Press, NY

RVP Press™ is an imprint of RVP Publishers Inc., NY

The RVP Publishers logo is a trademark of RVP Publishers Inc., NY

The publication of this book is supported by International Center for Western Values, Amsterdam.

Library of Congress Control Number: 2019948792

ISBN 978 1 61861 344 8

www.rvppress.com

Table of Contents

JEWISH COMMUNITIES

GREAT PEOPLE GONE

BOOK REVIEWS

ARTS & SCIENCE

Preface

Isi Leibler

This anthology of essays, book reviews and interviews provides a broad insight into Manfred Gerstenfeld's unique renaissance personality. It encompasses the extensive canvas of contemporary Jewry and the challenges it faces. It also includes some essays on subjects related to Gerstenfeld's other than exclusively Jewish interests such as architecture, science and the environment which reflect the breadth of his knowledge and scholarship.

Born in Vienna and forced to emigrate with his family to Holland, Gerstenfeld was educated in Amsterdam where his studies included organic chemistry and economics and then he achieved a PhD in environmental studies.

Subsequently his wideranging background in business and environmental strategies led to his becoming Europe's first financial analyst specializing in the pharmaceutical industry. When he settled in Israel in 1968, he became managing director of a major consultancy company.

Aside from this and other commercial interests, Gerstenfeld assumed leadership profiles in leading Israeli advisory boards. For twelve years he served as chairman of the Board of the Jerusalem Center for Public Affairs, the prestigious Jerusalem think tank. He was also the founder and director of the Institute for Global Affairs and edited the *Jewish Political Studies Review*.

His intimate knowledge of European political and social currents together with living in Israel have combined to making him one, if not the world's leading authority on Jew-hatred and anti-Israelism.

A prolific writer who passionately speaks out against the current explosion of antisemitism, he has authored many books, some of which have been translated into as many as four languages. His magnum opus *The War of a Million Cuts: The Struggle against the Delegitimization of Israel and the Jews and the Growth of the New Anti-Semitism,* a 500-page tome is probably the most comprehensive analysis of the world's oldest hatred. Gerstenfeld outlines the components of the new streams of Jew-hatred emphasizing the role of anti-Zionism and Holocaust inversion being employed to besmirch Jews by the Far Left and the radical Islamists.

Essays related to this theme comprise the early sections of this book in the categories entitled Holocaust, Anti-Israelism and Europe. In particular, the article "Are We Reliving the 1930s?" is an example of Gerstenfeld at his best. Combined, these essays provide a brutally realistic evaluation of the challenges confronting us and our failures to respond adequately.

In a later section titled Great People Gone, Gerstenfeld evaluates the work of a number of the most prominent scholars and activists who played a major role during their lives in combating and identifying the renewed tsunami of Jew hatred.

I consider this book a must read for those interested or engaged in contemporary politics.

December 2019

Interview with Manfred Gerstenfeld

René van Praag

Gersenfeld was—according to Israeli daily *Haaretz*—at one point "without doubt the greatest [living] authority on antisemitism." This persistent form of hatred and discrimination tends to mutate over time. Gerstenfeld passionately analyzed the roots and trends of Jew-hatred. He shared his findings and insights with a broad global audience in countless articles and books. A selection from these articles are presented in this tome, accompanied by texts touching upon other topics. I had the honor of publishing some of his books. Collaborating with Gerstenfeld on various projects has always been inspiring and led to a great friendship.

To shed some light on what made Gerstenfeld tick, we've decided to open this anthology with an interview. To conduct this interview, Gerstenfeld and I set up a special meeting at his apartment in the center of Jerusalem.

The text as presented below was composed a few months before Gerstenfeld died, on February 25, 2021. He insisted on seeing my final draft to fine-tune his answers. For him, detail and nuance were always key.

ॐ

Gerstenfeld lives in a tastefully decorated apartment, a stone's throw from the residence of the Israeli Prime Minister. The latter resides in a large walled white villa, which is guarded as if it were Fort Knox. This part of the city, the Israeli equivalent of the New York Upper West Side, contains the beautiful green districts of Rehavia and Talbiye and is a fifteen minute walk from the Old City.

Isi Leibler, a former long term leader of Australia's Jewry and a columnist at *The Jerusalem Post*, is among Gerstenfeld's close neighbors. A few blocks from Gerstenfeld's home we come across the former residence of Israel's grand old lady, Golda Meïr.

Gerstenfeld has lived at his current address since 1968, the year in which he, his wife Marianne and their two small sons, born in France, made aliyah from Paris. The interior of the house is clearly inspired by the style he and his wife learned to appreciate during the years Gerstenfeld's professional career took them to Italy. Gerstenfeld was employed for decades as a strategic consultant to the boards of several *Forbes* 500 companies, including Ford, Occidental Petroleum and Fiat.

There is figurative and non-figurative art on the wall, both more than century old Dutch as well as contemporary Israeli. A bright red lacquered cabinet, Italian design, immediately catches the eye while you sink into one of the comfortable fauteuils, also Italian made. Gerstenfeld serves tea. He takes his place under a cheerful wall sculpture by Israeli artist David Gerstein. It portrays a colorful mass gathering of birds, cut out of steel by laser.

A conversation with Gerstenfeld never bores. Although every train of thought is neatly completed, the sheer volume of themes that are reviewed at a rapid pace, require that you stay focused.

Gerstenfeld was raised and remained a Modern Orthodox Jew. He was born in Vienna in 1937. Soon after, his parents took him to the Netherlands to escape the Nazi regime. Gerstenfeld is an only child. The family went into hiding in Amsterdam. During these harsh times the family was able to stay together. His parents survived the Shoah.

The young Gerstenfeld grew up and studied in Amsterdam until he emigrated to Paris for work in 1964 with his wife. He was a very active member of the small post-war Amsterdam Jewish community. He took it upon himself to be chairman of the board of a national Jewish youth movement, Bnei Akiva. Gerstenfeld majored in chemistry at the University of Amsterdam. He was also chairman of the Amsterdam branch of the NZSO, the Dutch Zionist Student Association. He regularly wrote for the Jewish weekly, *NIW*.

Gerstenfeld has a broad mind. He loves researching topics related to Judaism, culture, sociology, history, economics and politics, to mention a few. For many years much of his audiences' makeup were CEOs of *Forbes* 500 companies, industrial decision makers, and board members who valued his experience as a business consultant and sought his advice on strategy.

After his retirement in 2000, he became the chairman of an influential think tank, the Jerusalem Center of Public Affairs. He held this office for twelve years. Over time, the settings did vary, but Manfred continued to create analyses, to the benefit of an ever changing, but always captive audience.

Gerstenfeld orates about 1001 themes with ease and immense authority. The subjects range from politics to finance and from science to art, but also touch upon the mundane. Gerstenfeld even follows major developments in Dutch professional soccer and Champions League football. "How else can I have a full conversation with my grandchildren," he explains.

Gerstenfeld, who is fluent in seven languages, is a true renaissance man. When he himself characterizes someone in such a fashion, he uses the gender-neutral variation "renaissance person." Yet anyone who would deduce from this politically correct jargon that Gerstenfeld prefers to avoid confrontation is hugely mistaken. To the contrary, Gerstenfeld is often accused of stirring up the debate by exaggerating current dangers. In my opening question I confronted him with this assesment.

Time and again, you sound the alarm in your articles and notice flaring antisemitism. Are you exaggerating to get people's attention, or is antisemitism really a growing problem, in a wide range of countries, virtually on all continents?
Gerstenfeld: "My articles, mainly written in English, have footnotes so that the reader can check my sources. Even if newspapers do not include them, the websites which translate my articles in French, German and Italian, do feature these points of reference for the reader.

"The state of affairs regarding the rise of antisemitism is actually worse than I usually indicate. This is a technique I picked up as a business consultant. You keep a few relevant facts in your back pocket for when you are criticized in order to be able to present some additional proof, to end the discussion, and win the debate for good."

While a few decades ago, Europeans were overwhelmingly pro-Israel, the fan base of the Jewish State has shrunk. BDS (Boycott, Divestment, Sanctions) is on the rise and countless opinion leaders spew nasty criticism of Israel, often bordering on blatant antisemitism. How was it possible for the climate to change so drastically, almost overnight?

"It took several decades, but the roots of antisemitism are woven into European and Western societies and have festered for over a thousand years. As European culture developed, the nature of antisemitism changed with it. The Holocaust has had two consequences. For several decades it has suppressed classic antisemitism, but it also opened the floodgates for a new strain of antisemitism: socially accepted anti-Israelism.

"It all began far more than a thousand years ago, with the first category, religious antisemitism, rooted in Christianity. In the nineteenth century, the second category, ethnic-nationalist antisemitism, exploded. This was aimed at Jews as a people. Nazi Germany and its allies took it further to the Holocaust genocide. In recent decades we notice a third wave, attacking Israel, the Jewish state. This antisemitism is disguised as legitimate political critique."

It is legitimate when people outside of Israel express unvarnished criticism of Israeli political leaders. But often foreign criticism of Israel borders on badly camouflaged Jew-hatred.

"In my book about anti-Israelism, *The War of a Million Cuts. The Struggle against the Delegitimization of Israel and the Jews, and the Growth of New Anti-Semitism*, I elaborate on the topic extensively.

"Let's for a moment talk about the Netherlands, where I came of age. According to a study by the University of Bielefeld, published in 2011, 38% of Dutch adults assume that Israel is waging a war of extermination against the Palestinian people. This suggests that 5 million Dutch citizens lack serious basic mental capacities. If Israel really would strive to destroy Palestinian society, why is it, that the population in the Palestinian territories has increased, not decreased, year after year?"

In your Dutch language book, The Decay *(Het Verval) you quote seasoned Dutch politician, Frits Bolkestein, who explains that he sees no future for Jews in the Netherlands, insofar as they manifest themselves recognizably as Jews, by wearing*

head coverings (kippot), and other physical symbols of the Jewish religion. Since the book was published, ten years have passed. Did his prediction become fact?
"At the time, Bolkestein's words caused a huge public stir in the Netherlands. Several Dutch politicians argued then that 'we should avoid this trend.' However, nothing has changed for the better. Since 2010, feelings of not belonging have only increased among Dutch Jewry. Jewish institutions are vanishing gradually. Today, little is left of the once flourishing Dutch Jewish subculture, which was already extremely damaged by the Shoah. The community cannot maintain all of its institutions. For instance, the only Jewish hospital has merged into a general hospital and the Amsterdam Jewish retirement home is now operating under non-Jewish management.

"For centuries, there were kosher butchers all over the Netherlands, with the exception of a short intermission under Nazi rule. But the ban on Jewish ritual slaughter is about to make a full comeback, if it's up to many of the current political leaders. Outlawing this Jewish practice failed in the Senate. But there was a majority in the House of Representatives that voted to ban kosher slaughter.

"The net effect: Dutch Jewry is gradually going up in thin air. Dutch Judaism is fading away and is already virtually absent in the Dutch public sphere. Similar developments can be observed all over Europe. For instance, there is a spike in French Jews emigrating. Part of them make aliyah to Israel."

May I conclude that you have a love-hate relationship with the Netherlands?
"I do not love or hate the Netherlands. I am a rational person. You cannot succeed as an analyst and strategic consultant in the world of finance and big business by using emotional thinking. Strategists cannot afford to hate. Board members of big companies do not like emotional statements. They want objective, fact-based assessments and recommendations.

"The Netherlands has changed over the years and not for the better. The near absence of critics from abroad has facilitated the arrogance of the political elites. But there are also good things about that country. There have been impressive architectural achievements. One example: a few years ago, Amsterdam added a new line to their subway network with a range of impressive underground stations. Quite an accomplishment."

In 2019, during a festive gala, organized by the Montreal based Canadian Institute for Jewish Research (CIJR), Manfred Gerstenfeld received the Lion of Judah Award for his extensive work as "the leading international authority in contemporary antisemitism." At this occasion, renowned international human rights lawyer Professor Irwin Cotler took the podium to compliment Gerstenfeld on his many achievements. Receiving praise from a man like Cotler can't be overestimated. Before Cotler became Minister of Justice in Canada, he played a crucial role in various historical legal battles. He counseled Nelson Mandela and Nathan Sharansky, among others.

In their communiqué CIJR referred to the many books Gerstenfeld wrote on antisemitism and related subjects, plus the impressive number of op-eds he authored, some of which have featured in media outlets such as *The Wall Street Journal, Newsweek, The Hill, Die Welt,* and *The Jerusalem Post,* and on platforms such as the website of Bar Ilan's University's Begin-Sadat Center and *Israel National News.*

For Gerstenfeld, taking home the Lion of Judah award was somewhat of a deja vu. In 2012, he received the Lifetime Achievement Award from the *Journal of the Study of Antisemitism* and in 2015 he was honored by the Simon Wiesenthal Center with their International Leadership Award.

The CIJR decided to honor you for your contribution to the debate on and the study of contemporary antisemitism. What are the three main developments or trends you have observed in the last few decades?
"Over the last decades, Muslim antisemitism has become the most important source of antisemitic trends. In France, Belgium and Denmark, Jews were murdered only because they were Jews. The perpetrators were Muslims, without exception. This does not imply that all Muslims are antisemites. Far from it. Israel recently made peace with several additional Arab countries in its region. That is a wonderful development and cause for optimism.

"A second trend and a huge cause for concern: Anti-Israel sentiment has become mainstream in Europe. Left and liberal media reinforce this trend.

"Thirdly, in Israel and among Jews abroad one finds a disproportional number of masochist and even self-hating Jews. There is a lengthy Jewish masochistic tradition, which starts with the patriarch Abraham. He strongly debated with God about the fate of Sodom and Gomorra, yet when he was told to sacrifice his son Isaac, he did not argue. One finds masochistic thoughts also in the Talmud as well as in later Jewish sources. This type of thinking now manifests itself in many places concerning Israel."

Being laureled is good for your ego, but does such recognition also serve another purpose? I'm sure it motivates you to keep going, but is that basically all these awards have accomplished?
"It does indeed feel good when you experience resonance and recognition. More importantly, when people who themselves are authorities in your field rally behind you, it also helps enormously in the battle you are waging. It becomes increasingly difficult for my opponents to ignore my arguments."

How did your style of writing change over time?
"For over fifty years, I have frequently written texts with a strong analytical content. Yet from 1964 until 2000 hardly any of my writing was in the public domain as I worked for and was paid by business clients. Almost everything I wrote was confidential and exclusive. This began when I joined Eurofinance, a Paris based firm, which undertook complex economic and financial research. Originally my work focused primarily on stock market analysis.

"In 2000, I fully retired from business activities. As chairman of the JCPA I initially focused on the impact of the Holocaust in post-war society. Soon antisemitism was added and began to dominate my work."

Can you elaborate on what it meant to be an analyst in a business environment?
"When I was charged to research and write a report about a company, I had to first distill the relevant points from the information available. I then prepared questions for an interview with the chairman, a board member or other senior executives of that company.

"When visiting top executives of corporations they usually provided me with an hour of their time, seldom more. The challenge was to obtain the information I needed within this restricted time frame. From doing hundreds of such interviews, I learned to focus on my goals. This skill became an invaluable tool for my research until today."

If I'm not misunderstanding, basically you're saying your career in business taught you how to become an effective activist and author of influential op-eds.

"As a strategy consultant for the likes of Fiat, I had to calibrate everything relevant. I learned not to be carried away by unsubstantiated suppositions or make prophecies of doom. In my stock market analyst days, the reliability of my writing was crucial to my clients.

"To come back to your question, yes, my professional career was the best possible education for my current occupation, analyzing and—to some extent—fighting current antisemitic trends."

What is the main difference between creating texts for CEOs and writing for the general public?

"My writing is still influenced by my business career. I try to provide many facts in a limited number of words. Yet there is a great difference between creating a business presentation and writing an op-ed. In the former case, your audience is captive but very small. The people to whom you present your findings want to hear what you have to tell them. When writing an op-ed for the general public, one has to raise interest with the opening sentences to captivate your audience. It is also preferable to conclude the article with something unexpected, an eye-opener."

Which type of writing gives you more satisfaction, the analyses you've created for the captains of industry or the op-eds in which you contribute to the well-being of the Jewish People?

"In my career, I covered four subjects which moved successively from one issue to the other: chemistry, corporate business strategy, environmental policy, and finally antisemitism. In each of these fields, the challenges were significant and unique. It is difficult to compare satisfaction at different time periods. I was totally immersed in each of these topics at various stages of my life."

Soon, we'll release an anthology presenting some of your essays, articles and lectures, under the intriguing title, Jewish Masochism. From Abraham the Patriarch to Woody Allen. *In a sense you provide the reader with a virtual roller coaster ride, pulling him in a variety of directions. You trust he or she won't get dizzy but will instead appreciate the vistas.*

"Yes, these texts touch upon a wide range of topics, not just antisemitism. My main focus, nowadays, is on trends relating to anti-Israelism and antisemitism. But during my life I've studied many other topics. I enjoy widening my horizon. It also keeps my mind alert. I was delighted when you suggested to create a book showcasing the variety of my writings. I hope the reader enjoys this journey."

In essence, are you an optimist or a pessimist? What does the future look like for 1) Europe, 2) the Jewish People and 3) Israel?
"The EU is clearly facing crises of all kinds. I'm not sure the future of Europe is bright. The future of the Jewish people largely depends on the State of Israel. Israel is developing itself relatively quickly into an industrial and R&D powerhouse.

"Yet there are still huge threats. Iran wants to destroy Israel. Many Western politicians are naive when it comes to curtailing Iran's atomic capabilities. This makes it difficult to predict Israel's future. Optimist or pessimist . . . an analyst has primarily to be a realist."

ISRAEL

Which Foreign Leaders Should Israel Welcome?

There were several negative reactions in Israel to the welcome Hungarian Prime Minister Viktor Orbán received during his visit in July 2018 to Israel.[1] The arguments brought forward included Orbán's rehabilitation of Hungary's antisemitic leader and ally of Hitler, Admiral Miklós Horthy.[2] There were also complaints about Orbán's illiberalism and the antisemitism in Hungary.

Eighty years earlier, in July 1938, the Evian conference took place to discuss the fate of the Jewish refugees, whom had nowhere to flee. Except for the Dominican Republic no country was willing to accept any. The democracies at that time were unsavory nations, the others were usually worse.

Democracies and other states are still partly unsavory, be it in a mutated way. The big difference in the world is the arrival of biased supranational bodies. For instance, the voting pattern at the UN General Assembly concerning Israel according to the prime definition of antisemitism—that of the International Holocaust Remembrance Alliance—leads to the conclusion that the UN is a frequently antisemitic institution.

In view of the superficial comments against Orbán's visit it is worthwhile to try to establish more rational political criteria—in addition to business considerations—for welcoming visiting state leaders. These could include issues such as: does the government of the visiting leader financially support the Palestinian Authority which enables it to free other monies to pay murderers of Israelis and their families? Does that country vote against Israel in the UN and where relevant in the EU? Does that country's government interfere in Israel's internal affairs? Has the country let in a massive number of Muslims without barring the antisemites among them? Are Jews in the visiting leader's country subject to violence? Do the country's leaders distort the Holocaust?

Other criteria could include: When country leaders visit Israel, do they also visit the Palestinian Authority thereby placing it at the same level as Israel? And does their government support BDS promoting organizations? As the level of sophistication in this investigating process increases, different weights can also be given to the various categories listed.

The reproach that Orbán has rehabilitated Horthy, the antisemitic leader of his country from 1920 to 1944 is justified.[3] Horthy applied antisemitic measures prior to the Second World War. However, Hungary does not finance the Palestinian Authority, it usually does not vote against Israel in supranational institutions, it has not let in Muslim refugees and thus avoided the import of extreme antisemites among them. There is sizable verbal incitement against Jews in Hungary, but little or no violence against them. Orbán's government does not interfere in Israel's internal politics. The Hungarian Prime Minister did not visit the Palestinian Authority. The Hungarian government does not give money to BDS supporting institutions.

Israel would gladly welcome French Prime Minister Edouard Philippe. The Israeli opposition politicians who came out against Orbán would most likely remain silent. On most of the other above criteria—except for the distortion of the Holocaust—France's reality is far more negative than that of Hungary. France is the West European country where the majority of murders of Jews for ideological reasons in this century have taken place. No Western European country has such a significant percentage of Jews emigrating as France. One does not have to sympathize with Orbán to welcome him. Neither does one have to like the illiberal character of his government. One should try to prevent further Holocaust distortion. Yet one has to close one's eyes to much more of France's behavior to cordially welcome a French prime minister.

One can apply the same criteria also for instance to the Netherlands. The Dutch government enacts Holocaust distortion in an indirect way. Its wartime predecessor in exile in London was totally disinterested in the fate of the persecuted Jews in the occupied Netherlands. It did not even do the minimum it could do. The Netherlands is the only country in Western Europe which has not admitted to its war time failures. In contrast, several Hungarian leaders have admitted their country's lethal and incomparably more severe Holocaust failures. Orbán has denounced the wartime alliance of Hungary with Germany.[4]

Israeli Prime Minister Benyamin Netanyahu calls Dutch Prime Minister Mark Rutte "a great friend of Israel."[5] If we look at the above criteria this qualifies as fake news. The Dutch cabinet concluded in July 2018 that it was unwise for Israel to deduct money from the Palestinian Authority equal to what it pays to murderers of Israelis.[6]

If governments employed psychiatrists for themselves, the opinion that Israel should indirectly pay the murderers of its citizens would be a valid reason for referral. On most of the above criteria the Netherlands comes out in a more negative light than Hungary. The fact that it is usually more pleasant to be on vacation in the Netherlands rather than in Hungary is not relevant in this context.

In this way one can go on investigating other EU member countries. In June 2018, Austrian Prime Minister Sebastian Kurz visited Israel. His country ranks quite positive on most of the above criteria. Yet the junior partner in the Austrian government is the Freedom party FPÖ, which has Nazi origins. Its leader Heinz-Christian Strache has called for a ban on unstunned ritual slaughter.[7]

The important issue here is not to analyze all EU members, but to demonstrate a methodology which enables better thinking than that used by the political opponents of Orbán's visit. To conclude the ranking: using this methodology the Czech Republic probably comes out at the top. Sweden on the other hand is near the bottom.

The Jerusalem Post, August 5, 2018

---

1   www.jpost.com/Israel-News/Viktor-Orban-Hungarys-controversial-prime-minister-set-to-begin-Israel-trip-562769

2   www.timesofisrael.com/hungarys-controversial-orban-to-begin-two-day-israel-visit-wednesday/

3   www.yadvashem.org/odot_pdf/Microsoft%20Word%20-%206429.pdf

4   www.smithsonianmag.com/history/holocaust-and-hungary-prime-minis-
    ter-180964139/

5   www.pmo.gov.il/English/MediaCenter/Events/Pages/eventPress060916.aspx

6   www.cidi.nl/kabinet-acht-dat-israel-niet-meebetaalt-aan-terroristenuitkerin-
    gen-onverstandig/

7   www.jta.org/2018/07/24/news-opinion/austrias-vice-chancellor-calls-for-ban-
    on-ritual-slaughter

Government Lags in Fighting Anti-Israelis Efficiently

To counter its enemies, Israel established three intelligence services: the Mossad, the Israel Security Agency (better known as Shabak or Shin Bet) and the military intelligence branch, Aman. Over the years the performances of these services have improved. They make major efforts to learn as much as possible about Israel's enemies in their respective fields. Their top people oversee the intelligence battleground in their area.

As a new field of aggression—cyber warfare—developed in recent years, the Israeli government recognized the danger and invested heavily in cyber defense. Israel is expected to be among the world's leaders as this field develops to confront increasingly sophisticated cyber warfare. Each of the bodies that counters the various types of aggression also develops specific organizational cultures among its employees. This greatly helps in confronting Israel's enemies.

Anti-Israeli propaganda themes have often developed from the many centuries-old core motifs of antisemitism. For many Europeans, anti-Israelism has become a substitute for a currently not very presentable antisemitism. It is easy to understand that defense against hate mongering should be structured via an organization in the anti-propaganda field, similar in concept to the bodies mentioned.

At least one foreign Jewish leader has raised the issue of a counter-propaganda agency with Prime Minister Benyamin Netanyahu in past years.

I have discussed it over the years with some politicians. They often understand the need for establishing such an agency. One also does not have to explain to them that one cannot fight propaganda with improved public diplomacy or as it is widely known, hasbara.

The possible reasons for not taking the logical and necessary step of establishing a counter-propaganda agency remain opaque. Over the years I have developed a number of arguments that together may provide some explanations for the failure.

One of these is that three ministries are devoted to fighting off some parts of propaganda attacks on Israel and/or antisemitism. Taking away their responsibilities in this area would mean yet another political battle, of which the Prime Minister already has many more than he likes.

A second reason is that, in order to take effective action against propaganda, one has to have a reasonable understanding of the various perpetrator categories. We no longer live in the ancient reality of Christian religious antisemitism, whose prime attacks came from a limited number of main perpetrators. Initially these were led by the Roman Catholic Church, then many centuries later also by followers of Martin Luther and some other Protestant denominations.

In the second major anti-Jewish hate outburst thereafter, ethnic-nationalist antisemitism, the Nazi movement and its followers became dominant. Their manifestations of antisemitism were horrible, yet easy to analyze.

No such transparency exists in today's, fragmented but major anti-Israelism. Huge perpetrators come from Muslim countries, Muslims in the Western world, media, politicians from different parts of the spectrum, academics, church leaders, NGOs, trade unionists, the social media, Jewish self-haters and other segments of society. This fragmentation is typical of the post-modern period.

A third reason has to do with the ancient tradition of Jewish masochism. One finds elements of it already in the Bible. This current of Judaism has greatly developed in the Diaspora over two millennia. Physical persecution and antisemitism were considered "normal" by many Jews. That attitude was an integral component of what is known as "galut mentality." Israel's immigrant society is partly permeated with such masochistic feelings. They are often expressed by pseudo-moralists who ignore the cruel nature of our enemies.

A fourth related reason is that some think that not too violent antisemitism in the Diaspora is good for Israel, because it may lead to aliyah even from Western countries. This has, for instance, been the case with some French Jews. If more research is conducted, it may bring additional reasons.

BDS is far from being the main threat to Israel; but the combined efforts to delegitimize the Jewish state are. Even the initiators of the BDS scheme, at the Durban NGO anti-racist conference in 2001, understood that its main purpose was as a propaganda tool against Israel. Had there been a counter-propaganda agency, most of BDS could easily have been stopped early on.

Perhaps the best hope for promoting the necessary establishment of a counter-propaganda agency lies in the Knesset. This could be achieved if a few of its members come together to systematically promote the establishment of such an agency.

There have been more than enough reminders over the years to stimulate this promotion. There is also no doubt that many important acts of incitement against Israel and defamation of it are on their way.

The Jerusalem Post, July 20, 2017

How President Rivlin Could Revive the Israeli Presidential Conferences

With the termination of Shimon Peres' presidency in 2014, his initiative of Israeli presidential conferences has ended as well. Five such gatherings took place between 2008 and 2013. President Reuven Rivlin would do well to reinstate these conferences annually. The potential to benefit Israel is enormous.

To obtain the maximum benefit for Israel, the formula devised under Peres would require significant changes. In the past, the conferences included a strange mix of both topics and invitees. By far, the best sessions of the past conferences were those that addressed the newest developments and expectations for the future in several advanced scientific fields. If one did not come early to the sessions the room was already packed. The panels consisted of both foreign and Israeli scientists. In those that I attended, the Israeli presentations were as insightful and impressive as those by scholars who came from abroad.

On the other hand, there were some sessions on world Jewry in which the panelists were mainly rehashing what one could regularly read in Jewish media. There are enough other gatherings where these issues can be discussed. One also got the impression that the organizers had minimized the number of orthodox and center-right speakers.

Once, absurdly enough, an extreme American Jewish critic of Israel, Peter Beinart, was invited. Also some of the goals announced were greatly overstated. Did the discussions at these conferences really—as suggested in

2013—"engage the central issues that will influence the face of our future: geopolitics, economics, society, environment, culture, identity, education, new media, and more"?[1] It would have been much better to have been a bit more modest.

What could be the best new strategy for these conferences? It would first be important to identify the areas in which Israel is at the world's forefront. There should be sessions on topics concerning recent advances and possible future directions. The panels should consist of leading foreign and Israeli participants.

Determining where Israel is a world leader or co-leader is crucial. Some very diverse areas are obvious candidates. For instance, cybersecurity, water technology, trauma treatment and the setting up of field hospitals. There are, however, many others which do not immediately come to mind. Identifying those areas of knowledge and expertise where Israel co-leads the world, by asking a number of well-chosen people who know Israeli society well, would rapidly create a long list.

Once one has identified the fields in which Israelis are among the world leaders, the next step would be to ask the country's top experts in these areas whom to invite from abroad. The conferences would be broadcast in real time to receive as wide an audience as possible. In previous conferences the speakers included politicians, writers, actors, a vulgar American comedian and so on. Such people could also attend, but there would be no opening session where well-known invitees express their truisms and platitudes. Distinguished cultural performances could however be a welcome addition.

The conference core of topics in the above categories could be complemented with discussions about crucial world issues. To mention a few almost at random: the future of liberal democracy, sovereignty versus globalization, which multiculturalism could be viable and truth versus fake news. It wouldn't take much effort to define a few more.

One of the huge advantages for the participants in the panels would be the greatly varied interdisciplinary character of the conference's speakers. Top people in a certain field usually participate in conferences where the attendees are mainly from professions close to their own. This diversity would increase the attractiveness of the conference for the panelists.

President Peres found generous patrons who financed the conferences he initiated. There is no reason why such a prestigious conference under the auspices of President Rivlin would not find similar donors. His international prestige would be enhanced by these gatherings as well. Regarding the technicalities of the conference, one could learn much from the experiences of staff members who had been part of the organization of the previous conferences.

There are many potential advantages for Israel. With the right public relations, these conferences would expose the world to a broad spectrum of Israeli knowledge and inventiveness including those which are greatly beneficial to many people worldwide. As Israel is frequently attacked by a wide range of enemies and opponents, the conferences could, to a certain extent, also be a counterweight to this hatred and defamation.

President Peres had a preference for interviewing some leaders of science during the conferences. This however was an extra and the conference could have proceeded easily without it. The important thing is that President Rivlin takes the initiative, that the invitations to the conference go out in his name, and that he presides over the conference.

The Jerusalem Post, November 25, 2017

1   mfa.gov.il/MFA/InnovativeIsrael/Conferences/Pages/Israeli-Presidential-Con-ference-2013.aspx

Should Israel Trust Germany?

German leaders and visiting politicians to Israel regularly make statements directed to Israel that a two state solution is the way to end the Palestinian-Israeli conflict. One such recidivist among many is former socialist leader and foreign minister Sigmar Gabriel, an extreme anti-Israel inciter.[1] The not so explicit underlying message of these German statements is: The genocide of the Jews during our grandfathers' generation is a horrible part of our past. Contemporary Germany is a democracy which has learnt the necessary lessons from its history. We are a powerful nation on the world map. We are thus entitled to tell you how you should act toward the Palestinians.

Already when I was a small child a democratically elected German government had a policy concerning me. In the first half of the 1940s, during the German occupation of the Netherlands I was in hiding. Had the occupiers found me they had two options. They could have either sent me to Sobibor to be gassed or to Birkenau where the same fate awaited me. Thereafter my body would be burned together with that of many other Jews and I would have had no individual grave. The post-war democratic German governments rightly recognized that they were the legal successors of the democratically elected Nazi government.

Germany's population has far from fully digested the horrible history of their grandfathers' generation. That means that its authorities should abstain from interfering in political recommendations which concern me. The major reason for this has just been mentioned. Yet there are several others. Indeed many Germans have nowadays radically different attitudes than the majority in their grandfather's generation. There is also a small number who identify with the policies of the Nazi regime.

Yet more important is another huge group. With them the demonic views about the Jews of the German grandfather generation have mutated into a similar perception of Israel. During the period from 2004 to 2014, seven representative polls were undertaken on this subject. Germans were asked whether they agreed with statements such as: "Israel conducts a war of extermination against the Palestinians," or "Israel is acting toward the Palestinians like Nazis acted toward the Jews." A poll conducted by the Bertelsmann Foundation in 2013 found 41 percent agreement among the German population to the latter statement. In 2007 the figure was 30 percent.[2] The 2013 figure translates into more than 25 million German adults who believe that Israel behaves like Nazis when it comes to the treatment of Palestinians.

In today's Western worldview behaving like Nazis represents absolute evil. So too does having genocidal intentions. The widespread agreement by Germans regarding these statements about Israel also reveals that large parts of the population do not understand the essence of their country's criminal history. Furthermore, it illustrates how large segments of German opinion-making media and journalists are morally corrupt in a major way. They have created the atmosphere for these beliefs.

However, this time round, it is not Nazi papers such as *Der Stuermer* of Julius Streicher or the *Voelkische Beobachter* of the NSDAP, the National Socialist Workers Party. Nowadays much of the incitement comes from a variety of German progressive media. Against the above background it doesn't matter whether demonization is caused by right wing or progressive perverts.

There are other reasons why German politicians should not tell Israel how to solve its conflicts. Democratic Germany has been unable to suppress antisemitism. Chancellor Angela Merkel keeps telling how ashamed she is about this.[3] A normal reaction to her statement should be: solve Germany's problems so that you do not have to be ashamed of your country.

Worse even, into a society where antisemitism cannot be eradicated, Chancellor Merkel has welcomed more than a million refugee immigrants. Many of these come from the most antisemitic countries in the world. Ultimately even Merkel had to admit that beyond the native antisemitism in Germany, imported antisemitism from Muslim immigrants has been added to the mix of the country's Jew-hatred.[4]

There are other reasons for Germans to remain silent about what Israel should do. No other country is better equipped to recognize that in Palestinian society large parts of the population have views which are mutations of what the many criminals in the German grandfather generation and their leaders thought. In the only Palestinian parliamentary elections—those of 2006—the genocidal Hamas movement received an absolute majority. Nevertheless the German government allows another genocidal movement Hezbollah to exist in its country. This attitude is supported by all parties except the populist AfD.

In part of the previous century out of Germany came a quantity of lethal hatred which should suffice for any country during more than a millennium. Germans are thus also best equipped to recognize similar hatred coming out of many Palestinian sources. That goes also for Iran which Germany is far too friendly with. It also goes for many other parts of the Muslim world and includes as well some Muslims in the European Union and elsewhere in the West. The Palestinian Authority rewards murderers of Jews and or their families financially. That is not so different from the Germans who rewarded civilians who betrayed Jews so that the Germans could murder them.

As the Germans did not find me in hiding I got my life as a bonus. I have made an effort to learn lessons for life from that fortunate circumstance in a very unfortunate environment. That lesson includes following attentively developments in Germany. This includes its participation in anti-Israel voting at the United Nations. Danny Danon, Israel's ambassador to the United Nations has pointed out that Israel represents 0.1 percent of the world population, but receives 78 percent of the UN condemnations.[5] Another lesson includes monitoring the profound hypocrisy of large parts of contemporary Germany and its government.

The Jerusalem Post, June 27, 2019

1   www.spiegel.de/politik/deutschland/gabriel-vergleicht-israels-palaestinenser-politik-mit-apartheid-regime-a-821601.html

2   www.bertelsmann-stiftung.de/fileadmin/files/BSt/Publikationen/GrauePub-likationen/Studie_LW_Germany_and_Israel_today_2015.pdf, 35–36

3   www.dw.com/en/germanys-merkel-warns-of-increased-anti-semitism-on-ho-locaust-remembrance-day/a-42336022

4   www.reuters.com/article/us-germany-holocaust/germanys-merkel-calls-for-zero-tolerance-of-anti-semitism-hate-idUSKCN1PKoEG

5   www.jpost.com/Israel-News/Danon-Ilhan-Omar-Jeremy-Corbyn-need-to-be-removed-from-office-592732

Israeli Masochism Versus Dutch Hypocrisy

There are radical cultural differences in how countries, even democracies, teach their past. I learned much at school in the Netherlands about the Dutch Indies—later Indonesia—which was then still the country's colony. Yet we were not taught at all about the Java war in the mid-nineteenth century when the Dutch military killed two hundred thousand locals, tens of thousands of whom were civilians.[1]

In contrast, my eldest grandson attended a Jerusalem high school and was asked to write about the 1948 Deir Yassin massacre. During intense fighting about 200 Arabs, including civilians, were killed by Irgun Zvai Leumi (National Military Organization) fighters. The atrocities were greatly exaggerated for political reasons by both Jews and Arabs. Why was my grandson given this assignment? Deir Yassin was not typical of the way Israel fought a war of survival.

Many extreme Dutch war crimes were hidden or minimized in history teaching in the Netherlands. I learned a bit about the 1873–1914 war in Atjeh in the Dutch Indies. The colonizers killed an estimated one hundred thousand locals and wounded half a million.

Hendrik Colijn was a lieutenant there. He would later become Dutch Prime Minister five times.[2] In November 1894 he wrote to his wife that in line with general policy he had ordered his soldiers to kill nine women and three children who asked for mercy.[3] This is just one example among many.

In 2017 the Dutch-Swiss historian Rémy Limpach published an 870 page book about Dutch war crimes that took place in the two so-called "police actions" in 1947 and 1948 in the Dutch Indies against independence fighters and criminal bands. He concluded that Dutch war crimes there were structural and not incidental as had been claimed before. The book gives many examples of the Dutch committing arson, torturing and shooting prisoners, as well as killing women and children. It received several reviews but there were no major reactions in Dutch society.

In the late 1960s a young Dutch historian, Cees Fasseur, was officially appointed to investigate these "police actions." He later admitted the superficial nature of the research.[4] Only now, when all Dutch perpetrators are dead or very old, has a major study on the decolonization period been started.

Over numerous decades hardly anybody cared about Dutch war crimes. Dutch captain, Raymond Westerling, was in charge of "pacifying" parts of the island of Sulawesi. In 1974 he told a journalist over a glass of diluted whisky that he had court-martialed 350 captives and executed them personally.[5] Dries van Agt, later to become Dutch Prime Minister, was Dutch Minister of Justice at that time (from 1971–till 1977). No action against Westerling was taken. Van Agt is the Netherlands' main anti-Israel inciter.

An interview with Westerling in which he admitted war crimes was filmed in 1969. All Dutch TV stations refused to broadcast it. It was finally aired in 2012.[6]

In 1987, historian Ad van Liempt wrote an article about a mass murder that resulted in the death of 364 locals.[7] He told me that there were no reactions. In 1997, he wrote a book, *The Train of Corpses* which tells how the Dutch starved to death close to half of the local captives being transported in a train. Van Liempt told me that many found it scandalous that he wrote a book about it.[8] A filmmaker I know made a movie in 1995 about the Dutch army's mass killings of hundreds of men in the village of Rawagede. He told me that the locals mentioned that similar crimes had happened in nearby villages.[9]

In his 2013 book, *My Promised Land,* Ari Shavit tells the story of an alleged intentional killing of Arab civilians by Israeli forces in July 1948 in Lod. Three Israeli academics, Martin Kramer, Efraim Karsh and Benny Morris debated Shavit's claims. None of the three considered his version to be accurate.[10] *The New Yorker* pre-published a shortened version of Shavit's chapter about this.[11]

The editor could have filled a year's worth of issues with murderous Dutch crimes that took place in Indonesia around the very same years.

In 1995, Dutch UN soldiers fled to the Croatian capital, Zagreb, from the Bosnian Muslim village of Srebrenica they were protecting. The Bosnian Serb occupiers committed genocide and killed 8 000 Muslims. A Dutch court found the Netherlands partly responsible for hundreds of the murders.[12] Dutch historian, Henri Beunders, wrote that while the Bosnians were standing up to their knees in blood, Dutch soldiers in Zagreb were standing up to their ankles in beer, being applauded by their crown prince, Prime Minister and Minister of Defense, who all knew about the knee-high blood.[13]

During a battle in Afghanistan near Chora in 2007, Dutch soldiers killed an estimated 50 to 100 civilians.[14] The Dutch government admits that it does not know how many civilians have been killed by its planes and helicopters between 2006–2010 in the Afghan province of Uruzgan.[15]

In 2018, the Dutch government admitted that its planes killed civilians in the war against ISIS in Iraq and Syria. While the US, the UK and Australia have provided information about the killing of civilians in this war, the Dutch refuse to do so.[16]

The Dutch hypocritical culture of dealing with their major black spots in the past greatly contrasts with the Israeli masochistic culture of stressing what they have done wrong, which pales next to Dutch crimes. In this culture fits that successive Dutch governments have obstinately refused to admit the huge failures of their government in exile in London during the Second World War toward the persecuted and murdered Dutch Jews. All other Western European countries, including Monaco and Luxemburg have done so. Several of them have also apologized to their Jewish citizens.

The Jerusalem Post, July 19, 2018

1   Manfred Gerstenfeld interviews Frank van Vree, "Hoe Nederlands collectieve Oorlogsherinnering zich ontwikkelde," *Aleh*, September 2018.

2   historiek.net/hendrikus-colijn-premier-crisisjaren/69176/

3   www.nrc.nl/nieuws/1998/06/18/colijn-en-de-koloniale-oorlog-7403557-a1118402

4   www.groene.nl/artikel/de-excessennota-moet-opnieuw

5	Rolf Boost, "Westerling spreekt voor de laatste maal: Ik was geen luitenant Calley," *Panorama*, 1971.
6	www.ad.nl/binnenland/kapitein-westerling-geeft-oorlogsmisdaden-1947-toe~ab110a1b/
7	Ad van Liempt, "De massamoord van Galoeng Galoeng," in: bijlage *Vrij Nederland*, January 31, 1987.
8	Manfred Gerstenfeld interviews Ad van Liempt, "Onvermoeibaar op zoek naar Feiten," *Aleh*, April 2018.
9	Personal communication Alfred Edelstein.
10	mosaicmagazine.com/essay/2014/07/what-happened-at-lydda/
11	www.reuters.com/article/us-warcrimes-bosnia-srebrenica-idUSKBN19I0XZ
12	retro.nrc.nl/W2/Lab/Srebrenica/130796opi.html
13	www.telegraaf.nl/nieuws/2168198/defensie-aangeklaagd-om-slag-bij-chora
14	www.volkskrant.nl/nieuws-achtergrond/onbekend-aantal-afghaanse-slachtoffers-door-nederlandse-bommen~b163feco/
15	www.rtlnieuws.nl/nederland/gevolgen-van-vernietiging-is-door-nederlandse-bommen-blijven-geheim
16	www.newyorker.com/magazine/2013/10/21/lydda-1948

A Year in the Palestinian Territories

Interview with Els van Diggele

"My first book which appeared in 2000 discusses Israel's internal conflicts regarding the state's identity. The Dutch title translates into English as *A People That Dwells Alone*. I published my next book in 2007 which deals with the divisions between Christians in Israel. The title translates as *Holy Quarrels*."

Els van Diggele was born in 1967 in the Dutch village of Warmond. After her history studies at Leiden University she followed a postdoctoral journalism course at Rotterdam's Erasmus University.

"I wanted to complete a trilogy by writing about the Palestinians. I resided in the Palestinian territories, carefully looking for people who would dare to tell the truth. Otherwise I would only hear: 'Everything is fine. The Israeli occupation is the problem.'

"My first insight occurred when a Palestinian asked me: 'Do you write about our occupation? We are occupied by our leaders. The Palestinian occupation starts in our family with our father and uncles. Afterwards we are occupied by our boss and our leaders. The individual does not exist.' He added: 'That is our greatest real problem and explains our society's stagnation.'

"I lived for a year in the Palestinian territories. I did not register as a journalist with the authorities. I was not hindered by the authorities in any way, though there were people who suspected me of being a spy.

"In Gaza I also did not encounter any hindrance. Interviewing there was even easier than in the West Bank. In Gaza people are also fearful and society is very hierarchical. Yet the people were more open, perhaps because they are poorer and more desperate. It became clear to me that there is no historical unity between the West Bank and the Gaza strip. It is as if living in different worlds.

"The sole hindrance I encountered was at Nablus University on the West Bank. I asked the students about a murder committed in 2007. I wanted to know what happened and where it took place. Some people reacted: 'What murder? I know nothing about it.' This response is characteristic for a culture of fear which frequently results in the denial of facts. A second time I visited with a Palestinian woman who had studied there. I was called to the university's management which forbade entry.

"Looking through history's lens at Palestinian society, I concluded that there was a century of stagnation, destruction and a power battle which was fought on the back of common Palestinians. Nobody asked them anything.

"This attitude runs as a common thread through Palestinian society. A strong example is the pushing out of former Prime Minister Salam Fayyad. I spoke with this moderate man and also with Hamas executives. The moderate voice cannot succeed in Palestinian society.

"The picture I obtained from conversations with cooperative Palestinians is greatly different from what we have been told during the past fifty years by the State News Service NOS and major Dutch newspapers. That obsolete picture tells us that the Palestinians are powerless victims of the Israeli occupation which has lasted for fifty years.

"The new picture I came to understand is the opposite of the one I had before I started my research. It was a shocking but interesting discovery. I realized that this new picture cannot be revealed in the Netherlands.

"I started to grasp this situation slowly. Many Dutch people are emotionally involved with the Palestinians. They believe that they live in an underprivileged society where one is not allowed to criticize. Journalists and experts are both so emotionally involved that they cease to practice their profession properly.

"Many journalists have become participants in what they report about. Thus facts are no longer relevant. This results from fifty years of one-sided reporting in Western Europe.

"The title of my 2017 book about the Palestinians translates as: *We Hate*

Each Other More Than the Jews. People in the Netherlands told me: 'You should not have allowed yourself to write this book. You know about the occupation. Everything results from the colonial rule. The Palestinians have never been able to form their own government because they were ruled by foreigners.'

"I replied: The stifling division among the Palestinians has already lasted for a century. One cannot blame England or Israel for that.

"It is strange that I cannot reason in the Netherlands with anybody in a serious well argumented and rational way about my book. People do not understand the nature of the Middle East. Weapons are widespread in Palestinian society.

"Fayyad wanted to create an orderly state by working together with Israel. He said: 'A state is not only our right but also our duty. We need law and order, disarmament and a fight against corruption.'

"The Palestinians did not want this. They preferred resistance. Abbas pushed Fayyad out."

Van Diggele concludes: "I am now working on a short book of which the title translates as: *The Misleading Industry. Dutch Media in the Iron Grip of Palestine.*"[1]

Israel National News, December 7, 2018

---

1   This publication was released June 2019.

ANTISEMITISM

The World's Mega Antisemites

In past centuries identifying the world's leading antisemites was not a problem. With respect to classic religious antisemitism, the Catholic Church dominated this type of hate mongering. Throughout generations Jews were accused of being responsible for killing God's alleged son Jesus. This was a lie. Only the Romans—during their occupation of Judea—could condemn somebody to death and then carry out the execution.[1]

In addition holding people responsible for what their ancestors have done—and in this case did not do—is a hate promoting approach which, when applied systematically, poisons any society. Later, some Protestant leaders joined the antisemitic inciters, Martin Luther was prominent among the worst.[2,3]

Upon this infrastructure of extreme Christian incitement against Jews a second type of classic Jew-hatred developed in the nineteenth century: ethnic/nationalistic antisemitism. In this area Germany had no competition when it—with the help of European allies and collaborators—carried out the Holocaust.

In today's ideologically fragmented societies, the sources of antisemitism are many and widespread. In this multitude some antisemitic perpetrators and incidents stand out because of what they do or say and who they are. Identifying these inciters provides a perspective on the severity of their acts.

Major areas of this problem include Muslim antisemitism, right and left wing antisemitism as well as anti-Israelism.

A speech given in 2003 by the Prime Minister of Malaysia, Muhammed Mahathir, stands out for its hatred of Jews and the widespread approval of it. He spoke at the opening session of the tenth summit of the Organization of Islamic Cooperation (IOC) held in Putrajaya, Malaysia.

Mahathir represented relations between Muslims and Jews as a worldwide frontal confrontation. He said: "1.3 billion Muslims cannot be defeated by a few million Jews." The meeting was attended by leaders of 57 countries representing almost the entire Muslim dominated world. They applauded his speech.[4]

Muslim mega-antisemitism is genocidal. Iran's leaders openly promote genocide against the Jewish state. They are also responsible for the largest terrorist attack against Jews in the post-World War Two period which took place at the Amia building in Buenos Aires in 1994.[5] Also Hamas and Hezbollah promote genocidal antisemitism.[6, 7]

Furthermore all ideological murders of Jews in this century in Europe of which the perpetrators are known have been committed by Muslims. Nothing is comparable to the extreme hate of Jews and Israel coming out of parts of the Muslim world. There are no other heads of state, right-wing or left-wing, who promote genocidal antisemitism or a total confrontation with Israel and Jews worldwide.

However unpleasant right-wing antisemitism is in the current environment of hate, no mega-organization towers above the others. The Greek Golden Dawn movement has never been in power. Some of its leaders are in jail and Greece is not a country with major influence.[8] Hungary's Jobbik is trying to become more moderate in order to attract additional voters.[9, 10]

Anti-Israelism is the third type of antisemitism. On the extreme left one can find many who would like Israel to disappear. This can only happen through genocide.

A major leftist current of thought is that the world is divided into oppressors and the oppressed. The oppressors are supposedly all white including Israel and the Jews. These people intentionally ignore the easily to be seen truth that most people killed in armed conflicts in this century are Muslims murdered by other Muslims. This group of antisemitic extreme leftists are not heads of state and do not have much influence.

In the mainstream left, we find extreme anti-Israel inciters in a variety of socialist parties. Currently, the worst Western example is the British Labour Party headed by Jeremy Corbyn who possibly may win the next parliamentary elections. Labour is however far from being dominated by antisemites. At the same time the majority of party members are whitewashers of antisemitism.[11]

The three main socialist leaders who compared Israel to the Nazis have died: Swedish Prime Minister, Olof Palme,[12] Greek Prime Minister Andreas Papandreou[13] and French President, François Mitterand.[14]

Media is another major source of left wing antisemitism which predominantly focuses its hatred on Israel. One of the vilest European antisemites was the German Literature Nobel Prize winner, Günther Grass. This leftist writer was in his youth a member of the Waffen SS.[15] In 2012, he claimed that Israel intended to commit genocide against the Iranian people with nuclear bombs.[16] He must have known that the reverse was true. Iranian leaders had regularly threatened Israel with eradication.

If another Nobel Prize winner had any chance in the mega-antisemites competition, Portuguese author, Jose Saramago, would also be a contender. He compared the most flourishing Palestinian town Ramallah to Auschwitz.[17]

Grass only became a mega-antisemite when his hate-poem received huge publicity from six European mainstream papers with millions of readers. These were the German *Süddeutsche Zeitung*,[18] the Italian *La Repubblica*,[19] the British *The Guardian*,[20] the Spanish *El Pais*,[21] the Danish *Politiken*,[22] and the Norwegian *Aftenposten*.[23]

One may also wonder about contemporary Christian antisemitism. In 1965, the Vatican issued the Nostra Aetate document, the declaration of the relations of the Church with non-Christian religions.[24] This statement greatly reduced Catholic antisemitism.

Substantial antisemitic hate, mainly focused on Israel, but also sometimes on the Jews comes out of parts of the Protestant world. However it is difficult to find very important Christian groups with extreme positions. The World Council of Churches incites against Israel.[25, 26] Two liberal American protestant denominations promote BDS. The number of members of both, the Presbyterian Church[27] and the United Church of Christ,[28] have been declining and are expected to continue to do so. Several Eastern Churches can also be mentioned as promoters of Jew-hate.[29] One should not forget Jewish anti-Israel organizations and individuals.[30] Fortunately, their influence is too small to make it to the premier league of antisemitism.

Finally there are those who indirectly support the Palestinian genocide promoters. Among these the United Nations and several of its associate organizations stand out.[31]

The Jerusalem Post, June 21, 2018

1   jcpa.org/article/the-origins-of-christian-anti-semitism/

2   www.momentmag.com/martin-luthers-anti-semitic-legacy-500-years-later/

3   jcpa.org/article/historical-roots-anti-israel-positions-liberal-protestant-churches-2/

4   www.jcpa.org/jl/vp506.htm

5   www.nbcnews.com/news/latino/anniversary-remembering-argentina-s-jewish-center-bombing-n611551

6   www.theguardian.com/world/2005/oct/27/israel.iran

7   www.timesofisrael.com/hezbollah-leader-rallies-shiites-with-highly-sectarian-speech/

8   www.theguardian.com/world/2013/oct/03/golden-dawn-leader-jailed-nikos-michaloliakos

9   www.huffingtonpost.com/entry/how-hungarys-right-wing-parties-are-trying-to-reform_us_58f4fc35e4b04cae050dc97d

10   www.haaretz.com/world-news/europe/head-of-hungarys-jobbik-denounces-partys-anti-semitic-ways-1.5628831

11   besacenter.org/perspectives-papers/uk-labour-antisemitism/

12   Per Ahlmark, *Det ar demokratin, dumbom!* (Stockholm: Timbro, 2004) 307.

13   www.nytimes.com/1982/06/26/world/israelis-assail-greek-leader-for-likening-them-to-nazis.html

14   www.nytimes.com/1982/08/11/world/begin-hints-that-mitterrand-remark-paved-way-for-terrorists-attack.html

15   www.spiegel.de/international/nobel-prize-author-guenter-grass-i-was-a-member-of-the-ss-a-431353.html

16   www.theguardian.com/books/2012/apr/04/gunter-grass-poetry-attack-israel

17   jcpa.org/article/holocaust-inversion-the-portraying-of-israel-and-jews-as-nazis/

18 www.theguardian.com/books/2012/apr/05/gunter-grass-israel-poem-iran
19 ricerca.repubblica.it/repubblica/archivio/repubblica/2012/04/04/una-poesia-contro-israele-ultima-provocazione.html?refresh_ce, Günter Grass, "Quello che deve essere detto," *La Repubblica*, April 4, 2012. (Italian)
20 www.theguardian.com/books/2012/apr/05/gunter-grass-israel-poem-iran
21 elpais.com/internacional/2012/04/03/actualidad/1333466515_731955.html
22 politiken.dk/kultur/fakta_kultur/art5415477/Dokumentation-L%C3%A6s-G%C3%BCnter-Grass-digt
23 www.aftenposten.no/meninger/i/QoBnx/Det-som-ma-sies
24 www.vatican.va/archive/hist_councils/ii_vatican_council/documents/vat-ii_decl_19651028_nostra-aetate_en.html
25 www.economist.com/erasmus/2017/03/12/the-world-council-of-churches-clashes-with-israel-over-a-ban-on-boycotters
26 www.camera.org/article/the-world-council-of-churches-supports-christian-anti-zionist-in-jerusalem/
27 www.jpost.com/Christian-News/Pro-BDS-Presbyterian-church-set-to-lose-400000-members-444376
28 www.ngo-monitor.org/reports/united-church-of-christ/
29 www.jpost.com/Opinion/Op-Ed-Contributors/Middle-Eastern-Christians-and-anti-Semitism
30 israelandtheacademy.org/wp-content/uploads/2016/06/progressive_jewish_thought.pdf
31 www.gatestoneinstitute.org/7813/israel-moral-equivalence

Jewish Dual Loyalty: The Classic Antisemitic Stereotype

The murder of 11 Jews in a synagogue in Pittsburgh in October 2018 was followed by the release of a FBI publication which reported that in 2017 60 percent of all religiously biased hate crime incidents in the United States were anti-Jewish, far exceeding the figure for other religions. These and a variety of other manifestations of antisemitism necessitate an analysis of the main negative stereotypes of Jews in the US against the background of the international situation.[1]

Statistics show that the main antisemitic hate motif worldwide is that diaspora Jews are more loyal to Israel than to the country in which they live. The Global 100 study released by the ADL in 2014 found that 30 percent of adult Americans—or 75 million people—believe this canard.[2] A 2015 ADL study found an even slightly higher percentage.[3]

The 2014 ADL Global 100 study also found that the false accusation of dual loyalty is the main international antisemitic stereotype. Forty one percent of the world's populations included in this survey believe this to be true[4] which translates into approximately 1.7 billion people. This huge figure provides a fertile infrastructure for many other antisemitic accusations. If the interests of Israel are opposed to those of the country where a Jew lives, the Israeli interest may take precedence. A priori this undermines confidence in Jews. One can put it as: "you are not really one of us." In its most extreme form, dual loyalty is a veiled accusation of treason.

JEWISH DUAL LOYALTY: THE CLASSIC ANTISEMITIC STEREOTYPE

The accusation that Jews are not loyal to the society or country where they live existed long before the State of Israel was founded. During the mid-fourteenth century it facilitated, at the time of the Black Death plague, the burning of Jews accusing them of poisoning food, wells and streams. There were a number of variations on this theme of dual respectively lack of loyalty. One version was that Jews were cosmopolitans, a people without a motherland who were only loyal to other Jews. That provided a convenient base for the accusations of treason and subsequent conviction in 1894 of French officer, Alfred Dreyfus. Being a Jew he was the ideal candidate to blame for espionage against France which in reality had been committed by a non-Jewish officer.

Accusing Jews of dual loyalty facilitates creating further antisemitic stereotypes. One is: "Jews want to control the world." The 2014 global ADL study shows that 29 percent of those interviewed worldwide believe that Jews have too much power over global affairs.[5]

In the US a 2015 ADL study revealed that 16 percent of the country's population or 40 million Americans believe that Jews have too much power in the business world.[6] The same number of Americans considered that Jews have too much power in international financial markets. Twelve percent or 30 million were of the opinion that Jews have too much control over the US government while the same number thought that Jews have too much control over global media. Twenty five million adult Americans believe that Jews have too much control over global affairs.[7]

Under the Obama administration a substantial disagreement occurred between the US and Israel regarding the Iranian nuclear agreement. Jewish Senator Chuck Schumer voted against it and was then accused of being more loyal to Israel than to America.[8] Jews often fear of being accused of double loyalty when one of them makes a major misstep. The most extreme case was Jonathan Pollard's spying for Israel. He is the only person to have received a life sentence for spying on the US on behalf of an ally.[9]

It is easy to show that on basic issues of great importance to Israel the dual loyalty accusation of American Jews is a major falsehood. So far Donald Trump has been the most pro-Israeli US president. If there was dual loyalty of Jews, the great majority of American Jews should today be supporting him. In 2016, 71 percent of Jews voted for Hillary Clinton as compared to 48 percent of the national vote. Only 24 percent of Jews voted for Trump.[10] In the newly elected Congress, a variety of Jewish Democrat committee heads attack the President in a major way.[11]

There is much further proof that the concept of dual loyalty of American Jews is false. Barack Obama was among the least friendly US presidents to Israel, yet Jews voted for him in huge numbers. In 2008, 78 percent of Jews voted for Obama as opposed to 53 percent of the national vote. In 2012, 69 percent of Jews voted for him as opposed to 58 percent nationally.[12, 13] A majority of American Jews voted for Obama seemingly against their own interests. He and his wife were longtime members of a church whose then pastor, Jeremiah Wright, is an antisemite.[14]

The shakiness of dual loyalty claims against Jews can also be shown in other countries. In a poll in the Netherlands conducted during the 2017 election campaign, it was found that 19 percent of Dutch Jews intended to vote for the anti-Israeli Labor Party (PvdA) whereas, only 6 percent of the general population voted for them.[15]

In the UK, 13 percent of the Jews said that they would still vote for Labour in the 2017 parliamentary elections.[16] This despite the fact that the leader of the party, Jeremy Corbyn is a sympathizer of genocidal terrorist attackers of Israel and an anti-Israel inciter.[17] Several people around him are extreme anti-Israel inciters.

Very diluted versions of dual loyalty can be found in many countries. Immigrants may cheer on their country of origin in a sport game against the country they live in. Sometimes however, this gets radically out of hand. A well-known case is the "friendly" soccer match in 2001 in Paris between France and Algeria. Algerians living in France whistled when the French anthem was played. The match had to be ended prematurely as Algerians invaded the field.[18]

Many countries have problematic Diasporas. Accusations of dual loyalty is however a typical and widespread anti-Jewish stereotype. There are cases of other ethnicities where the problem of dual loyalty is evident. One example results from the fact that Turkey allows its citizens living abroad to participate in its elections. More than 450,000 Turks or 65 percent of those participating in the vote in Germany, supported Erdogan's AKP in the 2018 parliamentary elections. This is substantially higher than the percentage of those who voted for it in Turkey. Yet, this did not lead to general anger in

Germany about these people backing a party abroad whose views are incompatible with democratic norms and values.

The former leader of the Green Party, Cem Ozdemir, was almost the only German politician who drew the obvious conclusion. He said that "The German Turkish Erdogan fans do not only cheer their autocrat, with this they also express a negation of our liberal democracy. That should preoccupy everybody."[19]

Finding intelligent ways to expose the false double loyalty claims against Jews may be the beginning of a new type of fight against antisemitism.

Besa Center, November 28, 2018

1   ucr.fbi.gov/hate-crime/2017/topic-pages/tables/table-1.xls
2   global100.adl.org/public/ADL-Global-100-Executive-Summary.pdf
3   global100.adl.org/#country/usa/2015
4   global100.adl.org/public/ADL-Global-100-Executive-Summary.pdf.
5   Ibid.
6   global100.adl.org/#country/usa/2015
7   Ibid.
8   www.timesofisrael.com/us-jewish-group-slams-dual-loyalty-smears-on-iran-deal/
9   www.theguardian.com/world/2015/nov/20/spy-jonathan-pollard-to-be-free-after-30-years-but-still-a-thorn-in-us-israeli-ties
10   www.jewishvirtuallibrary.org/jewish-voting-record-in-u-s-presidential-elections
11   www.jpost.com/Diaspora/Jewish-Americans-are-now-the-face-of-Trump-resistance-571399
12   Ibid.
13   www.jta.org/2018/10/17/news-opinion/politics/poll-shows-jewish-voters-favor-democrats-midterms-dislike-trump
14   www.israelnationalnews.com/Articles/Article.aspx/19883
15   www.niw.nl/enquete-joods-nederland-kiest-555/
16   www.thejc.com/news/uk-news/labour-support-just-13-per-cent-among-uk-jews-1.439325
17   besacenter.org/perspectives-papers/corbyn-against-jews-israel/

18   www.leparisien.fr/sports/france-algerie-pourquoi-le-match-a-degene-
     re-08-10-2001-2002494338.php
19   www.zeit.de/politik/ausland/2018-06/reaktionen-tuerkei-wahl-cem-oezdemir

Antisemitism Is Deeply Woven into the European Fabric

Saying that antisemitism is integral to European culture does not make one popular in Europe. That does not change if one adds that stating this is radically different from saying that most Europeans are antisemites.

Yet this claim about European culture is not difficult to prove. This mindset kept developing in a dominating hostile Christian environment over more than a millennium. Major incitement against Jews initially stemmed from the Catholic Church. Later, several Protestant churches including Lutherans promoted Jew-hatred.

If powerful institutions and elites promote hatred over a very long period, they permeate the culture. In the 1960s, Christian historian and clergyman James Parkes analyzed the conflict between Christians and Jews during the first eight centuries of the Christian era. Concerning that period he concluded, "There was far more reason for the Jew to hate the Christian than for the Christian to hate the Jew—and this on the evidence of Christian sources alone."

Parkes also considered that the Christian theological concept of the first three centuries created the foundations for the hatred, on which an "awful superstructure" was built. The first stones for this were laid at "the very moment the Church had the power to do so, in the legislation of Constantine and his successors." Parkes attributed the full responsibility for modern antisemitism to those who prepared the soil, created the deformation of the people and so made these ineptitudes credible.[1]

During the Enlightenment and thereafter many other leading Europeans thinkers expressed hatred against Jews with partly mutated arguments. Voltaire, several German philosophers, early French socialists, Karl Marx and many others took part in what can only be described as an antisemitic hate fest.[2]

The Holocaust was executed by Germans with the help of many Nazi allies. It was facilitated by the mainly Christian infrastructure of antisemitic feelings in Europe which had accumulated over centuries.

After Second World War, many thought that the Holocaust had taught Europeans a hard lesson. Antisemitism seemed to fade away, especially after some highly acclaimed movies including NBC's 1973 series *Holocaust*,[3] as well as Steven Spielberg's 1993 *Schindler's List*.[4] These reached a huge audience. Yet another one was Claude Lanzmann's 1985 documentary, *Shoah*.[5]

Nevertheless, classic antisemitism targeting Jews continues to exist. Polls by the Anti-Defamation League (ADL) exposed that the evil myth that Jews are responsible for the death of Jesus is alive and well in Europe. It was found that 46 percent of Poles, 38 percent of Hungarians, 21 percent of Danes and Spaniards, 19 percent of Norwegians and Belgians believe this. So do 18 percent of Austrians and British, and 16 percent of the Dutch, 15 percent of Italians and 14 percent of Germans.[6, 7]

Once an attitude is so ingrained in a culture, it takes a long time to "wash it out." Classic antisemitism had targeted Jews initially as a religion and later also in national/ethnic antisemitism as a people. On the other hand, political correctness made it impossible in recent decades for "respectable Europeans" to self-define as antisemites.

In this context the hatred mutated increasingly. A third major generation of antisemitism developed: anti-Israelism which targets the Jewish state. The inroads this has made in Europe was proven by a 2011 study conducted by the German University of Bielefeld.[8] From this study it emerged that at least 150 million adult EU citizens agreed with the statement that Israel is conducting "a war of extermination against the Palestinians."

If that were indeed the case, hardly any Palestinians would still be alive. To the contrary, the number of Palestinians has increased over the past decades. The persistent myth of Jews being responsible for the killing of Jesus has partly mutated into a new myth: Israel committing a—non-existent—genocide of Palestinians.

In another new mutation of antisemitism, European Jews are nowadays accused of being responsible for Israel's actions. A December 2018 study by the Fundamental Rights Agency (FRA), shows that this idea ranks among the most frequent expressions of antisemitism in many European countries.[9] Another aspect of antisemitism in Europe is the return of the word "Jew"—without an adjective—as a curse. It is also often used as an invective by non-Jews against other non-Jews.

There are also examples of real and fictitious Jewish characters which have become negative symbols in European subcultures. The name Rothschild has become a symbol if one wants to denounce destructive capitalism. Shakespeare's mean-spirited Shylock from the *Merchant of Venice*, is still used to symbolize Jewish greed.

The way that ingrained antisemitism manifests itself varies not only from subculture to subculture but also from country to country. In January 2014, a mass rally in Paris took place. This "Day of Anger" was not related to any specific Jewish topic. Part of the protest was against French President François Hollande's economic plans. However, various groups of participants started to shout antisemitic slogans. These included, "Jews, France doesn't belong to you" and [the Holocaust denier] "Faurisson is right," as well as "the Holocaust was a hoax."[10]

The same happened in the 2018 "yellow vest" demonstrations. These were a protest against French President Emmanuel Macron's raising of fuel prices. Again, this had nothing to do with Jews. During some demonstrations there were signs which described Macron as a "whore of the Jews" and as their "puppet."[11]

The late leading academic historian of antisemitism, Robert Wistrich said, "Antisemitism in Great Britain has been around for almost a thousand years of recorded history. Medieval England already led in antisemitism. In the Middle Ages, England pioneered the blood libel. The Norwich case in 1144 marked the first time Jews were accused of using the blood of Christian children for the Passover unleavened bread (matza).

"In the twelfth century, medieval Britain was a persecutory Catholic society, particularly when it came to Jews. In this environment, the English Church was a leader in instituting cruel legislation and discriminatory conduct toward Jews, unparalleled in the rest of Europe.[12] Wistrich devotes an entire chapter to how British antisemitism has developed over the centuries into contemporary antisemitism in his book *A Lethal Obsession*.[13]

State antisemitism against Jews has become marginal in the EU If one applies the definition of the International Holocaust Remembrance Alliance (IHRA) however, both the EU and many of its member countries commit antisemitic acts. One of the most frequent such acts of state antisemitism is voting for anti-Israeli resolutions at the United Nations, which is a hotbed of discrimination. No similar resolutions are passed there in anywhere near such large numbers against other countries.

Despite all this there are currently hardly any non-Jewish personalities pointing out that antisemitism is part of European culture. One of the very few such voices is the head of the Anglican Church, the Archbishop of Canterbury Justin Welby. He said that antisemitism is entrenched in British culture.[14]

In 2017 at Yad Vashem, Welby observed that "Within European culture, the root of all racism, I think, is found in antisemitism. It goes back more than 1,000 years in Europe. Within our Christian tradition, there has been century upon century of these terrible, terrible hatreds in which one people . . . [are] hated more specifically, more violently, more determinedly, more systematically than any other people."[15] One can only conclude that he is right.

Besa Center, January 28, 2019

1   James Parkes, *The Conflict of the Church and the Synagogue* (Cleveland, New York: Meridian Books, 1961) 375–376.

2   www.israelnationalnews.com/Articles/Article.aspx/14217

3   www.imdb.com/title/tt0077025/

4   www.imdb.com/title/tt0108052/

5   www.imdb.com/title/tt0090015/

6   "ADL Survey: Attitudes Toward Jews in 12 European Countries: Country by Country Results," Anti-Defamation League, June 7, 2005. www.jewishvirtuallibrary.org/european-attitudes-toward-jews; "Attitudes toward Jews In Ten European Countries," Anti-Defamation League, March 2012.

7 library.fes.de/pdf-files/do/07908-20110311.pdf

8 European Agency for Fundamental Rights, Experiences and perceptions of antisemitism, Second survey on discrimination and hate crime against Jews in the EU Luxembourg 2018. fra.europa.eu/en/publication/2018/2nd-survey-discrimination-hate-crime-against-jews

9 Jerome Gordon, "Gurfinkiel: France may have joined 'Europe's league of fringe anti-Semitic countries,'" *The Iconoclast*, January 29, 2014.

10 www.jpost.com/Diaspora/Antisemitism/Antisemitism-among-Yellow-Vest-protesters-demoralizes-Frances-Jews-577261

11 www.lemonde.fr/idees/article/2018/12/24/gilets-jaunes-en-matiere-d-antisemitisme-tout-est-a-craindre-et-les-strategies-d-occultation-sont-un-leurre_5401843_3232.html

12 www.israelnationalnews.com/Articles/Article.aspx/11230

13 Robert S. Wistrich, *A Lethal Obsession* (New York: Random House 2010) 362–395.

14 www.christiantoday.com/article/justin-welby-antisemitism-entrenched-in-uk-culture-and-church-is-partly-to-blame/96384.htm

15 www.theguardian.com/world/2017/may/03/justin-welby-archbishop-canterbury-israel-christians-unite-jews-halt-rise-antisemitism

Antisemitic Conspiracy Theories Proliferate in Labour

Jointly written with Irene Kuruc

Conspiracy theories can usually be found in antisemitic environments. Labour leader since 2015 Jeremy Corbyn is a terrorist sympathizer, supporter of Holocaust distorters, anti-Israel inciter and part-time antisemite.[1] He has also promoted conspiracy theories about Israel. Already years ago some senior Labourites promoted antisemitic conspiracy theories. Nowadays conspiracy theories appear among Labour members targeting Jews, Israel as well as others.

Conspiracy theories can usually be found in environments where antisemitism is substantially present. The classic most extreme case—a fallacy originating from Tzarist Russia—is the Protocols of the Elders of Zion. Many extreme antisemitic conspiracy theories flourish in the Arab world.

In publications about the antisemitism scandal in the UK Labour party, a slew of conspiracy theories by elected party members have come to the fore. Corbyn has promoted conspiracy theories about Israel. He was interviewed in 2012 by the Iranian propaganda outlet *PressTV.* There he commented on a terrorist attack at an Egyptian Army base in the Sinai Peninsula where sixteen Egyptian soldiers were killed. The Labour leader suggested that Israel was behind the attack because it had an interest in increased violence in the Sinai and a destabilization of the Muslim Brotherhood regime. Corbyn said: "In whose interests is it to kill Egyptians other than Israel, concerned about the growing closeness of relationships between Palestine and the new

Egyptian government." He added: "I suspect the hand of Israel in this whole process of destabilization."[2]

In 2010, Corbyn spoke at a meeting of the Palestinian Solidarity Campaign in London in which he mentioned the shooting by Israeli commandos of Turkish activists on a ship of the Gaza flotilla. Corbyn remarked that British MP's made speeches in parliament on this issue with a pre-prepared script. He said that he was sure that then Israeli Ambassador Ron Prosor wrote it, saying: "They all came with the same key words. It was rather like reading a European document looking for buzz-words. These were: Israel's need for security, the extremism of the people on one ship and the existence of Turkish militants on the vessel." The *Daily Mail* checked the transcript of the Commons debate in question and was unable to find any evidence that these buzz-words were used by MPs.[3, 4]

There are several classic cases of conspiracy theories in Labour. One of these concerns former mayor of London Ken Livingstone, who resigned from the party earlier in 2018 after having been suspended for some time. Sociologist David Hirsh defined his statements that antisemitism claims against individual Labourites and the party are raised to smear the left and silence criticism of Israel as the "Livingstone formulation."[5]

In 2003, veteran Labour MP Tom Dallyel said that Prime Minister David Blair was unduly influenced in his policy on the Middle East in favor of Israel by a cabal of Jewish advisers. He specifically mentioned Peter Mandelson, Lord Levy and Jack Straw. The latter, who was Foreign Secretary at the time, is an evangelical with one Jewish grandfather.[6]

In 2013, Labour peer Lord Ahmed claimed that Jewish lawyers and media were responsible for the length of the prison term he received after causing a fatal car crash. He resigned after the party suspended him.[7]

In recent years, some Labour officials claimed that Israel was behind ISIS. One of the perpetrators was Blackburn councilor and former mayor, Salim Mulla. He was also suspended by Labour.[8]

Corbyn has never apologized for his conspiracy claims. Some lesser Labour officials however apologized for the conspiracy theories they promoted about fake issues including Jewish world control and terrorism.

Mohammad Pappu, a local councilor in the London borough of Tower Hamlets, was praised by Corbyn for his help to create a "fair, just and decent society." It was found that Pappu shared messages on Facebook in which he accused Britain of attacking Syria "to install a Rothschild bank."[9] He had also shared posts on social media which claimed that Israel had staged 9/11, the London terrorist bombings and the Paris terrorist attacks.[10]

In December 2015, Labour councilor, Irfan Mohammed from the London borough of Lambeth, posted on his Facebook page, "Jews working in the World Trade Center received a text message before the incident, 'Do not come to work on September 11th.'" When this was exposed he resigned his post as councilor and apologized.[11, 12]

In 2017, John Clarke, a city councilor and prospective Labour parliamentary candidate, shared a tweet by a neo-Nazi containing slurs against the Rothschild family. "The Rothschilds have used usury alongside modern Israel as an imperial instrument to take over the world and all of its resources, including you and I." John Clarke commented that the tweet contained a great deal of truth.[13]

Andy Slack, a Labour city councilor in Chesterfield shared: "The modern State of Israel was created by the Rothschilds, not God, and what they are doing to the Palestinian people now is exactly what they intend for the whole world." He later apologized.[14]

The trade union leader, Mark Serwotka, head of the Public and Commercial Services Union (PCS), is an avid supporter of Jeremy Corbyn. While referring to the antisemitism row within Labour he told a conference that it was possible "that Israel could have created a story that doesn't 'exist' in order to distract attention from atrocities."[15] Serwotka had been expelled from Labour in the 1990s as an extreme leftist but was allowed to rejoin after Corbyn became its leader.

Ian Hilpus, a former BBC producer and Corbyn supporter, wrote about the Labour leader that the Zionists are "part of a conspiracy to undermine the most honest man in politics today."[16] He posted this on a Facebook group called "We Support Jeremy Corbyn" that has 70,000 members.

Where conspiracy theories about Jews and Israel proliferate, others are also attacked. Andrew Murray, policy advisor to Corbyn, suggested in an article that the British security services were undermining Corbyn.[17, 18]

It is difficult to surpass the incitement by Mendy Richards, selected as the prospective Labour parliamentary candidate for the constituency seat of Worcester. She was banned from bringing claims to the court without the judge's permission after she made nonsensical accusations against the security services, the Metropolitan Police, the army, the postal service, her water company, her gas, electricity and broadband providers and so on.[19] The above examples illustrate one more facet of hatemongering, mainly antisemitic, in the British Labour party.

Besa Center, October 29, 2018

1   besacenter.org/perspectives-papers/corbyn-against-jews-israel/
2   www.jpost.com/Diaspora/UK-Labour-leader-Corbyn-voices-conspiracy-theory-against-Israel-in-2012-563714
3   www.dailymail.co.uk/news/article-6105741/Corbyn-claims-Israel-controls-speeches-British-MPs-remarks-slammed-anti-Semitic.html
4   www.ynetnews.com/articles/0,7340,L-5337016,00.html
5   David Hirsh, *Contemporay Antsemitism* (London: Routledge, 2018) 19.
6   www.scotsman.com/news/politics/dalyell-zionist-cabal-runs-policy-on-israel-1-1385178
7   www.thejc.com/news/uk-news/lord-ahmed-quits-labour-party-before-jewish-conspiracy-hearing-1.44912
8   www.itv.com/news/granada/2016-05-02/former-mayor-of-blackburn-zionist-jews-are-a-disgrace-to-humanity/
9   www.thetimes.co.uk/article/labour-rising-star-mohammed-pappu-put-antisemitic-posts-on-facebook-qhnrmw6vm
10 www.dailymail.co.uk/news/article-6263161/Rising-Labour-star-Mohammed-Pappu-26-accused-spreading-antisemitic-conspiracy-theories.html
11 www.thejc.com/news/uk-news/labour-councillor-says-sorry-for-sharing-racist-conspiracy-theory-about-jews-1.468179
12 www.thesun.co.uk/news/7469062/labour-anti-semitism-councillor-quits/
13 www.independent.co.uk/news/uk/politics/labour-anti-semitism-claims-candidate-fair-right-twitter-meme-a7570181.html
14 order-order.com/2017/02/07/labour-ppc-says-far-right-rothschilds-conspiracy-contains-great-deal-of-truth/
15 www.independent.co.uk/news/uk/politics/labour-antisemitism-israel-corbyn-mark-serwotka-tuc-trade-union-pcs-a8535986.html

16 www.timesofisrael.com/jeremy-corbyns-supporters-see-a-conspiracy-against-him/

17 www.newstatesman.com/politics/uk/2018/09/deep-state-trying-undermine-corbyn

18 www.telegraph.co.uk/politics/2018/09/20/left-wingers-love-conspiracy-theory-distraction-real-reasons/

19 www.standard.co.uk/comment/comment/paranoia-rules-the-waves-as-labour-takes-the-art-of-conspiracy-theories-to-a-whole-new-level-a3820891.html

Categorizing Corbyn's Wrongdoings Against Jews and Israel

There is now so much information about the misdemeanors of British Labour leader, Jeremy Corbyn that classifying his wrongdoings against Jews and Israel is even possible without using all available material.

The first category of Corbyn's misdemeanor is his support for genocidal terrorists. He welcomed representatives of Hezbollah and Hamas in the British parliament in 2009 and called them his "friends." It took him until 2016, when Corbyn was challenged in the House of Commons by Conservative Prime Minister David Cameron to hesitantly renounce his words.[1]

In 2012, on the Iranian Press TV channel he praised Israel's release of 1000 Hamas terrorists who between them killed 600 people. He called them "brothers."[2] Corbyn has also commemorated terrorists of the Irish IRA.[3] In November 2012, he hosted a meeting in parliament with Musa Abu Maria, a member of the banned terrorist group, Palestinian Islamic Jihad. In addition, Corbyn once shared a platform with the Black September terrorist and hijacker Leila Khaled.[4] In August 2018, the *Daily Mail* discovered that in 2014 in Tunisia Corbyn was photographed standing with a wreath in his hand next to a plaque in memory and the graves of members of the Palestinian Black September movement. This terrorist organization perpetrated the murder of 11 Israeli athletes at the 1972 Munich Olympics.[5]

The Telegraph has reported that one of the three main donors to Corbyn's leadership campaign was Ibrahim Hamami, who is a supporter of stabbing

Jews in Israel. He is a general practitioner living in London and founder of the pro-Hamas group, the Palestinian Affairs Center. Hamami has also been a columnist in an official Hamas newspaper.

He furthermore helped organize the UK visit of Raed Saleh, who has described Jews as "bacteria" and "monkeys." Saleh has also promoted the blood libel, saying that Jews use the blood of gentile children to bake their bread. Hamami acted as his spokesman during the UK visit. When Saleh was jailed in the UK Corbyn called him "a very honored citizen who represents his people extremely well" and said he "looked forward to giving you tea on the [House of Commons] terrace." Corbyn has shared public platforms with Hamami.[6] Soon after his election as Labour leader in 2005, Corbyn hired Seamus Milne as his communications director. The new appointee had praised Hamas for their spirit of resistance.[7]

A second category of misdemeanor is Corbyn's relationships with Holocaust distorters. He participated annually in gatherings of a charity led by Holocaust denier Paul Eisen and gave a donation.[8] Thereafter, it became known that in 2010, on Holocaust Memorial Day, Corbyn held a meeting in parliament where the Netherlands' best known Jewish antisemite Hajo Meyer compared Israel to the Nazis. The latter has done so frequently including in Germany. A Holocaust survivor claims that Corbyn told a policeman which protesters he wanted removed from that meeting.[9, 10] Only eight years later Corbyn apologized for attending the meeting.[11, 12, 13] Both Corbyn and Labour Shadow Chancellor of the Exchequer, John McDonell signed a parliamentary motion proposing that Holocaust Memorial Day be renamed Genocide Memorial Day.[14, 15] In 2012, McDonell accused Israel of attempting to commit genocide against the Palestinians.[16]

A third category of Corbyn's wrongdoings concern extreme anti-Israel incitement. Scattered through Dave Rich's 2016 book, The Left's Jewish Problem, is substantial information about this. Corbyn, for instance chaired a conference which included talks on apartheid in Israel and Western imperialism and anti-Arab racism.[17] Rich also writes that Corbyn sponsored and supported throughout the 1980s the Labour Movement Campaign for Palestine (LMCP). This group wanted "to eradicate Zionism while it supported a democratic secular state in place of Israel."[18]

In 2011, Corbyn presented his opinion on the BBC on a state-funded

Iranian TV program. He said about the British broadcaster that "there is a bias toward saying that Israel is a democracy in the Middle East, Israel has a right to exist, Israel has its security concerns."[19]

In 2012, Corbyn promoted a conspiracy theory about Israel aired on an Iranian channel. He suggested that it was in "Israel's interest to kill Egyptians in an attack by Islamic Jihadists." He also said: "I suspect the hand of Israel in this whole process of destabilization."[20] In 2018, Corbyn attended a Passover seder with members of the small Jewdas Group. This radical anti-Zionist Jewish organization has called Israel a "steaming pile of sewage which needs to be properly disposed of."[21] In August 2018, information about a video was disclosed which shows Corbyn in a 2013 speech for the Palestinian Return Centre where he drew comparisons between the actions of the Israeli government and Nazism.[22]

In 2018, the outgoing president of the British Jewish umbrella organization the Board of Deputies Jonathan Arkush, mentioned that Corbyn had been chairman of Stop the War, an organization "which is responsible for some of the worst anti-Israel discourse."[23] Arkush added that Corbyn has antisemitic views and was making Jews question their place in Britain.[24]

A fourth category of Corbyn's wrongdoing concerns antisemitism. In 2012, he endorsed an antisemitic mural on Facebook. For doing this he apologized in 2018.[25] He also was a member of various Facebook groups where antisemitic material was posted.[26]

Corbyn is not the only member of his family who is highly problematic as far as antisemitism is concerned.[27] His brother Piers tweeted that "Jewish conspiracy will force Trump into war just like they did to Hitler."[28] The *Daily Mail* discovered a Nazi cartoon on his youngest son Tommy's Facebook page. The latter also was a member of several antisemitic Facebook groups.[29]

If only previous Labour leaders and their staff had been more alert, Corbyn would have been expelled from the party already a number of years ago. Among them is the main culprit for this failure, Corbyn's predecessor as Labour leader Ed Miliband. A mainstream party should not have selfdefined "friends" and "brothers" of terrorists in its ranks. The same is true for those who support Holocaust distorters. Corbyn belongs in both categories.

Besa Center, August 16, 2018

1   www.timesofisrael.com/cameron-demands-corbyn-renounce-friends-hamas-hezbollah/; www.theguardian.com/politics/2016/jul/04/jeremy-corbyn-says-he-regrets-calling-hamas-and-hezbollah-friends

2   www.dailymail.co.uk/news/article-6016733/Jeremy-Corbyn-praises-release-Hamas-terrorist-brothers-video.html

3   www.dailymail.co.uk/news/article-4571924/Corbyn-s-30-years-talking-terrorists.html

4   www.telegraph.co.uk/news/politics/Jeremy_Corbyn/11938212/Jeremy-Corbyn-campaign-part-funded-by-Hamas.html

5   www.dailymail.co.uk/news/article-6048807/Photos-Labour-leader-Corbyn-tribute-event-Palestine-martyrs-linked-Munich-massacre.html

6   www.telegraph.co.uk/news/politics/Jeremy_Corbyn/11938212/Jeremy-Corbyn-campaign-part-funded-by-Hamas.html

7   www.theguardian.com/politics/2016/jul/04/jeremy-corbyn-says-he-regrets-calling-hamas-and-hezbollah-friends

8   www.dailymail.co.uk/news/article-3187428/Jeremy-Corbyn-s-links-notorious-Holocaust-denier-revealed.html

9   www.thejc.com/news/uk-news/holocaust-survivor-jeremy-corbyn-had-police-remove-protestors-at-event-comparing-israel-to-nazis-1.467842

10 www.dailymail.co.uk/news/article-6017199/Holocaust-survivors-anger-day-Corbyn-shut-dissent.html

11 www.mirror.co.uk/news/politics/jeremy-corbyn-john-mcdonnell-called-13017046

12 www.timesofisrael.com/corbyn-sorry-for-attending-holocaust-memorial-event-comparing-israel-to-nazis/

13 www.theguardian.com/politics/2018/aug/01/jeremy-corbyn-issues-apology-in-labour-antisemitism-row

14 www.dailymail.co.uk/news/article-6016733/Jeremy-Corbyn-praises-release-Hamas-terrorist-brothers-video.html

15 jewishnews.timesofisrael.com/corbyn-led-motion-rename-holocaust-memorial-day-genocide-memorial-day/

16 www.telegraph.co.uk/politics/2018/08/08/john-mcdonnell-condemned-claiming-israel-attempting-carry-genocide/

17 Dave Rich, *The Left's Jewish Problem. Jeremy Corbyn, Israel and Antisemitism* (London: Biteback Publishing Ltd, 2016) 147.

18 Ibid., 148.

19 www.thejc.com/news/uk-news/new-footage-shows-corbyn-saying-bbc-has-bias-towards-saying-israel-has-a-right-to-exist-1.468101

20 www.jpost.com/Diaspora/UK-Labour-leader-Corbyn-voices-conspiracy-theory-against-Israel-in-2012-563714

21 www.theguardian.com/politics/2018/apr/03/jeremy-corbyn-called-irresponsi-ble-after-attending-radical-jewish-event

22 news.sky.com/story/labour-anti-semitism-row-jeremy-corbyn-faces-new-claims-he-compared-israel-to-nazis-11469216

23 news.sky.com/story/jeremy-corbyn-has-anti-semitic-views-says-jewish-leader-jonathan-arkush-11390816

24 www.thejc.com/news/uk-news/jeremy-corbyn-has-antisemitic-views-says-jonathan-arkush-1.464806

25 www.theguardian.com/commentisfree/2018/mar/25/jeremy-corbyn-regret-antisemitic-incidents-jews

26 www.jpost.com/Diaspora/Jeremy-Corbyn-deletes-personal-Facebook-page-amid-antisemitism-crisis-547650

27 www.dailymail.co.uk/news/article-4597490/Internet-swoons-Jeremy-Corbyn-s-son.html

28 antisemitism.uk/piers-corbyn-tweets-jewish-conspiracy-will-force-trump-into-war-just-like-they-did-to-hitler/

29 www.dailymail.co.uk/news/article-5560181/The-vile-anti-Semitic-Facebook-sites-endorsed-Jeremy-Corbyns-Labour-activist-son.html

Widespread Muslim Antisemitism in France

In most European countries, no quantitative data is available on Muslim antisemitism. Yet it is known that members of the Muslim community are behind much aggression and conduct extreme verbal attacks and slurs against Jews. A number of Jews have been murdered by Muslims in France over the past decades. There have also been attempts at pogroms.

A 2014 study by Fondapol titled *Antisemitism in French Public Opinion* and authored by Dominique Reynié provides many insights into antisemitism in France. Muslims are one segment of society on which the study focuses. The authors have also investigated the extreme right and extreme left. These however require separate analysis.

In French general society, 25 percent of the population has antisemitic prejudices. The study concludes that such prejudices against Jews among Muslims are two or three times as widespread. The study's authors have divided the Muslim population into three categories: practicing Muslims, who both believe and practice Islam, those who only believe, and those who are of Muslim origin. The category of those who practice Islam, accounts for 42 percent of Muslims in France. Those who believe are 34 percent and those of Muslim origin are 21 percent. Another 3 percent self-define as not being religious.

The Fondapol researchers asked six questions for this particular study:

1   Do Jews use the stories of victims of Nazi genocide during the Second World War for their own purposes?
2   Do Jews have too much power in the field of economy and finance?
3   Do Jews have too much power in the media?
4   Do Jews wield too much political power?
5   Is there a Zionist conspiracy at world level?
6   Are the Jews responsible for the current economic crises?

A few examples of the study's findings will serve to show the strong anti-semitism among Muslims in France. Nineteen percent of the general French population are of the opinion that Jews have too much power in politics. Among all Muslims, the percentage is 51 percent. Yet, if we break this figure down by category, among those who self-define as only of Muslim origin, the figure is 37 percent. For those who believe in Islam it is 49 percent and for practicing Muslims the figure is 63 percent.

The percentage of Muslims who answered negatively to all six questions about antisemitic prejudices is small. Only 17 percent of the Muslims answered "no" to all questions. There is hardly a distinction between practicing Muslims and those who just believe, respectively 13 percent and 14 percent. For those of Muslim origin, the percentage is substantially higher, yet again they are only a minority, 27 percent.

A study in France in 2005 had already shown that anti-Jewish prejudice was prevalent particularly among religious Muslims. Forty-six percent held such sentiments compared to 30 percent of non-practicing Muslims. Only 28 percent of religious Muslims in France were found to be totally free of such prejudice. Even though the studies are not comparable, their main findings about Muslim antisemitism point in the same direction.

The high percentages of antisemitism among French Muslims shouldn't come as a surprise. The great majority of these are immigrants from North African countries or descendants from such immigrants. The population of these countries is among the most antisemitic in the world.

The French comedian, Dieudonné, is considered one of the most extreme French antisemites. Finally many cities decided to prohibit his performances. Fifty seven percent of French Muslims consider that this antisemite was right in saying that Zionism is an international organization which tries to influence the world and society for the benefit of the Jews; 64 percent of practicing Muslims agree with this.

Forty six percent of Muslims think that Zionism is a racist ideology as opposed to 23 percent of the French general population. Sixty-six percent of Muslims think that Zionism is an ideology that serves Israel to justify a policy of occupation and colonization of Palestinian Arab territories. All the above answers group Jews as a collectivity which is typical of antisemitic thinking. In reality, attitudes concerning many issues and political convictions among Jews vary greatly.

Concerning attitudes toward individual Jews, prejudices of Muslims are also more pronounced than of the general population. Thirty three percent of Muslims and 43 percent of those who practice do not want a Jew as president of France as opposed to 21 percent of all French citizens. Twenty six percent of Muslims and 33 percent of those who practice do not want to vote for a Jewish mayor as opposed to 14 percent of the French. Twenty two percent of Muslims and 30 percent of those who practice do not want a Jewish boss as opposed to 10 percent of the general population. Eighteen percent of Muslims and 23 percent of those who practice do not want a Jewish banker as opposed to 10 percent of the general population.

Twelve percent of the French do not agree with teaching the Holocaust in schools. Twenty four percent of Muslims and 28 percent of those who practice do not agree with such Holocaust education. Three percent of the French population are Holocaust deniers either to a certain extent or totally. Among Muslims overall the figure is 5 percent agreeing to the false claim that the number of victims is greatly exaggerated. Yet among those who practice the figure is 8 percent.

All this leads to a clear conclusion: over the past decades French governments, whether socialist or right of center, have let huge numbers of antisemitic immigrants into their country.

Israel National News, March 27, 2018

Fifteen Years Too Late: French Manifesto Against Muslim Antisemitism

Jointly written with Irene Kuruc

Some fifteen years too late, more than 250 French personalities, both Jews and non-Jews have signed in 2018 a strong manifesto against Muslim antisemitism. This document sums up the main elements of violence and incitement against Jews emanating from parts of this immigrant community.

The manifesto starts off by stating that antisemitism isn't an issue of the Jews, but of the French people. It praises the French for their resilience after each Islamist terror attack. It should be noted here that "Islamist" is a politically correct expression used instead of "Muslim." Yet Islam's adherents are a continuum between two extremes. On the one outmost side there are radical violent Muslims who call for murder. On the other there are individuals who are Muslims in name only because they were born as such.

The document goes on to say that France has become a theatre of murderous antisemitism. It adds that terror is expanding, condemned by the public while the media practice silence. The manifesto then refers to the rhetoric of the previous Prime Minister Manuel Valls, who at that time was still a socialist. In parliament, he said, "France without Jews will no longer be France."[1] It sounds meaningful, but what is France really?

In Vichy France, the Jews were excluded and persecuted. Yet the government of this entity without Jews was a fully legitimate expression of France as has been stated by the last four French presidents; Jacques Chirac, Nicolas Sarkozy, François Hollande, and Emanuel Macron. The France of today, with an estimated 6 million Muslims, is very different from the country it was before most of these immigrants came in.

The document then refers to the murder by radical Islamists of eleven Jews and the torture of others because they were Jews. The names of most murdered are not given. The actual number is twelve. The manifesto probably doesn't include the murder in 2003 of Sebastien Selam by Adel Amastaibou.[2]

The manifesto's next paragraph explains that the societal emphasis on Islamophobia hides the fact that French Jews are twenty five times more at risk to be attacked than French Muslims. It adds that 10 percent of Jewish inhabitants of the central region of France had to move because they were no longer safe in their neighborhoods nor could their children attend public schools. This is called "silent ethnic cleansing."

Another hard-hitting paragraph follows. After asking why all this is occurring, the answer given is Islamist radicalization and the antisemitism it promotes. The document also exposes part of the French elites who see this as an expression of a social revolution, however, the same phenomena can be found in such diverse societies as Denmark, Afghanistan, Mali and Germany.

The signatories' conclusion is that in addition to the classic antisemitism of the extreme right, there is also antisemitism of the radical left. In anti-Zionism it has found its alibi of transforming murderers of Jews into victims of society. This is possible because of the electoral reality that the French Muslim vote is ten times more numerous than the Jewish vote.

The last section of the manifesto deals with what is expected from Islam in France. The first paragraph recalls the demonstration after the murder of Mireille Knoll by a Muslim in March 2018.[3] It mentions that there were also imams among the demonstrators. It is stated that these imams were aware that Muslim antisemitism is the greatest danger to Islam as well as to the world of peace and freedom in which they have chosen to reside. Yet, most of these imams require police protection. This reflects the terror Islamists exercise against French Muslims.

Unfortunately, the next poorly thought through paragraph taints what could have been a flawless description and accusation of the major antisemitic criminality and hatred coming out of parts of the French Muslim community. The document asks Muslim theologians to declare obsolete the texts of the Quran which call for the murder and punishment of Jews, Christians and non-believers. This change is considered necessary so that Muslim believers can no longer base their actions on a holy text when committing crimes.

Non-Muslims should not however involve themselves in Islamic theological issues. The signatories could have made a far more compelling statement saying: "It is the moral duty of all Muslim religious and lay leaders in France to come out forcefully against terror and criminality committed by members of the Muslim community against Jews as well as against others." The document concludes by demanding that the fight against antisemitism becomes a national cause before it is too late.

The manifesto was written by a non-Jew, Philippe Val, the former director of the weekly, *Charlie Hebdo*. In January 2015, Muslim murderers killed 12 of its staff members and injured 11 others.[4] Among the manifesto's signatories are former President Nicolas Sarkozy, former Prime Minister Manual Valls and Laurent Wauquiez the leader of the Republicans, the country's second largest party. Others include former Republican Prime Minister Jean-Pierre Raffarin and the former Paris mayor, Bertrand Delanoe, a socialist. The French Minister of Justice, Nicole Beloubet, said that she would have been willing to sign the document as well.[5]

One must regret its shortcomings, but despite them the manifesto is one of the most forceful documents against the widespread antisemitism among Muslims and their non-Muslim allies.

The Jerusalem Post, May 20, 2018

1   www.youtube.com/watch?v=k9M1Cq9nQoI
2   www.ynetnews.com/articles/0,7340,L-3829946,00.html
3   www.liberation.fr/france/2018/03/29/hommage-a-mireille-knoll-une-marche-blanche-mouvementee_1639751
4   edition.cnn.com/2015/01/21/europe/2015-paris-terror-attacks-fast-facts/index.html
5   fr.timesofisrael.com/belloubet-aurait-pu-signer-le-manifeste-contre-le-nouvel-antisemitisme/

Contemporary American Antisemitism

Interview with Alvin Rosenfeld

Professor Alvin H. Rosenfeld holds the Irving M. Glazer Chair in Jewish Studies at Indiana University and is Director of the university's Institute for the Study of Contemporary Antisemitism. He has written widely on the Holocaust, Jewish literature, and antisemitism.

"While American history is not free of antisemitism, there is a substantial contrast to the situation of Jews in several European countries today. American Jews do not typically encounter any ongoing, seriously threatening anti-Jewish hostility. Unlike Jewish residents of Christian and Muslim lands who suffered over the centuries from more systematic intolerance and persecution, Jews in the US have never faced large-scale pogroms or other organized forms of mass violence.

"In earlier decades, social antisemitism restricted Jews from certain forms of employment, residential areas, some universities, social clubs, holiday resorts and so on. By and large, such discriminatory exclusion of Jews no longer exists in the US Acts of aggression against individual Jews and Jewish institutions occasionally occur, but these tend to be episodic and not chronic or continuous. The great majority of American Jews go about their daily lives without having to deal with overt antagonism directed against them. They are however aware of the upsurge of antisemitism elsewhere in the world. One cannot take for granted that America will remain immune from such hatreds.

"A few previously unknown or marginal figures, mostly affiliated with the newly vocal white supremacist movement, are currently running for political office and have made outrageously antisemitic statements. They are always quickly denounced by their political parties for doing so. Yet the fact that they have a public platform at all for voicing wild conspiracy theories about Jewish "power" and other anti-Jewish canards seems to reflect a weakening of the taboos previously in place against the open expression of Jew-hatred. Alert to these hostile developments abroad and, now, also to some degree at home, many American Jews live with feelings of social and political unease that are new to most of them.

"According to annual reports by the FBI, Jews are the most targeted religious group in America. By contrast, the most recent Pew poll found that Jews are also the most admired religious group in the country. The picture is thus mixed. The most recent report of the Anti-Defamation League records a 57 percent increase in antisemitic incidents in 2017 over the previous year. Some 1,986 events and activities were directed against Jews and Jewish institutions. The numbers are troubling, although almost all incidents involved acts of vandalism and verbal abuse and not physical assaults.

"Campuses are probably the main areas of antisemitism. America has over 4,000 colleges and universities. The great majority of these are free of chronic antisemitic activities and anti-Israel incitement. However, at some of the country's more elite universities, especially on the east and west coasts, BDS, Israel Apartheid Week, and other manifestations of extreme antagonism to Zionism and Israel take place. This has introduced what many observers see as a hostile environment for Jewish students, faculty members, and others.

"Such antagonisms, when they occur, are never campus-wide. They tend to originate among activist students and some faculty members within several humanities and social science departments. Campus science departments, business schools, medical schools, agricultural colleges, etc., are rarely, if ever, hospitable to such hostility. Activists include people in some radicalized Muslim student organizations, left-wing political groups, Jewish Voice for Peace, and others allied with these.

"White nationalist and white supremacist groups have long existed on the margins of American society. More recently, they have felt emboldened and are making efforts, as in the much-publicized 2017 Charlottesville rally, to enter the mainstream. Their numbers are small, but they have an active on-line existence and, more recently, a negligible but visible public presence. The so-called 'alt-right' refers to a loose, diverse, and still amorphous collection of white populist and nationalist groups. They range from Ku Klux Klan and overt Nazi groups, which are proudly antisemitic, to less militant and to date, less openly antisemitic white 'pride' groups. All bear watching.

"There is no well-defined, well-organized 'left wing' in the US as in the European model. Yet some Americans who identify as political 'progressives,' including numbers of Jews, devote a lot of time and energy to actively opposing Israel's present government, policies, and actions. At their most extreme, as in Jewish Voice for Peace, they are passionately and determinedly 'anti-Zionist.' They oppose Israel's very existence as a Jewish majority state. They often collaborate, on campuses and elsewhere, with BDS supporters and other extreme anti-Israel and sometimes, antisemitic political allies. Ultra-Orthodox Jewish anti-Israelism is a minor affair and lacks any appreciable political weight.

"As far as Muslims are concerned, their current presence in America is relatively small. For the most part they are not apt to take to the streets, as in Paris, London, and elsewhere in large and hostile anti-Israel demonstrations. From time to time, imams in some American mosques voice extreme Jihadist sentiments, sometimes even calling for the death of Jews and the destruction of Israel. A number of such events have been recorded by the MEMRI organization. To date, these voices seem untypical and unrepresentative of majority American Muslim sentiment.

"Louis Farrakhan, the leader of the Nation of Islam is one of America's most vocal and tireless antisemites. He persists in giving speeches about 'Satanic Jews,' Jewish 'evil' and 'corruption.' Farrakhan is more than a minor irritant but also less than a major influence. His immediate following in Chicago is not large. Yet it is possible that some of those who hear his impassioned words may be sympathetic to his calls to put an end to the Jews and may be inclined to act on those ideas.

"One has to realize that America is a polarized society. That divisiveness long precedes President Trump. There is no doubt that it has increased since he took office. There are many social, cultural, religious, anti-religious, economic and political reasons for these sharp and angry divisions. It would be simplistic and wrong to pin them all on the present incumbent in the White House. Nevertheless, he is an extremely unconventional political leader and has introduced an angry, hostile, often aggressive rhetoric into mainstream discourse. Many others now do the same. As a result, the social and political climate is overwrought.

"To date, President Trump's policies toward Israel have been extremely supportive. His recognition of Jerusalem as its capital and the move of the American embassy to Jerusalem were diplomatically bold and courageous steps. Most American Jews, but by no means all, favor these actions.

"American Jews are overwhelmingly liberal in their political attitudes, do not favor President Trump, and many are also at odds with Netanyahu and Israeli policies. This is especially the case with Reform and secular Jews. Most Conservative Jews and Orthodox Jews appreciate President Trump's stance toward Israel and applaud the diplomatic moves he has taken to date. At the same time, he is a mercurial political leader, and there is some concern about his next moves regarding Israel and other nations in the Middle East.

"Liberal anti-Israelism is a prominent force. Its presence, especially within the left wing of the Democratic party and among younger Jews, is growing. American Jews are badly split along both religious and political lines. One can no longer speak of anything like a unified American Jewish 'community.' As poll after poll reveals, the fracture lines are obvious. Among the splits, conflicting attitudes among American Jews toward the Jewish state have intensified and are especially worrisome. To date, no American Jewish leader of any stature has emerged to address these divisions in any compelling and healing way. That's very much needed, but I see no signs of it happening anytime soon."

Israel National News, June 22, 2018

The Mahathir Affair:
A Case Study in Mainstream Islamic Antisemitism

Muslims and Jews: A Worldwide Confrontation?

In October 2003, in Putrajaya, Malaysia, the 10th Summit of the Organization of the Islamic Corporation (OIC), took place. In his speech, there Malaysian Prime Minister Mahathir Mohamad represented relations between Muslims and Jews as a worldwide frontal confrontation. Though he only devoted a few sentences to Jews, he presented some new examples of what antisemitism studies call "the theory of Jewish conspiracy." Mahathir said: "1.3 billion Muslims cannot be defeated by a few million Jews. There must be a way. And we can only find a way if we stop to think, to assess our weaknesses and our strength, to plan, to strategize and then to counter-attack.

"We are actually very strong. 1.3 billion people cannot be simply wiped out. The Europeans killed six million Jews out of 12 million. But today the Jews rule this world by proxy. They get others to fight and die for them.

"We are up against a people who think. They survived 2000 years of pogroms not by hitting back, but by thinking. They invented and successfully promoted Socialism, Communism, human rights and democracy so that persecuting them would appear to be wrong, so they may enjoy equal rights with others. With these they have now gained control of the most powerful countries and they, this tiny community, have become a world power. We cannot fight them through brawn alone. We must use our brains also."[1]

Creating Myths

The worldwide attention given to Mahathir's antisemitic remarks overshadowed the rest of his speech which contained a number of observations that are typical of much of contemporary discourse by Islamic leaders. Mahathir said: "We are all Muslims. We are all oppressed. We are all being humiliated."

Mahathir added: "We are now 1.3 billion strong. We have the biggest oil reserve in the world. We have great wealth. We are not as ignorant as the *Jahilliah* [the ignorant of the pre-Islamic period] who embraced Islam. We are familiar with the workings of the world's economy and finances. We control 50 out of the 180 countries in the world." He concluded that because Islamic countries do not unite against the outside world, they are not using their power efficiently.

Many of the "facts" Mahathir expressed concerning Muslims were misrepresentations. It is difficult to claim that all Muslims are being humiliated. Many inhabitants of oil-rich countries are quite well-off, where it is Muslims who humiliate other Muslims, sometimes almost treating them like slaves. Mahathir avoided mentioning the near absence of democracy and the presence of major corruption in the Islamic world, responsible for much of its problems. Mahathir replaced these facts with myths.

International Reactions

Mahathir's antisemitic attacks led to many reactions from the Western world. US State Department spokesman Adam Ereli said: "We view them with the contempt and derision they deserve."[2] A few days later at the Asia-Pacific Summit in Bangkok, President Bush told Mahathir—according to White House spokesman Scott McClellan—that his words about the Jews controlling the West by proxy "were wrong and divisive . . . It stands squarely against what I believe."[3] Mahathir, however, denied that Bush had rebuked him.[4]

Australian Prime Minister John Howard commented on Mahathir's OIC speech: "Any suggestion from anybody anywhere in the world of dividing the world into Jewish and non-Jewish groupings is historically indefensible and wrong and something that most Australians would regard as quite repugnant."[5]

Later, at the Asia-Pacific Summit, Australian Foreign Minister Alexander Downer declared: "We regard antisemitism as unacceptable and the Australian government hopes that there won't be further comments of this kind."[6]

The Foreign Minister of New Zealand, Phil Goff, said: "We're concerned about language that brings back memories of so-called Jewish conspiracies."[7]

Outgoing Canadian Prime Minister Jean Chrétien, who also attended the Asia-Pacific Summit, refused to condemn Mahathir personally when asked to do so at a press conference in Bangkok, and referred to an earlier statement by his foreign ministry. The *Toronto Star* wrote, "Jean Chrétien suffered an unexpected casualty yesterday. He lost his tongue . . . Chrétien greeted Mahathir with a warm handshake, as many leaders did. But he kept his mouth shut on the subject of antisemitism."[8]

European Union Divisiveness

British Foreign Minister Jack Straw summoned the Malaysian high commissioner to complain about Mahathir's remarks. The Foreign Office stated: "It is particularly regrettable that some positive and welcome messages in Mahathir's speech, such as the emphasis on negotiation being the path to peace, were obscured and overshadowed by racist remarks."[9] Also, the German Foreign Office summoned Malaysian diplomats in order to complain.[10]

Italy at the time held held the presidency of the European Union. Italian Foreign Minister Franco Frattini told reporters: "The [Malaysian] Prime Minister used expressions that were gravely offensive, very strongly antisemitic and . . . strongly counter to principles of tolerance, dialogue, and understanding between the Western world and the Islamic world."[11]

Since an EU summit was being held at the same time, it was proposed to include a condemnation of Mahathir's remarks in the summit's 19-page final statement. According to *Haaretz*, the draft stated: "his unacceptable comments hinder all our efforts to further inter-ethnic and religious harmony, and have no place in a decent world. Such false and antisemitic remarks are as offensive to Muslims as they are to others."[12]

However, French President Jacques Chirac opposed the inclusion of these lines in the summit statement, and Greek Prime Minister Costas Simitis supported Chirac, *Haaretz* reported. According to a statement issued by the

French Embassy in Israel, Chirac condemned Mahathir's remarks but considered the EU summit an inappropriate place to state this. French Embassy spokesman Pierre Filatoff told Agence France-Presse that "the EU rules did not allow such declarations (condemning antisemitism) to be integrated in such documents."[13] Apparently, the leaders of most EU countries thought differently.

Thus, it was decided that the Italian presidency of the Council of the European Union would post a statement on its website, saying: "The EU deeply deplores the comments made earlier today by Dr. Mahathir in his speech at the opening of the 10th session of the Islamic Summit conference in Putrajaya, Malaysia . . . Such words hinder all our efforts to further inter-ethnic and religious harmony, and have absolutely no place in a tolerant world."[14]

Chirac's Ambiguity Toward Jews Exposed

By now President Chirac had much reason to be satisfied. He had once again proven his friendship for the Islamic world. He vetoed the condemnation of one of their leaders in a major EU meeting, and substituted instead an Italian statement on an EU website, as well as a statement by the French Embassy in Israel.

It was Mahathir's reaction, however, which exposed Chirac. The Malaysian Prime Minister thanked Chirac for blocking the EU summit declaration which intended to deplore his speech. The Malaysian daily *The Star* quoted Mahathir on Chirac: "I think he understands better. Anybody who reads the whole speech through will understand what I said. In fact, I was worried that the Muslims would be against me, but it was the Europeans who were against me. I can't understand them."[15]

Chirac was now caught in a situation where he had to minimize the damage. Had he not reacted, this would have exposed him as condoning antisemitism and would have shown the statement of the French Embassy in Israel to be a minor, meaningless gesture toward the Jews.

Thus, Chirac replied to Mahathir on October 19, saying, "your remarks on the role of Jews provoked strong disapproval in France and around the world."[16] Chirac also expressed his approval of Mahathir's calling for an end to Palestinian suicide attacks on Israelis. Yet the French were three days late in making a specific statement from Paris, thus further exposing Chirac's ambivalence toward the Jews. Chirac is facing increasing difficulty in maintaining the facade that he is critical toward Israel but friendly toward the Jews.

In an interview shortly thereafter, Israel Singer, Chairman of the World Jewish Congress Executive, noted that during the restitution negotiations of the 1990s, Chirac's behavior followed a classic pattern of being anti-Israel and then trying to compensate by being supportive of diaspora Jewry. On a later occasion, however, Chirac told Singer that Jews are the cause of antisemitism in France and everywhere else.[17]

In May 2003, at a meeting in Paris with leaders of the Simon Wiesenthal Center (SWC), Chirac denied the existence of antisemitism in France. He claimed that attacks on Jews were only suburban hooliganism. Chirac also mentioned that a year earlier he had invited a Palestinian student in France to lunch at the Elysee Palace after the student had told him he wanted to return to Palestine to kill Jews. When the SWC leaders went to their next meeting not far from Chirac's residence, some of them who wear *yarmulkes* were insulted by bystanders' antisemitic remarks, such as: "Jews get out of France."

The Greek Role

France's allies in the Mahathir affair—the Greek Socialists—have a long history of anti-Jewish racism. Already in 1982, Socialist Prime Minister Andreas Papandreou—father of the Foreign Minister George Papandreou at the time—publicly compared the Israelis to the Nazis.[18]

Widespread antisemitism among Greek politicians, the press, and throughout society is being increasingly exposed by the SWC. At the OSCE/ODHIR Human Dimension Meeting in Warsaw on October 14, 2003, Dr. Shimon Samuels of the SWC presented a lengthy report entitled, "Twenty Months of Anti-Semitic Invective in Greece, March 2002–October 2003." He called for the Greek government to take appropriate measures against the antisemitic offensive in its country, which violates the EU's provisions and international conventions.[19]

Press Reactions

The Western press reported extensively on the Mahathir affair. *The New York Times* wrote in an editorial: "Sympathy for the Muslims' plight must not be confused with the acceptance of racism. Most Muslims have indeed been shoddily treated—by their own leaders, who gather at feckless summit meetings instead of offering their people what they most need: human rights, education, and democracy. The European Union was asked to condemn Mr. Mahathir's speech in its statement yesterday ending its own summit. It chose not to, adding a concern that displays of antisemitism are being met with inexcusable nonchalance."[20]

A few days later, the paper balanced these views with a column by Paul Krugman largely blaming the United States for the anti-Americanism in the Muslim world. Krugman called Mahathir's remarks "inexcusable," yet tried to explain them.[21] Krugman was smarter than Mahathir. When he stated that Bush backs Sharon unconditionally, this is a much more elegant way of stating the fallacy that the Jews run the world by proxy.

Columnist Richard Cohen in the *Washington Post* referred to the standing ovation the summit's audience gave Mahathir for his speech: "Mahathir's claque included Saudi Arabia's Crown Prince Abdullah, Pakistan's President Pervez Musharraf, our guy in Afghanistan, Hamid Karzai, and even Russia's Vladimir Putin, representing his country's large Muslim minority . . . But what corrupts and enfeebles large parts of the Islamic world is not Jews in either New York or Tel Aviv but its own self-serving and inept leadership—in other words, some of the very people who stood and cheered the speech."[22]

Singapore's *Straits Times* political editor Zuraidah Ibrahim commented on the speech: "To give it the kindest spin possible, one could say that he was only trying to rally Muslims to learn from the Jews as they seek to slough off the humiliation and oppression of centuries. That he was lauding the Jews for setting a positive example: they responded to persecution by using their brains, not just their brawn. But to leave it at that would be to gloss over his dangerous and irresponsible portrayal of Muslims as being in an epic confrontation against the Jews. The sad truth, however, is that it is a line one has heard said among Muslims. Must it be that way? Must Muslims view the world in such foreboding terms, of them versus us? . . . It is easy to reduce all of the world's problems to either Islamic terrorism or a Jewish conspiracy. But that doesn't mean it is right."[23]

The French daily *Le Monde* wrote in an editorial that nobody had left the hall when Mahathir voiced his antisemitic comments. The author wondered why nobody had left and suggested: "Not out of courtesy for the host of this tenth summit. Not out of apathy. For a much more severe reason. Because the audience approved. Because such words are common currency in the Arab Islamic world where they pass for evident truth and are regularly uttered by government, the press—which is most often controlled—and teachers . . . and this direct form of racism, purely and simply is practiced as a normal category of the 'political debate'—which alas has penetrated some of our [French] suburbs." The paper concluded that Mahathir has allowed himself to announce peaceful means to fight against the "Jews." He should know that his speech nourishes terrorism.[24]

Jewish Reactions

The Israeli Foreign Ministry condemned Mahathir's speech. So did Minister Natan Sharansky, saying: "This is the first time since World War II that antisemitism in its most primitive and vulgar form constitutes the official agenda of a respected international political forum which, in this instance, is composed of nearly one-third of the world. This occurrence is made possible only because of the indifference and lack of concern demonstrated by the Western world when confronted by blatant antisemitism. We all know how these things begin—always with Jews—but history has taught us again and again that it never ends with the Jews."[25]

David Harris, executive director of the American Jewish Committee, said: "This kind of language, which attributes to Jews a variety of demonic powers, is reminiscent of the crudest and most vile antisemitism in history."[26] Later he said: "This is a good test in terms of international reaction to bigotry. Is it condemnation followed by business as usual, or are there teeth to the denunciation?"[27]

The SWC condemned Mahathir's speech as: "A diatribe that would have made Hitler and Goebbels proud . . . Rabbi Abraham Cooper, associate dean of the SWC, blasted Mahathir as a 'dangerous racist whose hateful rhetoric is a virtual invitation for further antisemitic attacks.'"[28]

The Anti-Defamation League (ADL) in a press release "expressed appreciation to those countries and leaders who strongly condemned the vehemently antisemitic speech by Mahathir . . . but called those who acquiesced or were silent in their reaction to the speech, 'willingly complicit in spreading Mahathir's hate.'"[29]

ADL national director Abraham Foxman expressed specific appreciation to the EU, Italy, Spain, and Germany, and added, "We are especially outraged by the actions of French President Jacques Chirac and Greek Prime Minister Costas Simitis to block the inclusion of a condemnation of Mahathir's antisemitic speech in the official statement of an EU summit. By their disgraceful behavior, these countries are willingly complicit in spreading these words of hate."[30]

Colin Rubenstein, executive director of the Australia/Israel and Jewish Affairs Council (AIJAC), said that Mahathir's "vile assertions were probably the most blatant and viciously antisemitic remarks made publicly by any major world figure in decades."[31]

Amnon Dankner, editor of the Israeli daily *Maariv,* published a harsh criticism of Chirac's behavior. In a more moderate yet still critical way, the French-Jewish umbrella organization CRIF came out against the EU and French government's attitude, saying: "It seems to us that the protest of the European Union is insufficient and purely formal. Beyond a formal letter to the Prime Minister of Malaysia, we expect from France a strong, solemn statement of global impact against barbarous utterances."[32] Some French-Israeli tensions were a further fall-out of the Mahathir affair.

Mahathir's Antisemitic Past

Mahathir has a long history of making antisemitic remarks. According to the *BBC News* website, already in 1970—long before he became Prime Minister—Mahathir said, "The Jews, for example, are not merely hook-nosed, but understand money instinctively."[33]

In December 1997, the World Jewish Congress (WJC) published a policy dispatch devoted to Malaysian antisemitism under Mahathir. It said, inter alia, "in 1983, the *Protocols of the Elders of Zion* was printed in Malaysia . . . In a 1986 speech at a meeting of the Non-Aligned Movement, Mahathir stated that 'the expulsion of Jews from the Holy Land 2,000 years ago and the Nazi oppression of Jews have taught them nothing. If anything at all, it has transformed the Jews into the very monsters that they condemn so roundly in their propaganda material. They have been pupils of the late Dr. Goebbels.'"[34]

In May 1998, *Business Week* published a letter from ADL national director Abraham Foxman entitled, "Mahathir's Anti-Semitism is an Old Story," in which he wrote: "Although Malaysian Prime Minister Mahathir Mohamad attempts to justify anti-Jewish remarks he made earlier this year, we must remember that those distasteful comments are consistent with his long history of antisemitism and belief in a Jewish conspiracy to bring about the downfall of Malaysia. So his recent comments blaming a Jewish conspiracy for Malaysia's economic fall came as no surprise."[35]

At the 1999 Davos economic conference, Mahathir criticized the Jews using arguments reminiscent of the *Protocols of the Elders of Zion*. He blamed the Jewish connection for Asia's economic problems.[36]

Retired Israeli ambassador Moshe Yegar, who in the 1960s lived in Malaysia for more than a year, published an essay in summer 2003 entitled: "Malaysia: Anti-Semitic Policy Without Jews." In it, he mentioned how in June 1983 the country's Prime Minister condemned Israel for the campaign in Lebanon, calling it "the most immoral government in the world."[37] In 1997, Mahathir claimed his government was afraid the Jews were planning to destroy Malaysia's economy and that of other Muslim countries.[38]

Malaysia's Three-Fold Strategy of Reaction

In view of the unexpected major criticism, Malaysia developed a three-fold strategy of reaction. The first element was to try to create a smokescreen through contradictory declarations of senior politicians. In an interview with Australian television's Nine Network, Malaysian Foreign Minister Syed Hamid Albar said that Mahathir had been misunderstood. He added: "I am confident he has no anti-Jewish feeling."[39] Yet the next day, Mahathir said: "I have been accused of being antisemitic when what I said was only based on facts. That is my perception of things." He added: "These are facts of history and to tell me that I cannot mention facts of history is to deny me my right to free speech."[40] He also continued to fan the antisemitic flames on the following days.

A second element in the Malaysian strategy of reaction was to mobilize other Islamic leaders to support Mahathir or explain that he was misinterpreted. Iranian President Mohammad Khatami claimed that accusing Mahathir of being antisemitic was "Western propaganda . . . No Muslim is antisemitic."[41]

Pakistani President General Pervez Musharraf said at a press conference, "I don't think he called for war against the Jews or anything like that, he expressed his own thoughts but I'm very sure he did not ask Muslims to go to war with anyone."[42] The President of Afghanistan, Hamid Karzai, said: "Dr. Mahathir was just talking about issues confronting the Muslim world and what Muslims should do."[43]

Egyptian Foreign Minister Ahmad Maher argued that Mahathir's remarks had been taken out of context. If one read the entire speech, it would show that he "had in fact made a shrewd and deep assessment of the problems facing the Muslims."[44] Farouk Kaddoumi of the PLO observed that Mahathir spoke the truth, "but Israel and their sympathizers tend to regard any statement against them as antisemitic. They accuse us while they occupy our country, kill our people, and claim that we are terrorists."[45]

Abdikassim Salad Hassan, President of Somalia, stated: "My entourage and I found Dr. Mahathir's speech very straightforward and in-depth. He was not trying to incite hatred or incite the Muslims to go to war against the Jews, but in fact his speech was about unity to face the threats from the Jews."[46]

Megawati Sukarnoputri, the Indonesian president, took a similar line. She claimed the foreign media had misinterpreted Mahathir's speech, which was indicative of the information gap between Muslim and non-Muslim countries: "That is why there should be more communication between these two sides, to put through the real message of Islam, which is essentially one of tolerance and moderation. We have to put across our own values."[47]

The third element in the Malaysian government's strategy, the Malaysian media, pointed out that Mahathir had been misinterpreted,[48] while criticizing the reactions of Western leaders. Ahmad A. Talib wrote in the *New Straits Times:* "Imagine. These are reactions from so-called world leaders who have often declared that they are promoters of freedom of speech and a democratic way of life . . . Some of us flipped when we read the news item datelined London: 'UK summons Malaysian diplomat over comments on Jews.' Someone in Kuala Lumpur makes a comment on Jews and a representative of the government is hauled up by a foreign government."[49]

Another of the paper's columnists, Shamsul Akmar, wrote that the question remained whether the Jews controlled the world. He added: "Should the rest of the world also ignore the genocide waged by Israelis against Palestinians just because Washington is silent about it?"[50]

Very few voices in the Islamic media condemned Mahathir's statements, further proving how deep-seated antisemitism is in what is called the "moderate" Islamic world.

Conclusion

The smokescreen the Malaysians tried to create around their Prime Minister's words didn't last very long. On October 21, 2003, Mahathir told the *Bangkok Post:* "Just recently in Japan, the Japanese newspapers put down my talk to me being antisemitic . . . they pick up one sentence in which I said the Jews control the world. Well, the reaction of the world shows that they control the world. The Europeans and the Americans and others want to condemn me when, in fact, one chap said all Muslims are terrorists. Did the EU pass a resolution to say that this is against Muslims?"[51] He added that he has Jews among his friends, thus using a classic line of those who have to explain away their antisemitism. Mahathir has also frequently attacked the United States, Australia, the Europeans, homosexuals, and many others.[52]

The importance of the Mahathir affair is that it has exposed in a short time and in a concentrated way the profound antisemitic thought present among major layers of both Muslim elites and society. There is no shame in publicly using the most vile antisemitic expressions including those from the *Protocols of the Elders of Zion.* This work of falsification is regularly republished throughout the Islamic world.

Mahathir has thus generated a wide-ranging demonstration of mainstream Islamic antisemitism. The Mahathir affair now serves as the core proof of this antisemitism, while the remainder of the abundant anti-Jewish material from the Islamic world serves as supporting evidence for this mainstream racism.

Finally, Mahathir's words at the Islamic summit were applauded and later backed by many others. These reactions show that the Islamic world—in which hardly anybody is democratically elected—is dangerous not only for the Jews but for the rest of humanity as well. Beyond those extremist Muslims who preach genocide using the Arab expression *jihad,* the Mahathir affair has demonstrated how problematic the world of ideas of mainstream Islamic society is for the West. It is also an important case study for the analysis of Western reactions to Islamic antisemitism.

Jerusulam Center for Public Affairs, November 2, 2003

1   News Desk, "Dr. Mahathir Opens 10th OIC Summit," *The Star*, October 16, 2003. (This article contains the full text of the speech.)

2   "What They Say about Mahathir's Remarks on Jews," *Straits Times*, October 19, 2003.

3   Darren Schuettler, "Bush Tells Mahathir His Jew Remarks are 'Wrong,'" Reuters, October 20, 2003.

4   Nirmal Ghosh, "Mahathir Downplays Bush Criticism," *Straits Times*, October 23, 2003.

5   Ibid.

6   "Anti-Jewish Remarks May Mar Mahathir's Political Swan Song," *Sydney Morning Herald*, October 20, 2003.

7   Ibid.

8   Martin Regg Cohn, "Chretien Has No Comment on Mahathir," *Toronto Star*, October 21, 2003.

9   John Aglionby, "West Accuses Malaysian PM of Racism," *The Guardian*, October 18, 2003.

10 Ibid.

11 *Straits Times*, October 19, 2003.

12 Sharon Sadeh, Yoav Stern, and Amiram Barkat, "EU Condemns Malaysian PM's Remarks on Jews, But No Apology is Forthcoming," *Haaretz*, October 19, 2003.

13 "Chirac Backed EU Condemnation of Malaysian PM: Spokeswoman," *EU Business*, October 19, 2003.

14 Italian Presidency of the Council of the European Union [website], October 16, 2003.

15 Devid Rajah and Clarence Chua, "Mahathir Thanks Chirac for Support," *The Star*, October 19, 2003.

16 "France Condemns Mahathir Speech on Jews," Reuters, October 19, 2003.

17 Manfred Gerstenfeld interview with Israel Singer, "Restitution: The Second Round," *Post-Holocaust and Anti-Semitism*, no. 14, November 2, 2003.

18 Daniel Perdurant, "Anti-Semitism in Contemporary Greek Society," *Analysis of Current Trends in Anti-Semitism*, no. 7 (Jerusalem: Hebrew University, 1995) 10.

19 Simon Wiesenthal Center, "Twenty Months of Anti-Semitic Invective in Greece, March 2002–October 2003," October 14, 2003.

20 Editorial, "Islamic Anti-Semitism," *The New York Times*, October 18, 2003.

21 Paul Krugman, "Listening to Mahathir," *The New York Times*, October 21, 2003.

22 Richard Cohen, "Return to Wannsee," *Washington Post*, October 21, 2003.

23 Zuraidah Ibrahim, "Insight: Drop that Jews vs Muslims Worldview," *Sunday Times*, October 18, 2003.

24 "L'editorial du Monde, Antisemitisme," *Le Monde*, October 19, 2003.

25 As communicated by Minister Sharansky's office.

26 American Jewish Committee Press Release, "AJC Condemns Anti-Semitic Remarks by Malaysian Prime Minister," October 16, 2003.

27 Ron Kampeas, "After Mahathir's Anti-Semitic Remarks, Jews Wonder If Outrage Will Yield Change," JTA, October 21, 2003.

28 Simon Wiesenthal Center Press Information, "Mahathir's OIC Diatribe Would Make Hitler and Goebbels Proud and Is a Warrant for Anti-Semitic Terrorism," October 16, 2003.

29 "ADL Statement on World Reaction to Mahathir's Speech," Press Release, October 17, 2003.

30 Ibid.

31 "Jews Condemn Mahathir," News.com.au, October 17, 2003.

32 CRIF, "Chirac Explains He Condemned Malaysia's PM, Denies He Blocked EU Move. Jewish Leaders Not Convinced," October 22, 2003.

33 *BBC News*, August 10, 2003.

34 "The Protocols' Malaysian Style: The Case of Prime Minister Mahathir Mohamad," *World Jewish Congress Policy Dispatch*, no. 24, December 1987.

35 Abraham Foxman, "Mahathir's Anti-Semitism Is an Old Story," *Business Week*, May 14, 2003.

36 Israel Ministry of Foreign Affairs, "The Anti-Semitism Monitoring Forum, Gov-

ernment Secretariat: Report of Anti-Semitic Incidents—February 1999."

37   Moshe Yegar, "Malaysia—Anti-Semitic Policy Without Jews," *Gesher*, Summer 2003, 81.

38   Ibid., 87.

39   "Malaysian Defends PM's Statement on Jews," AP/*The New York Times*, October 19, 2003.

40   "Dr. M Hits Out at the West for Distorting His Speech," *The Star*, October 18, 2003.

41   "Leaders Rally to Defend Dr. Mahathir," *New Straits Times*, October 17, 2003.

42   Ibid.

43   Ibid.

44   Ibid.

45   Ibid.

46   "To the Defense of Dr. Mahathir," *The Star*, October 18, 2003.

47   Ibid.

48   Ashraf Abdullah, "International Media Twisting Dr. M's Words," *New Straits Times*, October 18, 2003.

49   Ahmad A. Talib, "Outcry Over Dr. Mahathir's Remarks Makes No Sense," *New Straits Times*, October 19, 2003.

50   Shamsul Akmar, "The Question Still Is: Do Jews Control the World?" *New Straits Times*, October 18, 2003.

51   Pichai Chuensuksawadi, "Exclusive Interview/Mahathir Mohamad," *Bangkok Post*, October 21, 2003.

52   *BBC News*, August 10, 2003.

The Animalization of the Jews by Its Enemies

On April 25, 2019, *The New York Times* International Edition published a cartoon depicting US president Donald Trump and Israeli Prime Minister Binyamin Netanyahu.[1] A number of its antisemitic characteristics have been described in the paper itself by columnist Brett Stephens.[2] One aspect of the cartoon which merits much wider discussion is the dehumanization of Netanyahu by presenting him as a dog. This 'animalization'—or 'zoomorphism'—is a widespread and ancient antisemitic motif applied both verbally and visually.

In its most extreme form, Jews are depicted as even lower than animals. Nazis called them "microbes" and "vermin,"[3] or just parasites. Dehumanization served as a marketing tool for the Germans' future genocidal extermination campaign. The most extreme Nazi paper, *Der Stürmer*, published a cartoon depicting a Nazi spraying a tree covered in vermin. The caption read: "When the vermin are dead, the German oak will once again flourish."[4] This motif of Jews as a pest has been adopted by America's leading antisemite, Louis Farrakhan. He has referred to Jews as "termites."[5]

The world's leading expert on antisemitic cartoons is Belgian scholar Joël Kotek. He says that in zoomorphic antisemitism Jews have traditionally been drawn as animals or insects:[6] "In Nazi, Soviet and Romanian caricatures, the Jew is often depicted as a spider, perceived as an evil insect. [The cartoonist] Stavro in the [Lebanese] *Daily Star* portrays Ehud Barak with a Star of David on his breast as a spider interrupting the peace process."[7]

Kotek adds: "The two other predominant antisemitic zoomorphic motifs are the blood-thirsty vampire and the octopus. The vampire image is a classic theme used by antisemites. I have not found any other people besides the Jews represented in such a way. This genocide-preparing design originates in Christian imagination."[8]

By far the main contemporary abuse of portraying Jews as animals occurs in parts of the Muslim world. Calling Jews apes and pigs is a recurring motif. It is even used by prominent religious preachers. In a weekly sermon in April 2002, Al-Azhar Sheikh Muhammad Sayyid Tantawi, the highest-ranking cleric in the Sunni Muslim world, called the Jews "the enemies of Allah, descendants of apes and pigs."[9]

In one of his sermons, Saudi sheikh Abd Al-Rahman Al-Sudayyis, imam and preacher at the Al-Haraam mosque—the most important mosque in Mecca—beseeched Allah to annihilate the Jews. He also urged the Arabs to give up peace initiatives with them because they are "the scum of the human race, the rats of the world, the violators of pacts and agreements, the murderers of the prophets, and the offspring of apes and pigs."[10]

In another sermon, Al-Sudayyis called contemporary Jews "evil offspring, infidels, distorters of [others'] words, calf-worshippers, prophet-murderers, prophecy-deniers . . . the scum of the human race 'whom Allah cursed and turned into apes and pigs . . .'"[11]

In an August 2001 sermon, Sheikh Ibrahim Madhi, a Palestinian Authority official and imam of the Sheikh Ijlin mosque, Gaza City's main mosque, said: "Lances must be directed at the Jews, the enemies of Allah, the nation accursed in Allah's book. Allah described [them] as apes and pigs, calf-worshipers, idol-worshippers . . ."[12]

In the framework of the Gaza Return March in 2018 a preacher delivered a sermon in which he said that the "blessed land" was being "trampled by the accursed descendants of apes and pigs, the remnants of the brutal, savage, and barbaric colonialism." The sermon was broadcast by Hamas' Al-Aqsa TV.[13]

Arab political leaders also use the apes and pigs dehumanization to attack the Jews. Former Egyptian President Mohammed Morsi said: "Either [you accept] the Zionists and everything they want, or else it is war." He added: "This is what these occupiers of the land of Palestine know—these bloodsuckers, who attack the Palestinians, these warmongers, the descendants of apes and pigs."[14]

Hassan Nasrallah, head of Hezbollah, said in one of his speeches ". . . We reaffirm the slogan of the struggle against the Great Satan and call, like last year: 'Death to America.' 'To the murderers of the prophets, the grandsons of apes and pigs,' we say: . . .'Death to Israel . . .'"[15]

The dehumanization of the Jews has permeated Arab societies. Ordinary citizens, having followed opinion leaders, also consider Jews to be apes and pigs. A well-known example concerns a 3½ year old Muslim girl who was interviewed in 2002 by the Saudi-Egyptian satellite television station Iqraa. After she answered an earlier question saying that she did not like Jews, the interviewer asked her why that was so. She replied that Jews were apes and pigs. When questioned further about who had said so, she answered that Allah said so in the Koran.[16]

One also finds many indications that these demonizing ideas are brought into the Western world by some Muslims living there. I once interviewed a young academic from the Netherlands who used the pseudonym Samar. Unbeknownst to her Muslim colleagues she had secretly given up her religion. Samar said that she had met approximately 150 Muslim students during her university days. She remarked: "These students also believe that Muslims are superior to other people. In particular, they look down on Jews in contempt. They believe Jews descend from apes and pigs. This is stressed in particular by those who know where this is written in the Koran. It's not that they think Jews change into monkeys during a full moon. Rather, they believe that Jews are not fully human. This message is also broadcast on Arab TV stations."[17]

Mohammed al-Khaled Samha is an imam at a mosque run by the Islamic Society in Denmark (Islamisk Trossamfund) in the Odense suburb of Vollsmose. He was among a group of imams who travelled to the Middle East to stir up anti-Danish sentiment in the aftermath of the *Jyllands-Posten* newspaper printing of the series of Mohammed cartoons.

In a sermon, he said: "How can we—or any free Muslim with faith in his heart—accept the division of Palestine between [the Palestinians] and a gang of Jews, the offspring of apes and pigs?"[18]

Various Canadian imams have also called Jews "apes and pigs." In 2014, Mostafa Saad Hannout, an imam at the Masjid Toronto mosque, posted on his

Facebook page: "O Allah, [show] your kindness to our brothers in Gaza O Allah, give them victory [help] over your enemy and their enemy O Allah, destroy [take revenge against] the grandchildren [descendants] of the apes and pigs."[19]

In its recently published cartoon, *The New York Times* dehumanized Netanyahu. Yet however severe, it was a one-time occurrence. The "animalization" of Jews in a variety of Muslim circles, including in the Western world, is a recurrent event. It is yet further proof of the fact that Muslim antisemitism is more extreme and more widespread than homegrown antisemitism in the West.

Israel National News, May 6, 2019

1   www.nytimes.com/2019/04/28/business/ny-times-anti-semitic-cartoon.html

2   www.nytimes.com/2019/04/28/opinion/cartoon-nytimes.html

3   See for instance: www.jta.org/1933/02/15/archive/nazi-leader-would-rid-germany-of-jewish-vermin

4   www.facinghistory.org/resource-library/image/when-vermin-are-dead-der-strmer-antisemitic-cartoon

5   www.jpost.com/Diaspora/Farrakhan-compares-Jews-to-termites-says-Jews-are-stupid-569627

6   jcpa.org/article/major-anti-semitic-motifs-in-arab-cartoons/

7   Joel Kotek, *Cartoons and Extremism: Israel and the Jews in Arab and Western Media* (Edgware: Vallentine Mitchell, 2009) 47.

8   Ibid.

9   As quoted in www.jewishvirtuallibrary.org/muslim-clerics-jews-are-the-descendants-of-apes-pigs-and-other-animals

10 Ibid.

11 Ibid.

12 Ibid.

13 www.memri.org/tv/gaza-friday-sermon-return-march-blessed-land-trampled-accursed-descendants-apes-and-pigs/transcript

14 www.forbes.com/sites/richardbehar/2013/01/11/news-flash-jews-are-apes-and-pigs-so-why-is-egypts-morsi-the-elephant-in-americas-newsrooms/#5587cff63ca2

15 As quoted in www.jewishvirtuallibrary.org/muslim-clerics-jews-are-the-descendants-of-apes-pigs-and-other-animals

16   www.illinoisreview.com/illinoisreview/2014/11/three-year-old-egyptian-girl-jews-are-apes-and-pigs-video.html

17   www.israelnationalnews.com/Articles/Article.aspx/15450

18   www.thelocal.dk/20141014/video-danish-imam-calls-jews-apes-and-pigs

19   jcpa.org/article/why-do-canadian-imams-call-jews-the-sons-of-the-pigs-and-apes/

Diplomats at The United Nations Commit Antisemitic Acts

Global antisemitism can best be observed at the General Assembly of the United Nations. Senior diplomats of many democracies participate actively in these major annual antisemitic activities.

The widely accepted definition of antisemitism agreed upon by the International Holocaust Remembrance Alliance (IHRA) states that an antisemitic manifestation: ". . . might include the targeting of the state of Israel, conceived as a Jewish collectivity. However, criticism of Israel similar to that levelled against any other country cannot be regarded as antisemitic."[1]

Despite its genocidal past against Jews in their "grandfather generation," contemporary Germany participates wholeheartedly in these antisemitic manifestations at the UN. This issue came to the fore in March 2019. Germany's largest daily, *Bild* published that in recent years the General Assembly accepted more than 500 resolutions against Israel and not a single one against the Palestinian terror group, Hamas.

Bild gave some examples for the period 2014–2017. In 2014, of all resolutions directed against a specific country, 87 percent were against Israel. In 2016, the number was 77 percent. In 2017, 78 percent. In the United Nations Human Rights Council (UNHRC), more than half the resolutions were against Israel. *Bild* pointed out that Germany regularly sides with Israel's enemies. In November 2018, of 21 General Assembly resolutions against Israel, 16 were supported by Germany and on 4 it abstained.[2]

There are no similar resolutions anywhere near these numbers against any other country at the General Assembly. This makes the anti-Israeli votes of Germany and other countries supporting the condemnations of Israel manifestations of antisemitism.

The German liberal party, FDP, at the beginning of 2019 proposed a motion in the country's parliament, the Bundestag, to change its policy of voting against Israel. The motion said that the ongoing disproportionate condemnation by numbers of Israel in its total picture goes far beyond legitimate criticism.

In the parliament, 408 members voted against the resolution, 150 agreed and 63 members abstained.[3] Only the populist AfD sided with the FDP and supported the motion. With one exception Chancellor Angela Merkel's Christian Democrats and its Bavarian allies of the Christian Social Union, the Socialists and the Left party all voted in favor of maintaining the country's antisemitic voting at the UN. The Green party abstained.

In German politics, there is a 'cordon sanitaire' around the AfD. This implies from the side of the boycotters: "We are good and white, the AfD is bad and black." The vote in parliament however, showed that concerning parties which opposed the FDP resolution the difference with the AfD, may only be a different shade of grey. After the vote, US Middle East expert Daniel Pipes tweeted: "Merkel just talks, AfD delivers."[4]

German Foreign Minister Heiko Maas, a socialist has often said that Auschwitz inspired him to go into politics.[5] He defended the government's attitude claiming that it was better to participate in drafting the text of these anti-Israeli resolutions and make them more moderate rather than not participate in the discussion and vote against them. Insiders claim that this attitude is part of a game. The Palestinians prepare a radical resolution knowing well that the ultimate text will be less extreme. The Europeans negotiate a more moderate text and then claim that they have succeeded in weakening the original resolution.[6]

After the Holocaust and many other huge crimes, the United Nations agreed on the Universal Declaration of Human Rights in 1948.[7] Its first article says that "All human beings are born free and equal in dignity and rights. They are endowed with reason and conscience." After the Second World War many Germans and others who had participated in criminal activities claimed that they had followed the orders of superiors. This argument was frequently used by defendants in the post-war Nuremberg trials. The German expression for "order is order," Befehl ist Befehl became an international expression. The courts did not consider superior orders a valid claim for those who had committed crimes to go free.

Jewish religious law already understood the nature of the issue more than a millennium ago. If somebody charges another to carry out a sin, the messenger who follows these instructions is responsible for the sin he has committed.[8]

The United Nations Human Rights Council (UNHRC) is even worse in its anti-Israel incitement. An alien from Mars who comes to earth in order to get a quick idea of what human rights means would probably focus on a visit to the Council in Geneva. He could then report back to those who sent him that the inhabitants of the earth have developed a perfect immoral system to condemn states. Every country transgresses what they call "human rights." Thus a majority in the UNHRC of those who misbehave on human rights—including some which do so severely—can target any country they want.

Foreign ministries decide whether to support the wholesale condemnations of Israel at the General Assembly. If they do, they are committing antisemitic acts. Their diplomats at the UN who execute these orders have a personal responsibility. These people "are endowed with reason and conscience." They cannot deny their responsibility by saying "I am just an elite messenger who carries out the orders from my superiors." No human being can claim that he is a robot without morality.

For each democratic diplomat who has participated in the massive UN and UNHRC condemnations of Israel a file should be established of how often he or she has participated in such manifestations of antisemitism. Carrying out antisemitic acts is frequently not a crime, yet it is always an expression of an individual's defective character.

The Jerusalem Post, April 4, 2019

1   www.holocaustremembrance.com/sites/default/files/press_release_document_antisemitism.pdf

2   www.bild.de/politik/ausland/politik-ausland/deutschland-bei-der-uno-fdp-will-anti-israel-irrsinn-stoppen-59894948.bild.html

3   www.mena-watch.com/mena-analysen-beitraege/bundestag-und-israel-lippen-bekenntnisse-statt-solidaritaet

4   twitter.com/DanielPipes/status/1106568848008982529

5   www.timesofisrael.com/most-horrible-place-on-earth-german-foreign-minister-visits-auschwitz/

6   www.mena-watch.com/mena-analysen-beitraege/bundestag-und-israel-lippen-bekenntnisse-statt-solidaritaet

7   www.un.org/en/universal-declaration-human-rights/

8   www.etzion.org.il/he

HOLOCAUST

Are We Reliving the 1930s?

Elie Wiesel noted that Iranian President Mahmoud Ahmadinejad's speech at the 2008 United Nations General Assembly calling for the destruction of Israel demonstrates that the world has learned nothing from the Holocaust. The upcoming 70th anniversary of Kristallnacht on November 9 and 10 provides an occasion to grapple with the question of whether, in the current decade, the Jewish people are reliving the 1930s.

To answer that, one has to look at issues such as genocide and hate promotion, appeasement of totalitarians, Western leadership and so on. The correct answer must then be: "Yes, but only in certain aspects." The existence of the State of Israel is the main difference between the two decades. In the 1930s, the Jews were an incoherent, leaderless group, with no tools to defend itself against enemies. Today there is a Jewish state, which is threatened by substantial parts of the Muslim world and others, but is not helpless.

There is furthermore no country today like Nazi Germany with systematic state-promoted antisemitism and state-sponsored violence against its Jewish citizens. There is, however, an explicitly genocidal antisemitic power—Iran, which proclaims that it intends to annihilate the Jewish state and is developing an atom bomb to do so. Extermination policies have mutated as a result of technological development.

There are few Jews within the borders of Iran. Its allies and the countries it might invade have even fewer. Iran aims mainly at Israelis. It instrumentalizes its own Jews for political purposes and was at the origin of the murder-ous attack against Jews in Buenos Aires in 1994. In the 1930s, Germany, ruled by Hitler, together with its future allies and the countries it would invade, had many millions of Jews within their borders, and they were an easy target. Today, Israel can probably prevent attacks and certainly retaliate.

Israel also has an ally in the United States, and other states are willing to support it to varying degrees. This is radically different from the structural disarray of the Jews in the 1930s and the unwillingness of any nation to help them. That became fully clear at the 1938 Evian Conference, where no major country was willing to commit to receiving Jewish refugees.

While widespread antisemitism—disguised as anti-Israelism—has made a major comeback in this decade, it has not been turned anywhere into dis-criminatory legislation. Another major departure from the 1930s is that the radical improvement in international communications impacts on societies in so many ways that it is difficult to analyze which one is most important.

Yet ominous similarities between the 1930s and now do exist. First of all, there is totalitarianism. Leading Holocaust scholar Prof. Yehuda Bauer has said, "In Islam, there are major forces which are mentally prepared—given the power—to carry out genocide against all others . . . Islamic radicalism is the desire for a global utopia, to be achieved through violent means, which aims at global dominance. This is equally true for National Socialism and communism. Every universal utopia is murderous and every radical universal utopia produces radical murderers."

As in the 1930s, Western leadership is weak and hardly aware of loom-ing dangers. British Prime Minister Neville Chamberlain was reviled for his appeasement of Nazi Germany for decades. Nowadays a rehabilitation of Chamberlain is indirectly on its way, as more and more revisionist historians claim that the Second World War could have been avoided and that Churchill was a warmonger.

Today, many in the West favor both external and internal appeasement of radical Muslims. In foreign policy, Europe is pushed toward appeasement because it possesses little military force. Domestically, it seeks to placate its resident Muslim extremists through proposals that Sharia be allowed to operate within the framework of national legal systems.

Some appeasement movements and motifs are the same as in the 1930s.

Pacifists have frequently been of use to totalitarians. Moral relativists, fearing to be judgmental, are another type of appeasers. There is also a parallel between those in the 1930s in Western Europe, who felt guilty about the severe conditions of the Versailles peace treaty regarding Germany, and those who nowadays feel guilty toward the Third World for the sins of colonialism. Similarities also abound between those who were willing to sacrifice Czechoslovakia for an illusionary peace and those who want to pressure Israel to make concessions to the Palestinians on the false assumption that once this conflict is solved, Western relations with the Islamic world will improve permanently.

One phenomenon that may be unique to our time is what can best be called "humanitarian racists." One finds many of these in NGOs, whose number has exploded in recent decades. Left-wing politics, the media and the academic world are also hotbeds of this poorly recognized form of racism. Humanitarian racists believe, to varying degrees, that only whites must be held accountable for their acts, whereas Third Worlders or non-whites are mainly victims. By diminishing non-whites' responsibility for their criminal deeds, one is in effect ranking them somewhere between "real" humans and animals, which live by their urges. The behavior of the NGO gathering at the 2001 UN Durban Conference against Racism, Racial Discrimination and Xenophobia made humanitarian racism visible internationally.

Humanitarian racism can often be discerned in the debate on the Palestinian-Israeli conflict, where it consists of systematically ignoring the criminal character of large parts of Palestinian society, such as its many promoters of genocide and its education of children to become "martyrs" through murdering Jews.

In a globalized society, the forces of radical Islam, genocide promotion and appeasement of totalitarians are increasing—as are those in opposition to them. Their relative strengths will determine whether the similarity of our world to that of the 1930s will grow or decline.

The Jerusalem Post, November 5, 2008

The Lockdown and Hiding During the Shoah

Usually in the days before Yom Hashoah, I recall my year and a half in hiding during the Holocaust. During this time I was holed up in a small apartment in Amsterdam with my parents. Until today I do not understood where they found the mental and emotional strength to withstand this situation. As a child of 6 and 7 years of age, I did not grasp the full importance or the risks involved. I now know that somewhere between 30–40 percent of the Jews in hiding were betrayed to the German occupiers, mainly by Dutchmen.

My parents had rented an apartment in the center of Amsterdam in the name of an unmarried mother. I know now that this apartment was about a kilometer from where Anne Frank and her family were hiding. This was the place we intended to go into once it became clear that Dutch Jews were being transported to the transition camp, Westerbork. We did not know that trains were departing every week to the east from there. Those people who were sent to Sobibor were murdered upon arrival. Part of those on the trains sent to Auschwitz/Birkenau were gassed immediately. Other Dutch Jews had a small chance of survival there if they were put to work. Yet most of these died from the horrible conditions in the camps.

The apartment we hid in had three rooms. The woman in whose name the apartment was rented occupied the front room. Her son was a mariner who rarely visited. The middle room was very small without windows. This is where I slept. We lived in the back room during the day and my parents slept there at night. Below us was a shop selling typewriters. The people who worked there knew that there was a single woman living above them who went out to work during the day. We were therefore barely able to move or make a sound during shop hours.

The courageous resistance organization supplied us with food stamps. Without this the lady would have been unable to purchase food for us. A cousin of my father, himself in hiding, supplied us with the money to pay the rent and buy basic necessities. Under usual local circumstances we would not have had electricity. However, someone from the resistance linked us up to the electricity from a shoe store a few houses further owned by Dutch Nazi collaborators. Radios at that time were fairly large and depended on electricity. It was illegal to own a radio, but then again, we ourselves were illegal.

Many Jews in hiding were traumatized for their entire life from that period. The isolation period had a huge lasting psychological impact on them. Yet the isolation influenced my father in the opposite way. In hiding, he made a vow that if he survived the war, he would devote the rest of his life to helping Jewish survivors.

That is indeed what he did. After the war, he established a social and pastoral department at the Amsterdam Ashkenazi community. This organization assisted survivors in a variety of ways. Even though a Jewish umbrella body had been created to help people out with financial problems, my father's department also helped many poor people to some extent.

Besides poverty, there were also huge social problems. Many Jews had lost all or most of their relatives. My father arranged communal activities specifically for survivors where they came together, sometimes to listen to lectures, or to get together to engage in arts and embroidering activities. He also started to organize joint trips, initially to other Jewish communities in the Netherlands, and later to Jewish communities elsewhere in Western Europe. Eventually, there were annual trips to Israel. These activities were financially supported by Jews who had rebuilt their businesses after the war and saw it as a worthwhile charitable cause.

The condition of the surviving Jews—three-quarters of the 140,000 pre-war Dutch Jews had been murdered by the Germans—was radically different from that of society at large. Dealing with the problems of part of them made my father a pioneer in Dutch social work, a profession which was only at the beginning as a field of scholarly study. A Dutch professor of contemporary history, Isaac Lipschits, wrote my father's biography. It became a commercial book.

During this time in lockdown in Israel, I have started to reflect more than usual, and in more detail, on my life during the Shoah. My personal history gives me a radically different perspective on the contemporary situation from many Israelis. Even though the current isolation entails a variety of handicaps, they are very minor compared to those in my days of hiding.

The Coronavirus risk is unpleasant, but minimal compared to the probability of being gassed. I am not alone being in lockdown, but together with many Israelis. I am also in this together with many people in the Western world. My children bring food. It is of very superior quality to what I ate during the last years of the Shoah. Did I also eat tulip bulbs and sugar beets toward the end of the war? I don't remember. I do recall that thanks to the Swedes, we received the first piece of white bread I ever ate a few days after the war ended.

Today there are pleasant surprises. Friends call to enquire how I am. I call other friends to find out how they are doing. I have received some calls come from people I don't generally hear from. Friends from abroad also write. In many of these conversations, I learn very interesting things, not specifically related to the lockdown.

One of the highlights of my lockdown took place on Friday night, a few weeks ago. Neighbors and their children sang Kabbalat Shabbat from their windows. Others joined in from their balconies. A week later, there was much progress. Shabbat and evening prayers have become a collective experience. More than the 10 people required for a minyan gather in the streets, keeping distance from each other, while several including myself participate from the balconies.

We are now in the fourth week of Shabbat services. They have become formalized. People come out into the street over a stretch of 100 meters and stand at the required distance from each other. The Chazzan who leads the services has a very loud voice. During Pesach and last Shabbat we also ad a reading from the Torah as well as the priestly blessing. During the weekdays of Pesach, there were afternoon and evening prayers, which have since continued on regular week days. At the end of the Shabbat morning service, a woman across the street puts out glasses and a bottle of—I guess—wine so that people can make kiddush. I cannot go to synagogue, yet I am fortunate that synagogue has come to me.

As I am thinking about this, I fully realize how crucial it was that more than 50 years ago my late wife and I decided to leave Europe and settle in Jerusalem.

Israel National News, april 21, 2020

The Ignored Lessons of Evian 1938

This year marks the 80th anniversary of the 1938 Evian Conference whose purpose was to discuss the plight of the increasing numbers of Jewish refugees fleeing persecution by Nazi Germany. There, hardly any places of refuge were offered to the half million Jews from Germany and Austria.[1] The anniversary of this failed event has drawn scarce attention. Yet there are important actual lessons—and not only historical ones—to be learned from its failure.

The ten-day conference could not take place in Switzerland as the government feared upsetting Hitler.[2] Instead it was held a few kilometers from the Swiss border in the French resort town of Evian on Lake Geneva. When I visited Evian in 2017 there was no indication of this conference. During a symposium in the summer of 2018 a plaque was finally presented to Evian's Royal hotel to be placed close to the 1938 conference's rooms.[3]

The conference was the initiative of American President Franklin Delano Roosevelt. Thirty two countries participated in the ten-day long discussions. Rhetoric dominated and hardly any solutions were offered by the various democracies and dictatorships, including the initiator, the United States. The Australian delegate who spoke on the second day said that his country did not have a racial problem.[4] The underlying message was clear: Australia believed that it would create a racial problem if it allowed a significant number of Jews to immigrate. After the war, Australia did however let in many Holocaust survivors who went on to make significant contributions to the country.

Of all the countries present at the conference, it was only the small Dominican Republic ruled by dictator Rafael Leónidas Trujillo whose representative concretely offered refuge to a number of the Jewish asylum seekers. Trujillo's government had massacred between 8000–12000 Haitians in an ethnic conflict. A German Jew who came to Haiti, the neighboring dictatorship on the same island, is quoted as saying: "When a murderer saves your live, you still have to be grateful to the murderer."[5]

Had the persecuted Jews been spread proportionately over the countries present, they would have at most represented two tenths of a percent of their respective populations. Financing the exodus from Germany and Austria was also not an insurmountable problem.

To put this in a contemporary perspective the refugees let in by Germany during the past three years, represent about two percent of the country's population. It might be offensive to some, yet it is true that Jewish refugees have made larger contributions to those countries which accepted them before the Holocaust and caused less problems than part of the recent immigrants to Germany. A segment of those do not even want to integrate.

The main characteristic of the Evian conference was pervasive rhetoric. Hitler's name was not mentioned. In the current century, antisemitism has substantially grown and is increasing further. This is not only the case in Europe, but also in the United States and Canada.[6,7] Most reactions by the leaders of democracies to this hate mongering is once again rhetoric. The current lack of practical solutions to antisemitic incidents stresses the importance of the existence of Israel. The Zionist idea is nowadays again demonstrating its relevance.

As populism and nationalism increase in Europe, the generosity of Israel's Law of Return becomes even clearer. Israel continues to welcome Jews to immigrate even if they may have publicly opposed its policies and are unlikely to contribute to its society in future.

Some of the few articles devoted this year to the Evian conference, suggested that the many asylum seekers admitted into Germany and Sweden are proof that Western Europe has learned from the 1938 conference failure. This is a false conclusion. A large part of the recent immigrants come from Muslim countries where antisemitism is part of the culture promoted by political and religious leaders, the media and many others of their elite. All polls available show that the percentage of antisemites among Muslim immigrants is substantially higher than among native populations.

Is this the distorted lesson of the Evian conference: letting in more antisemites? The due to the Holocaust greatly reduced European Jewish population is now increasingly subjected to antisemitism and violence.

The main actual lesson from Evian is more likely to be in line with what Winston Churchill said in the House of Commons in 1947. "No one pretends that democracy is perfect or all-wise. Indeed, it has been said that democracy is the worst form of Government except all those other forms that have been tried from time to time."[8]

The hostile voting patterns concerning Israel of EU countries, including Germany, at the United Nations are only a small reflection of contemporary democracies failing Israel and occasionally even discriminating against it.

Indeed those who think that Israel should rely exclusively on the support of democracies are greatly mistaken. Because of this conclusion and the other abovementioned reasons, the failure of the Evian conference should take a much more central place in Jewish and Israeli discourse.

The Jerusalem Post, December 13, 2018

1   www.ec4i.org/80th-anniversary-of-evian-conference-asked-why-did-the-nations-fail-the-jewish-refugees-in-1938/
2   Jochen Thies, *Evian 1938. Als die Welt Die Juden Verriet* (Essen: Klartext, 2017) 9.
3   www.ec4i.org/80th-anniversary-of-evian-conference-asked-why-did-the-nations-fail-the-jewish-refugees-in-1938/
4   Thies, *Evian 1938*, 47.
5   Ibid., 85.
6   www.ushmm.org/educators/teaching-materials/national-history-day/research-topics/the-evian-conference
7   www.thecanadianencyclopedia.ca/en/article/holocaust
8   Winston Churchill, the House of Commons, November 11, 1947.

Why Apologies for the Shoah Are Important

More than many decades after the Shoah, official apologies from countries and institutions which collaborated with the Nazis during the Shoah still trickle in. Eastern European heads of state have almost turned these into a ritual when they visit Israel.

Yet also in Western Europe the phenomenon continues. The Netherlands provide in particular contrasting attitudes. In 2005, entirely unexpectedly, Aad Veenman, president of the Dutch Railways offered an apology to the Jewish community for his company's behavior during the Second World War. The railways transported, on German orders, most of the Dutch Jews to the transit camp Westerbork and from there to the German border on their way to extermination.

In 1945, a few months after the war ended, Steef van Schaik, the minister of transport and energy, in the first post-war democratic government in the Netherlands expressed the opposite view. He publicly praised the Dutch railway workers for not going on strike rather than transporting the Jews, saying: "It was the duty the Dutch government asked of you, because the railways are one of the pillars on which the economic life of the Netherlands rests, and that should not be put at risk too early." On the occasion of the railways' recent apology Frans Peeters, an editor of the Amsterdam daily *Het Parool*, called Van Schaik's remarks "the most cruel sentence ever pronounced by a Dutch minister."

The Dutch Government has still not offered its apologies for the misbehavior of its war-time predecessors. The Dutch authorities in the Netherlands
collaborated with the German occupiers in many illegal measures against the
Jews without the government in exile in London reacting. There are many
proofs that that government had hardly any interest in the fate of the Dutch
Jews.

When Queen Beatrix visited Israel in 1995, she said in the Knesset: "The
people of the Netherlands could not prevent the destruction of their Jewish
fellow-citizens." She admitted there that the minority of Dutchmen who
had resisted the Germans behaved exceptionally compared to their fellow-
citizens.

At the major Stockholm Holocaust conference in January 2000, Swedish
Prime Minister Goran Persson apologized for his country's attitude toward
the Jews during the Second World War. There, on the same day the then
Dutch Prime Minister, Wim Kok of the Labor Party, spoke and did not offer
any apologies. A few days later, he apologized under pressure, but only for the
behavior of the post-war Dutch democratic governments mainly concerning
the failures of the restitution process.

A further development came when in March 2005, Dutch Prime Minister, Jan Peter Balkenende, a Christian Democrat, visited Jerusalem on the
occasion of the opening of Yad Vashem's Holocaust museum. He called the
deportation of the greater part of Dutch Jewry, "a pitch-black" chapter in
Dutch history.

Balkenende was criticized for not apologizing for the war time government's failure by several major Dutch papers, and was compared unfavorably
with Belgian Prime Minister, Guy Verhofstadt, who at the same event said:
"Two years ago I recalled the share of responsibility of my country by mentioning the role that some Belgian civil servants and administrations have
played in this tragedy. I want to repeat these apologies today."

In April 2005, on the occasion of the thirtieth anniversary symposium of
the Dutch Center for Documentation and Information on Israel, Balkenende
became, after sixty years, the first Dutch Prime Minister to finally mention
the collaboration of the Dutch authorities during the war with Nazi Germany,
again without apologizing for it.

Why are formal apologies for misbehavior during the Holocaust so important? Some critics stress that those who apologize are not the ones who misbehaved. While that is true they do represent the same institutions. Other critics say that many of the apologies made—for instance those during the restitution negotiations—were not morally motivated, but rather represented political pressure or fear of economic boycotts in the United States.

Yet other critics of apologies say that the main thing is to tell the history as it was. Stressing the painful truth once again in 2006 then Austrian President Heinz Fischer said that the 1955 Declaration of Independence of his country falsely represented Austria as a victim of the Nazis rather than as a co-perpetrator of crimes.

Despite all, criticism, apologies by governments, institutions and companies for their war-time behavior remain extremely important. Once these have not only recognized their guilt, but have also offered apologies a common basis of what is normative has been established. They constitute a clear declaration of irrevocable guilt toward their Jewish counterparts. These apologies will remain well-documented for future generations, after all Holocaust survivors have passed away.

At a time when the President of Iran and others, not only in the Arab and Muslim world, unashamedly deny the Holocaust while at the same time promoting a new one, official apologies and the historic mark they make assume an even greater importance than in the past.

The Jerusalem Post, April 23, 2006

Stiffnecked Netherlands Finally Apologizes for Holocaust Failures

Dutch Prime Minister, Mark Rutte, has rather suddenly offered much belated apologies on behalf of his government for the failures of the Dutch authorities toward the Jews during the second World War.[1] He did so in a speech at the National Holocaust commemoration in Amsterdam on January 26. It was a radical departure from yearlong policies where he—and his predecessors—had found various reasons to refrain from admitting the truth about the widespread Dutch wartime misbehavior. This fits an ingrained Dutch elite culture, which often avoids admitting failures, including major ones. This attitude enables the Dutch elite to arrogantly moralize to others.

With that, be it very late, the only Western European government which had not done yet so started telling the truth about how their nations' leaders failed their Jewish citizens during the German occupation. In Western Europe, the Netherlands was the country with the highest percentage of Jewish victims during the Holocaust. When the Germans conquered the Netherlands in 1940, there were 140,000 Jews living there; 102,000 of them were murdered by the occupiers during the war.

Those who were deported to the death camps in Poland were arrested by Dutch policemen, transported by the Dutch railways and guarded by the Dutch military police in the transit camp Westerbork. Most of these Jewish deportees came from families that had lived in the Netherlands for several centuries.

In 1995, French President Jacques Chirac said in a far more detailed admission of the truth than Rutte's recent one: "France committed the irremediable. It broke its word and delivered those it protected to their executioners. We maintain toward them an unforgivable debt."[2] Two years later, French socialist Prime Minister Lionel Jospin was even more explicit and said, "Not even one German soldier was necessary to carry out this disgrace."[3]

In March 1995, a few months before Chirac's admission of the truth, then Dutch Queen Beatrix visited Israel. She spoke in the Knesset and said that there were many Dutch who had resisted the Germans, but they were the exceptions and that "the people of the Netherlands could not prevent the destruction of their Jewish fellow citizens."[4] This was a whitewashed version of the truth. She should have added something like: "Even the limited things our authorities could do, they did not. Our government in exile in London refrained from giving instructions to Dutch officials in the occupied Netherlands for how to act on German orders concerning the persecution of the Jews. My Grandmother Queen Wilhelmina also greatly failed. She did not call upon the Dutch population to help Jews who wanted to go in hiding."

Rutte is Prime Minister of the Netherlands since 2010. He had stalled all efforts to offer governmental apologies to the Dutch Jewish community. In January 2012, the, now defunct Dutch daily, *De Pers,* devoted its front page and another one to the apologies issue.[5] This was based on two interviews from the Appendix of my 2011 book, *Judging the Netherlands: The Renewed Holocaust Restitution Process 1997–2000.*[6] There former Dutch Deputy Prime Ministers, Els Borst—who was murdered in 2014—and Gerrit Zalm, declared that they would publicly support the Dutch government if it offered apologies to the Jewish community.

That same day, Freedom party MP's Geert Wilders and Raymond de Roon posed parliamentary questions to the prime minister. They asked him why the Netherlands would not offer apologies to the Jewish community for the government's misconduct toward the Jews during the Holocaust. Soon thereafter on that day the Associated Press sent out two articles on the lack of apologies by the Dytch Government which were picked up by many media outlets all over the world from the US to China.[7]

Rutte got away with an irrelevant reply. He referred to a Dutch government declaration from 2000.[8] However, the apologies offered to the Jewish community by the government at that time were unrelated to the war period. They referred to the formalistic, bureaucratic and heartless Dutch post-war restitution process. Even those apologies were only half-truths, as they claimed that this unacceptable attitude had not been intentional except for one case. There were, however, already many documented cases in which Dutch post-war policy toward the Jews was quite deliberate.

Rutte also answered that his government saw no reason to apologize in part because there was no broadly supported advice from the Jewish community to do so.[9] This was an extremely misconceived answer. Victims do not have to ask for apologies from the legal successors of those who failed. Those who are at fault are expected to present apologies on their own initiative.

In 2012, a poll found that two-thirds of the Dutch people were opposed to their Prime Minister apologizing to the Jewish community for the misconduct of the wartime government in exile in London. Only 27 percent of those polled were in favor of such apologies.[10]

At the beginning of 2015, parliamentarians Joram van Klaveren and Louis Bontes, of the small Voor Nederland party, again asked Rutte to apologize to the Jewish community for the wartime government's failures.[11] In his answer Rutte curtly referred to the glib statement of then Dutch Queen Beatrix in the Knesset in 1995.[12] If there had then been at that time at least one Dutch journalist who verified what the Queen said, he could have published that his country's government stood behind nothing.

The recent sudden apologies are important. Now the successors of the deficient authorities and the victims—some of whom are still alive—agree about the history of the failure.

Rutte's apologies were of a rather general nature. One is still waiting for the apologies of the Head of the police—as many of them were major collaborators with the occupiers—and of the Supreme Court whose wartime predecessors radically failed the Jews. Rutte should also have mentioned that the government was responsible for the failure of Queen Wilhelmina and much more. These topics may be challenges for his future speeches.

1   nos.nl/artikel/2320304-excuses-rutte-overheid-schoot-tekort-tijdens-de-holocaust.html

2   Speech by the President of the French Republic, Mr. Jacques Chirac, during the ceremonies commemorating the Vel' d'Hiv' Roundup of July 16 and 17, 1942 (Rafle du Vélodrome d'Hiver) Paris, July 16, 1995. www.ambafrance-us.org/news/statmnts/1998/wchea/vel2.asp

3   Speech by Prime Minister Mr. Lionel Jospin, on the occasion of the Vel' d'Hiv' ceremony, Paris, July 20, 1997. www.info-france-usa.org/news/statmnts/1998/wchea/vel1.asp

4   Address by Her Majesty the Queen to the Knesset, March 28, 1995 (Rijksvoorlichtingsdienst).

5   Dirk Jacob Nieuwboer, "Excuses voor wegkijken," *De Pers*, January 3, 2012.

6   Manfred Gerstenfeld, *Judging the Netherlands: The Renewed Holocaust Restitution Process, 1997–2000* (Jerusalem: Jerusalem Center for Public Affairs, 2011).

7   Associated Press, "Lawmaker urges Dutch to apologize for WWII Jewish-deportations," Fox News, January 4, 2012.

8   Answers to questions posed by Dutch Members of Parliament De Roon en Wilders (PVV) provided by MP Rutte about the attitude of the Dutch government towards the Holocaust during the Second World War, January 12, 2012, https://zoek.officielebekendmakingen.nl/ah-tk-20112012-1226.html

9   Ibid.

10 J. Geerdink, "Twee derde: geen excuus jodenvervolging," *Spits*, January 7, 2012.

11 zoek.officielebekendmakingen.nl/ah-tk-20142015-1340.html

12 Ibid.

Kristallnacht Abuse
As a Political Instrument

This year as has often occurred in the past, some Kristallnacht memorial meetings in Europe were abused as political instruments rather than to memorialize Jewish victims. Memorial day manipulation in Germany goes back many years. In 1969 on the date marking Kristallnacht, an anarchist-leftist group painted graffiti on Jewish memorials stating, "Shalom and Napalm" or "El Fatah." Additionally, a firebomb was thrown at the Jewish community center in Berlin. The leftist groups' common perception was that, "Jews who were expelled by fascism became fascists themselves, who in collaboration with American capitalism, want to annihilate the Palestinian people."[1]

In 2010, Frankfurt's then-Christian Democrat Mayor, Petra Roth, invited Holocaust survivor Alfred Grosser to deliver the 2010 Kristallnacht speech in Paul's Church. This German-born French Jewish intellectual promoted reconciliation between Germans and the French. He is a notorious anti-Israel hate-monger. Grosser used his speech to draw parallels between the conduct of the Nazis and Israel.[2]

In 2013, another Kristallnacht manipulation drew much attention. *Jerusalem Post* reporter Benjamin Weinthal detailed the criticism of a memorial conference at Berlin's Jewish Museum. Jewish anti-Israel hate-monger Brian Klug was invited as the keynote speaker there.[3]

The abuse of Kristallnacht memory is far from limited to Germany. On November 9, 2003 in Vienna, a memorial meeting was disrupted by members of the Sedunia group, who shouted through loudspeakers. They had to be removed by participants of the meeting. Sedunia is an organization of Muslims and Austrian converts to Islam.[4]

In the same month a leading Dutch inciter against Israel, Gretta Duisenberg—the widow of a former president of Europe's Central Bank—took part in a demonstration in one of Amsterdam's main squares. A mock Israeli checkpoint for Palestinians was set up there. Only the participation of Palestinian suicide murderers would have made it more realistic.

A few years ago, the Dutch Jewish community started to organize its own Kristallnacht memorial meetings in Amsterdam. The other leftwing dominated commemoration downplays contemporary antisemitism and focuses on general racism. Muslim organizations also participate in it, often to promote the fight against Islamophobia. They do not speak out against the fact that the greatest violence in any religion in the world comes out of several Muslim societies. In 2013, at least 65,000 Muslims will be murdered by other Muslims in a number of Arab states. Nor will they mention that the involvement of Muslims in anti-Semitic incidents in Europe is far larger than their proportion of the population. This has again been confirmed in the study published in 2013 by the European Agency for Fundamental Rights.[5]

Muslim bodies and left-wing organizations sometimes play together a major role in this abuse of Kristallnacht. In Helsingborg, Sweden, the Jewish community refused to participate in the 2012 Kristallnacht memorial meeting. Local paper *Helsingborgs Dagblad*, noted that the community's leader Jussi Tyger said that the memorial meeting was organized by left-wing parties and Muslims, who are known to be the most racist against Jews.[6]

In the Norwegian town of Bergen, the November memorial day is not centered on Kristallnacht, but on the 26th of the month when cargo ship Donau left Oslo with 552 Jews—the great majority of whom were killed in extermination camps. They had been arrested by Norwegian police rather than by German occupiers. In 2012, the speakers were leader of the Socialist Left party Audun Lysbakken and former Prime Minster Kåre Willoch, both notorious anti-Israelis. This was another expression of abuse of Holocaust memory: extreme anti-Israelis attempting to whitewash their reputation. The local Jews decided not to participate.

An American-Norwegian Jew who has participated for years in the event with Jewish prayers and an original composition, wrote on his Facebook page: "I refuse to participate in the same program as Kåre Willoch. They could not have chosen a more inappropriate speaker at a ceremony commemorating the Holocaust." He explained to his American friends in English that Willoch is "extremely anti-Israel, and has made some terrible anti-Semitic comments."

In 2013, Florence Aryanik, a young gentile woman of Iranian descent, pulled out of the Oslo Kristallnacht memorial. She was meant to speak there, but received a death threat earlier that day.[8] At the Stavanger memorial, former Labor Party Deputy Mayor Odd Kristian Reme spoke. He wore a Palestinian *keffiyah* scarf. The Chairman of the Oslo Jewish community, Ervin Kohn, condemned this saying that the highlighting of other political issues was a misuse of what happened to the Jews.[9]

There is also wider abuse. UN watcher Anne Bayefski wrote: "The Algerian delegate at the 2002 and 2003 United Nations Commission on Human Rights said that Israeli actions repeat Kristallnacht daily. He also said that Palestinians have numbers put on their arms and wondered how long one was going to wait for the Israelis to commit a massacre like Babi Yar. No state, except for Israel, drew attention to that statement."[10]

Of a different distorting nature is the regular comparing of potential ecological disaster to the Holocaust. In 1989, then-Senator from Tennessee Al Gore, published an op-ed in *The New York Times* titled, "An Ecological Kristallnacht. Listen." Gore called upon all humankind to heed the warning: ". . . the evidence is as clear as the sounds of glass shattering in Berlin"[11] All these vignettes above have to be seen in a broader context: the widespread and increasing abuse of Holocaust Memory at large.

The Jerusalem Post, November 12, 2013

1   Bommi Baumann, *Wie alles anfing* (Frankfurt am Main, 1976). As quoted in Susanne Urban, Being Leftist and Anti-Semitic in Germany, P&A, 32, May 1, 2005.

2   Manfred Gerstenfeld interviews Benjamin Weinthal, "Germany Bestows Awards Upon Anti-Israel Inciters," *Israel National News*, January 27, 2013.

3   Benjamin Weinthal, "Inclusion of anti-Israel speaker at Berlin conference on ways to tackle anti-Semitism sparks uproar," *The Jerusalem Post*, November 6, 2013.

4   http://no-racism.net/article/1008/

5   europa.eu/en/publication/2013/discrimination-and-hate-crime-against-jews-eu-member-states-experiences-and

6   "Inget judiskt deltagande när Kristallnatten ska uppmärksammas," *Helsingborgs Dagblad*, November 7, 2012.

7   McGonagall, "No let-up for Norwegian Jews; Israel bashers Willoch and Lysbakken tapped to give speeches at Holocaust memorial event," *Norway, Israel and the Jews*, November 13, 2012.

8   Richard Orange, "Kristallnacht Speaker Receives Death Threats," *The Local-Norway*, November 11, 2013.

9   Conrad Myrland, "Prest holdt appell i Palestinaskjerf på jødemarkering," *MIFF*, November 11, 2013.

10   Manfred Gerstenfeld interviews Anne Bayefsky, "The United Nations: Leading Purveyor of Anti-Semitism," P&A, 31, April 1, 2005.

11   Al Gore, "An Ecological Kristallnacht. Listen," *The New York Times*, March 19, 1989.

ANTI-ISRAELISM

Israel and Isis, The Genesis of a New Antisemitic Motif

Jointly written with Leah Hagelberg

The libel that Jews are absolute evil is the core accusation of antisemitism for close to two thousand years. Since 2014, the Islamic State, the cruelest of the major Muslim terror groups, has started to replace Nazism as the symbol of absolute evil. In line with the tradition of antisemitism, a wave of accusations associating Israel with ISIS has rapidly sprung up.

This defamation has a number of variations including that Israel has helped to create ISIS, is behind ISIS, is comparable to ISIS, and is the reason for ISIS. The short time during which the image of ISIS has developed in the public domain, enables us to closely follow the genesis of a new version of the old core calumny that Israel is absolute evil. Most, but far from the only, promoters of this hate come from the Muslim world, the extreme left and the extreme right.

Some of the earliest propagators of the new hate motif were Iranian. Its Islamic Republic News Agency, cited in 2014 a supposed interview with the American whistle-blower Edward Snowden, that a US, British and Israeli plot to destabilize the Middle East, code-named Hornet's Nest, was the force behind the creation of ISIS.[1] Another rumor attributed to Snowden, but which he has claimed is a hoax, is the one that ISIS leader Al Baghdadi is really a Jewish Mossad Agent named Elliot Shimon or Simon Elliot.[2]

In June of 2014, shortly before ISIS proclaimed itself a caliphate, Iranian Army Chief of Staff Gen Hassan Firouzabadi stated, "ISIS is Israel's cover up for distancing the revolutionary forces from Israeli borders and creating a margin of security for the Zionists."[3] Iranian Deputy Minister Hossein Amir Abdollahian claimed in November 2014 that Israel helped to create ISIS.[4]

In Europe, one of those who spread the hate message early was non-practicing Dutch Muslim Yasmina Haifi, an employee of the Dutch counter terrorism agency NCTV. Haifi had been a candidate of the Labor party in the 2012 parliamentary elections, although of very low rank. In August 2014, she tweeted, "ISIS has nothing to do with Islam . . . it is a plan of Zionists who want to blacken Islam."[5] Haifi thus attempted not only to whiten the Islamic character of the world's most extreme Islamo-Nazi movement, but in addition, to spread a conspiracy theory about Jews. A Facebook site supporting her went up that had more than 11,000 likes.

In the same month, Mohammad Shabbir, aide to MP Naz Shah of the British Labour Party, tweeted the question, "Is ISIS serving a purpose to create a pretext for Israel to invade Syria and Iraq? Has quest for greater Israel started?"[6] Salim Mulla, a Labour councilor and former mayor of Blackburn also claimed that Israel was behind ISIS. As so often among Muslim antisemites around the world, in addition to attacking Israel they also incite against Jews. Mulla wrote: "Zionist Jews are a disgrace to humanity."[7] Beinazir Lasharie, a Labour councillor in Kensington posted a Facebook message saying: "Many people know about who was behind 9/11 and also who is behind ISIS. I've nothing against Jews . . . just sharing it!"[8]

On the extreme right of the political spectrum, David Duke, former Imperial Wizard of the Ku Klux Klan whose antisemitic slurs frequently involve conspiracy theories, wrote an article titled: "Horrors of IS created by Zionist Supremacy." It lists a "series of planned deliberate actions, all initiated by Zio-Supremacist fanatics who seek to spread disunity, infighting and turmoil among all non-Jews, and particularly those neighboring their international headquarters of Israel."[9]

Allegations are indeed being spread across the political spectrum and across the world. Top Putin aide, Alexander Prokhanov, claimed in 2014 that the Mossad is training IS in order to undermine Russian interests in the Middle East.[10] A Polish-Nationalist website called *Justice4Poland* posted a widely-circulated article by Makia Freeman that opens with the sentence "IS is a US-Israeli creation, a fact as clear as the sky is blue."[11] This same article has been posted on left-wing and free-press sites such as GlobalResearch[12] and that of Paul Craig Roberts, former associate editor of *The Wall Street Journal* and author of *The Neoconservative Threat to World Order*.[13]

Another totally unfounded charge originated in an article published by the Qatari based *al-Araby al-Jadeed*.[14] It alleges that Israel is the main buyer of ISIS oil. The British parliamentarian Lady Tonge is a frequent producer of antisemitic slurs. She did not miss out on ISIS, saying: "The treatment of the Palestinians by Israel is a major cause of the rise of extreme Islamism and Daesh [IS]."[15]

Yet another major series of accusations claims that Israel and ISIS are comparable. We find American Jewish author Max Blumenthal—who calls Israelis Nazis—among those who say this. He is credited with coining the term JSIL (Jewish State in the Levant).[16] He is the son of Sidney Blumenthal, a close advisor to Hillary Clinton, of whom it is known that he passed on articles of his Holocaust inverter son to the presidential candidate.[17] The anti-Israel Jewish site Mondoweiss' Dan Cohen also claims credit for launching the JSIL hashtag along with Rania Khalek.[18]

Chris Hedges, the former *New York Times* Middle East bureau chief, in an article for the independent media site Truthdig titled "ISIS- the New Israel," has compared IS's tactics in creating an "ethnically pure Sunni state" to those of the "Jewish guerillas who used violence, terrorism, foreign fighters, clandestine arms shipments and foreign money, along with horrific ethnic cleansing and the massacre of hundreds of Arab civilians, to create Israel."[19] This is an example of making a false-moral equivalency.

The extreme leftist leader of the British Labour Party Jeremy Corbyn presented the Israel-IS comparison indirectly when he said "Our Jewish friends are no more responsible for the actions of Israel or the Netanyahu government than our Muslim friends are for those of various self-styled Islamic states or organizations."[20] The underlying assumption here is that Israel's and IS' actions are comparable sources of evil. Former Chief Rabbi of England Lord Jonathan Sacks called Corbyn's comment "demonization of the highest order."[21]

The above selection shows how in a short time a very diverse array of people across the political spectrum, who meet antisemitism definitions or are on its periphery, create a vast gamut of accusations, lies, defamation, etc.

This is a preliminary selection of charges of those connecting Israel with ISIS and represent only some of the antisemitic smears linking the two. These include that Israel is the main buyer of IS oil, that ISIS' rise is due to Israel's treatment of the Palestinians, and that the tactics of Israel and ISIS are the same. As time passes on more will develop.

It is not surprising that there are so many accusations - that is in line with the age-old nature of antisemitism. Social media accelerates the process. The same themes in articles, graphics, and conspiracy theories are being shared among people from very different origins. Also in this case antisemitism brings together people at odds with each other, in their common cause of vilifying Israel.

The Jerusalem Post, September 21, 2016

1   time.com/2992269/isis-is-an-american-plot-says-iran/
2   www.globalresearch.ca/isis-is-a-us-israeli-creation-top-ten-indications/5518627
3   www.jpost.com/Middle-East/Iran-army-chief-accuses-Israel-of-creating-ISIS-359875
4   www.haaretz.com/middle-east-news/1.624626
5   "PvdA-ambtenaar: ISIS is complot van zionisten," *De Telegraaf*, August 13, 2014.
6   www.israelnationalnews.com/News/News.aspx/211496
7   www.itv.com/news/granada/2016-05-02/former-mayor-of-blackburn-zionist-jews-are-a-disgrace-to-humanity/
8   www.independent.co.uk/news/uk/politics/khadim-hussain-former-lord-mayor-of-bradford-suspended-by-labour-party-over-anti-semitism-a6948856.html
9   davidduke.com/horrors-isis-created-zionist-supremacy/
10   www.jpost.com/Breaking-News/Top-Putin-aide-Mossad-training-ISIS-terrorists-in-Iraq-Syria-383963
11   justice4poland.com/2016/04/18/indications-that-isis-is-a-usisraeli-creation/
12   www.globalresearch.ca/isis-is-a-us-israeli-creation-top-ten-indications/5518627
13   www.paulcraigroberts.org/2016/04/09/ten-indications-that-isis-is-a-us-israeli-creation/
14   www.alaraby.co.uk/english/features/2015/11/26/raqqas-rockefellers-how-islamic-state-oil-flows-to-israel/

15   www.independent.co.uk/news/world/middle-east/israel-isis-creating-terrorism-
     baroness-tonge-liberal-democrat-a7150161.html
16   www.algemeiner.com/2014/10/06/jsil-another-obscene-israel-analogy/
17   www.jpost.com/Opinion/No-Holds-Barred-Hillarys-Clintons-troubling-rela-
     tionship-with-Israel-hating-adviser-441158
18   mondoweiss.net/2016/01/suddenly-comparing-jewish/
19   www.truthdig.com/report/item/isis_--_the_new_israel_20141214
20   edition.cnn.com/2016/06/30/europe/uk-corbyn-israel-isis/
21   www.bbc.com/news/uk-politics-36676018

The Long History of Progressives and Perversity

Many progressive organizations and individuals claim that they promote a better world. The perverse elements among them assert moral positions while they themselves are immoral or corrupt. In September 2001, the World Conference against Racism (WCAR) convened in Durban, South Africa. It became this century's first major manifestation of a new type of progressive perversity. Adjacent to it, an NGO conference took place with thousands of participating organizations that can best be characterized as an anti-Israeli hate fest.

Irwin Cotler, former Minister of Justice and Attorney General of Canada, is a leading international human rights advocate. He described the WCAR as "a festival of racism against Israel and the Jewish people . . . a conference dedicated to the promotion of human rights as the new secular religion of our time increasingly singled out Israel as a sort of modern day geopolitical anti-Christ."[1]

Israel and/or Jews are overrepresented as targets of progressive perverts, but they are far from the only ones aimed at. In 2018, the hypocrisy of various international humanitarian aid organizations was exposed. Oxfam UK was a leader among the deceivers. The head of its mission to Haiti after the 2010 earthquake regularly engaged in paid sex with a minor.

An internal investigation in 2011 led to the voluntary or forced departure of seven employees involved in sexual abuse in Haiti. The detailed report was kept secret yet many had access to it. These included the heads of the Dutch sister organization, Oxfam Novib. The latter made the report available to the Dutch Foreign Office as well as to the National Accounting office.

The scandal only became public in 2018. Thereafter additional information about sexual abuse elsewhere by employees of Oxfam UK came to the light. The same happened at other aid organizations including Save the Children and Doctors without Borders. All three organizations have been pseudomoral inciters against Israel.[2]

Amnesty International released its annual report on 2017, it was titled: "'Politics of demonization' breeding division and fear."[3]

NGO Monitor's website contains a long list of the organization's biased positions against Israel. One can say that they add up to demonization.[4] Progressives usually see themselves on the left of the political spectrum. Communism also claimed to be a progressive movement. Its ideology led to giant mass murders mainly in Russia and China. In its margins there were peace movements whose members attended gatherings organized by communist front organizations.[5] Nowadays anti-fascist movements are supposedly also progressive. The Paris branch of the far left Antifa organization has called for Israel's destruction.[6]

Social Democrat and Labour parties are also on the progressive side of politics. Among their elected representatives one finds quite a few promoters of perverse statements. Once again Israel is a good example to uncover the hypocrisy. Leading politicians such as the late Social Democrat Swedish Prime Minister Olof Palme[7] and the late Greek Socialist Prime Minister Andreas Papandreou have accused Israel of using Nazi practices.[8]

The British Labour Party has among its representatives a number of classic progressives next to progressive perverts. Antisemitic incidents in the party are frequent and perpetrators are far from always expelled. Several green parties can also be included in the category discussed above. Peter Pilz, a veteran Austrian Green parliamentarian, left the party and ran in the 2017 elections with his own list which gained entry into the parliament. Pilz did not take up his seat due to sexual harassment allegations.[9] He called the Palestinians 'victims' that one should side with and promoted partial sanctions against Israel.[10]

The history of perverse progressives goes back many centuries. Erasmus of Rotterdam who lived at the end of the fifteenth and beginning of the six-teenth century was called the "Prince of the Humanists." Dutch theologian Hans Jansen investigated Erasmus' antisemitism which was extreme even for its time. This "humanist" called Judaism the "worst pest." He even turned down an invitation to Spain in 1517, 25 years after the last non-converted Jews had left Spain, saying there was no more "Judaized country" than Spain.[11]

The largest student exchange program of the European Union is named after this hardcore antisemite.[12] Erasmus College in Brussels and the Erasmus University in Rotterdam are well known as well. Many other institutions are also named after Erasmus.

The famous French eighteenth century enlightenment philosopher, Vol-taire, was an antisemite as were several of the French socialist precursors of the nineteenth century. So was Karl Marx. The late Robert Wistrich's book, *From Ambivalence to Betrayal. The Left, The Jews and Israel*,[13] provides many additional examples of progressive perverts.

Progressive perversity partly overlaps with the narrower "humanitar-ian racism." Progressive perverts often just lie about Israel as Palme and Papandreou did. Humanitarian racists may bring true claims against Israel but remain silent about huge crimes of Palestinians and their leadership. Pro-gressive perverts and humanitarian racists frequently find willing partners among those Israelis and Jews who continue the millennia long tradition of Jewish masochism.[14]

After the Second World War, ugly aspects of extreme right wing move-ments have been analyzed in many detailed studies. Similarly in depth assess-ments of contemporary perverse progressives are long overdue.

The Jerusalem Post, March 7, 2018

1   www.jpost.com/Opinion/Op-Ed-Contributors/Durban-and-911-ten-years-later
2   tundratabloids.com/2018/03/dr-manfred-gerstenfeld-international-charities-sex-abuse-and-israel/
3   www.amnesty.org/en/latest/news/2017/02/amnesty-international-annual-report-201617/
4   www.ngo-monitor.org/ngos/amnesty_international/

5   www.nytimes.com/1983/07/26/world/kgb-officers-try-to-infiltrate-antiwar-groups.html?pagewanted=all

6   www.timesofisrael.com/french-antifa-calls-for-striking-a-blow-in-paris-over-us-jerusalem-recognition/

7   Per Ahlmark, "Palme's Legacy 15 Years On," *Project Syndicate*, February 2001.

8   Moses Altsech (Daniel Perdurant, pseud.), "Anti-Semitism in Contemporary Greek Society," *Analysis of Current Trends in Anti-Semitism*, 7 (Jerusalem: Hebrew University, 1995) 10.

9   www.reuters.com/article/us-austria-politics-pilz/austrian-party-leader-quits-parliament-over-accusation-of-sexual-assault-idUSKBN1D40H5

10 derstandard.at/2000003933349/Peter-Pilz-und-die-Dummheit-Israels

11 heplev.wordpress.com/2014/07/28/erasmus-furst-des-humanismus-der-renaissance-und-antisemit/

12 www.erasmusprogramme.com/

13 Robert Wistrich. *From Ambivalence to Betrayal. The Left, the Jews and Israel* (Lincoln, NE: University of Nebraska Press, 2012).

14 www.jpost.com/Opinion/From-Abraham-to-Woody-Allen-The-Jewish-masochist-tradition-409614

The Widespread Anti-Israelism in the United Kingdom

Various studies have shown how widespread the dislike of Israel and anti-Israelism are in a number of European countries. The University of Bielefeld, for instance, published a widely publicized report of seven EU countries in 2011.

One of the questions in this report asked those polled whether they agreed with the assertion that Israel is carrying out a war of extermination against the Palestinians. The lowest percentages of those who agreed were in Italy and the Netherlands, with 38 percent and 39 percent respectively. The others were Hungary 41 percent, United Kingdom 42 percent, Germany 48 percent, and Portugal 49 percent. In Poland, the figure was 63 percent.[1]

More detailed data on the specific prejudices against Israel are occasionally obtained. This is the case in a report from the UK by L. Daniel Staetsky titled, "Antisemitism in Contemporary Great Britain, a Study of Attitudes toward Jews and Israel." The study was published in September 2017 by the Institute for Jewish Policy Research (JPR) and the Community Security Trust (CST).[2]

Twelve specific statements about Israel were submitted to those who were interviewed.[3] The first asked whether Israel has the right to exist. Sixty two percent affirmed Israel's right to exist and 6 percent denied it. The remainder of the interviewees refused to answer or had no opinion. This outcome seems very positive at first glance. Yet it means that there are three million hard core antisemites in the UK who are in favor of the destruction of Israel. This goal can only be realized by murderous violence.

Another extreme finding of the report was the answer to the statement "Israel is committing mass murder in Palestine." Twenty four procent agreed with the statement and 22 percent disagreed. This affirmation is however not about an opinion but about facts. Israel is not conducting mass murder in "Palestine." Those who agree—representing twelve million UK citizens—are either extremely misled people or liars. Their agreement to this statement is an indicator of how far the demonization of Israel in the UK has advanced.

Interviewees were also asked whether they agreed with a somewhat similar false statement: "Israel is deliberately trying to wipe out the Palestinian population." In this case, 23 percent agreed and 26 percent disagreed.

The huge numbers of those who agree with the last two statements cannot only be explained by the number of Muslims (4.5 percent), extreme leftists (3.6 percent) and extreme rightists (1.4 percent) in British society.[4] Many of them must belong to the British mainstream.

Regarding the statement "Israel is an apartheid state," 14 percent agreed and 19 percent disagreed." To another question "Israel has too much control over global affairs," 17 percent agreed and 30 percent disagreed. More than eight million British citizens thus agreed with the "Zionist variant" of the classic antisemitic claim that Jews control the world.

Ten percent agreed with the statement "Israel is the cause of all the troubles in the Middle East," while 44 percent disagreed. Nine percent of those interviewed were in favor of boycotting Israel. This opinion apparently has also some support in the British mainstream.

Other statements submitted to those polled were: The state of Israel is the historic homeland of the Jewish people; The state of Israel makes a positive contribution to global society; The interests of Israelis are at odds with the interests of the rest of the world and Israel is the only real democracy in the Middle East. In the general population the percentage of those holding some anti-Israeli prejudice is substantially higher than those holding some antisemitic prejudice.

Analysis of the answers to the 12 statements of the survey among Christians show that their opinions do not statistically differ from those of the general population.[5] The findings concerning Muslims are however very different. While 9 percent of the general population agree with between six and nine anti-Israel attitudes, among Muslims the figure is 34.7 percent.[6] Seventy five procent of Muslims hold at least one anti-Israeli attitude,[7] as opposed to 47 percent of the general population.[8]

The study also analyzes whether there is a significant difference between religious and non-religious Muslims. Indeed, a somewhat higher percentage of Muslims who pray five times a day are hard-core "third generation anti-semites" who agree with between six and nine of the anti-Israeli attitudes than the percentage of those Muslims who never pray.

As far as prejudices go, i.e., those with at least one anti-Israeli attitude, the difference between Muslims who pray five times a day and those who never pray—"heritage Muslims"—is not very significant. Often, when a Muslim commits a crime somewhere in Europe against Jews, the media mentions that he isn't religious. This study seems to indicate that there is not such great a difference as far as prejudice against Israel is concerned between the very religious Muslims and those who are not religious at all.

A disproportional part of the anti-Israel and antisemitic remarks by representatives of the Labour party are made by Muslims.[9] Several of the latter represent areas with large concentrations of Muslims. The above findings explain why anti-Israel incitement can be assured of a welcome reception in their constituencies. The UK has not screened immigrants for their anti-semitic or anti-Israeli prejudices. This despite the fact that it is well known how widespread the hatred of Jews and Israel is in many of their Muslim countries of origin. The UK has thus become willingly a major importer of antisemites and Israel haters.

The UK government would do well to have a detailed study undertaken about the sources in British society which have caused the demonic view of Israel among so many citizens. This is not only an Israeli problem but also a British one. Large numbers of demonizers of others in a country is a sign of its partial cultural degeneration. The areas of society to be investigated include Muslims, the far left, the far right, media, politicians, academia, trade unions, NGOs and some church denominations.

There is also an Israeli angle to all this. The Palestinians and their many Muslim allies have for decades spread extreme hatred against Israel as well as lies about it. The Israeli government has largely ignored this and has not put in place a counter propaganda agency. Nor has it stressed that the promotion of antisemitic hate, including violence, is widespread in the world of Islam and that the great majority of Palestinians who support Hamas and Fatah is an integral part of various extremist Muslim currents. As a supervisory institution of the government, the Knesset has equally failed to induce successive governments to counter these developments.

Israel National News, September 2, 2018

1   library.fes.de/pdf-files/do/07908-20110311.pdf
2   www.jpr.org.uk/documents/JPR.2017.Antisemitism_in_contemporary_Great_Britain.pdf
3   Ibid., 29.
4   Ibid., 30.
5   Ibid., 8.
6   Ibid., 59.
7   Ibid., 66.
8   Ibid., 30.
9   www.israelnationalnews.com/Articles/Article.aspx/18841

France Keeps
Blackening Israel

Relations between France and Israel have been ambivalent and complex for decades. Among the most prominent are those where the French government sets out to blacken Israel. President Emanuel Macron is seemingly a new type of Frenchman. He reached the presidency without having risen through the ranks of an existing political party. He is a suave, intelligent politician with an excellent education, an international outlook, many ideas, and good public relations.

However, analysis has to concentrate on facts and not packaging. A good point of departure are the French reactions to the 2018 Gaza border violence. When Israeli Prime Minister Netanyahu met Macron in Paris in April of that year, the French president told him that the relocation of the US Embassy to Jerusalem, "led to people dying and did not advance peace."[1] With this transparently false statement Macron showed his skills in greatly distorting the truth in a few words. What provoked the violence was the terror organization Hamas' initiative to send civilians to the border and mix terrorists among them. Among the more than 115 Gazans killed by Israel, more than half were confirmed terrorists.[2] That many of those killed were terrorists was confirmed by Hamas itself.[3]

France also supported an UN Security Council resolution which called for protective measures for Palestinians, but didn't mention Hamas. Deputy Israeli Minister Michael Oren summarized it in a tweet: "Shame on France for supporting it. French government cannot say it's against antisemitism and vote for this antisemitic resolution.[4] During the violence in April 2018 France urged Israel to show restraint and told Israel that it was its duty to protect civilians.[5, 6] Their spokesmen knew full well that Hamas had sent terrorists to mingle among the civilians and that many civilian demonstrators did not have peaceful intentions. This French behavior was in particular hypocritical because of the many deadly terrorist attacks by Arabs in their country. The most deadly violence took place in Paris in 2015 and resulted in 130 deaths. In 2016, 86 people were murdered in Nice.

When IDF spokesman Brigadier General Ronen Manelis spoke to French parliamentarians he reminded them that along with other countries, French donations had helped Hamas to build terror capabilities.[7]

French reactions to the Gaza violence have deep roots in Middle Eastern history. In 2008, David Pryce-Jones published his book *Betrayal: France, the Arabs and the Jews*.[8] He had access to the archives of the French Foreign Ministry, better known as the Quay d'Orsay. His conclusion can be summarized as: France throughout modern history has done more damage to the Middle East than any other country.

France's reactions to the Gaza violence reminded me of a visit to a conference in Paris in autumn 1961, a few weeks after French policemen had murdered an estimated 150–200 non-violent Algerian demonstrators in the French capital on October 17, 1961. Some of the corpses were found in the river Seine. Historians have called it the most violent repression of a demonstration by a Western European state in contemporary history.[9] After more than fifty years of government silence then French President François Hollande in 2012 finally acknowledged the killings.[10] The resulting publicity over the years about the killings was so major that Macron and those who issued the condemnations of Israel must have been familiar with many details of these mass murders by the French police.

There are other aspects which should be taken into account when judging France's blackening statements of Israel. France is the most dangerous country in Europe for Jews. Of the fifteen Jews killed for ideological reasons in Europe—of which the perpetrators, all Muslims, are known—twelve were murdered in France in six different attacks.[11] The two mass attacks by violent Muslims on synagogues in the EU were both carried out in France, in Paris and Sarcelles.[12, 13]

Frequently exposing the ongoing French hypocritical blackening of Israel is unlikely to stop it, but it may make it less worthwhile for the official perpetrators.

Besa Center, July 25, 2018

1   www.haaretz.com/israel-news/watch-netanyahu-and-macron-give-statements-after-meeting-in-paris-1.6153497

2   www.timesofisrael.com/idf-spokesman-to-french-mps-hamas-is-spending-your-money-on-terror/

3   www.timesofisrael.com/hamas-official-50-of-the-people-killed-in-gaza-riots-were-members/

4   www.timesofisrael.com/michael-oren-french-envoy-in-twitter-spat-over-un-gaza-vote/

5   www.haaretz.com/world-news/europe/.premium-france-urges-israel-after-gaza-border-deaths-to-show-restraint-1.5973351

6   www.reuters.com/article/us-israel-usa-diplomacy-france/france-tells-israel-to-show-restraint-disapproves-of-u-s-embassy-move-idUSKCN1IF1ZG

7   www.timesofisrael.com/idf-spokesman-to-french-mps-hamas-is-spending-your-money-on-terror/

8   David Pryce-Jones, *Betrayal: France, the Arabs and the Jews* (New York: Encounter Books, 2006).

9   www.lemonde.fr/cinema/article/2011/10/14/octobre-a-paris-et-ici-on-noie-les-algeriens-le-17-octobre-1961-la-justice-se-noya-dans-la-seine_1587857_3476.html; www.lemonde.fr/societe/article/2011/10/17/17-octobre-1961-ce-massacre-a-ete-occulte-de-la-memoire-collective_1586418_3224.html

10 www.reuters.com/article/us-france-algeria/frances-hollande-acknowledges-1961-massacre-of-algerians-idUSBRE89G1NB20121017

11 Manfred Gerstenfeld, *War of a Million Cuts The Struggle Against the Delegitimization of Israel and the Jews, and the Growth of New Anti-Semitism* (Jerusalem: JCPA, 2015) 163.

12 www.france24.com/fr/20140716-emeutes-rue-roquette-synagogue-paris-anti-semitisme-conflit-isra%C3%A9lo-palestinien

13 www.huffingtonpost.co.uk/2014/07/22/france-jewish-shops-riot_n_5608612.html

EUROPE

The Clouded Future of Western European Jewry

The future of Western European Jewry seems clouded. The further away one gets from the Holocaust, the less resistance there is to the reemergence of antisemitism. This hate mongering has been an integral part of European culture for more than a thousand years.[1] To avoid misunderstanding: this should not be confused with the false statement that most Europeans are antisemites.

The problems for many Western European Jews in their social environment have been greatly enhanced by the immigration of millions of antisemites from Muslim countries where the majority of inhabitants have extreme prejudices toward Jews.[2] Statistics available show that both classic antisemitic and anti-Israeli attitudes among European Muslims are far more widespread than among the native populations.[3, 4] Worse still, all lethal terrorist acts in the past decade against Jews in Europe, of which the perpetrators have been identified, have been committed by Muslims.[5] In addition, many of the most extreme antisemitic statements also evolve from members of Muslim communities.

Furthermore there are frequent campaigns against Jewish rituals. The primary one concerns unstunned religious slaughter which is required for kosher meat. Switzerland was the first European country in the late nineteenth century, to forbid this. Before the Second World War unstunned religious slaughter was also prohibited in Sweden and Norway under Nazi influence. In recent years, it has been forbidden in Denmark and large parts of Belgium.[6, 7] In several other countries this way of slaughter is opposed by strong pro-animal groups and sometimes anti-Islam movements. Halal slaughter accounts for the great majority of animals slaughtered without stunning in Europe.

Iceland has a population of less than 350,000. It is not a member of the European Union. The country has a long antisemitic tradition.[8] The number of Jewish citizens has always been tiny. Iceland became the first European country to ban male circumcision.[9] Possible prohibition of this ritual is also being discussed from time to time in other Western European countries. Religious Jews can eat imported kosher meat if unstunned slaughter is forbidden in their country. Yet a much larger percentage of Jews than those eating kosher have their sons circumcised. A prohibition of this ritual would make the survival of Jewish communities far more problematic.

When analyzing the future of European Jewry another important factor is the nature of Jewish bonding. Nowadays this includes bonding through participation in religion, holidays and customs, bonding to the Jewish community and bonding via interest in Jewish culture. Other types of Jewish bonding include Israel, sensitivity to antisemitism as well as through Holocaust experiences and history.

Where antisemitic aggression occurs in the public domain, the dangers are not equally spread amongst all Jews. The greatest risks face those who are recognizable as Jews, for instance by their clothing or physiognomy. The severity of the problem also depends on the city and neighborhood where one lives. Sweden's third largest city Malmö is often considered Europe's capital of antisemitism.[10] Aggression of Jews in Malmö by far exceeds that in communities like the North London borough of Barnet, where many Jews live. Some public schools where Jewish children study may also be risky environments.

Next in line for aggression are synagogues, Jewish schools and other Jewish institutions. Jewish events, restaurants and shops have also been attacked.

The factors to take into account when discussing the Jewish future in Europe are disparate. High percentages of mixed marriages dilute Jewish bonding. In the decades following the war, several Jewish communities were strengthened by immigration such as the massive influx of North African

Jews that came into France in the 1950s and 1960s.[11] Another wave of immigration was comprised of Russian Jews who came to Germany.[12] No similar mass immigration in Western Europe seems to be on the horizon. There may be much smaller movements of Israelis into some European towns. Many of them do not participate in Jewish communal activities.

Factors which prevent people from leaving their home country, even if they want to, include lack of professional and language skills necessary in Israel, the United States or Canada. Family circumstances are also often a reason not to leave.

 Jewish emigration is not evenly spread among European countries. Antisemitism is often not the sole motivating factor. The largest Jewish emigration in recent years in absolute terms took place from France.[13] In the decision to leave, the economic problems of the country played a role as well. If in the United Kingdom the Labour party—rattled by antisemitism and led by the extreme leftist Jeremy Corbyn—comes to power, emigration of British Jews may well increase.[14]

Though no data is currently available on this, it is reasonable to assume that the percentage of those leaving are highest among those who are most actively Jewish. The core of European Jewish life thus seems to be eroding faster than that of the more marginal participants.

Due to the many factors which are in play, few precise forecasts can be made. Yet one thing is clear. Among the many issues determining the Jewish future in Western Europe few are positive.

The Jerusalem Post, March 20, 2018

1   www.jpost.com/Opinion/Why-anti-Semitism-is-part-of-European-culture-407050
2   www.adl.org/news/press-releases/adl-global-100-poll
3   www.israelnationalnews.com/Articles/Article.aspx/21562
4   www.israelnationalnews.com/Articles/Article.aspx/21678
5   jcpa.org/book/the-war-of-a-million-cuts-the-struggle-against-the-delegitimiza-tion-of-israel-and-the-jews-and-the-growth-of-new-anti-semitism/ 163.
6   www.theguardian.com/commentisfree/andrewbrown/2014/feb/20/denmark-halal-kosha-slaughter-hypocrisy-animal-welfare

7   www.independent.co.uk/news/world/europe/belgian-region-walloon-bans-
     kosher-halal-meat-islam-jewish-a7723451.html

8   www.jcpa.org/text/nordic.pdf, 219-239

9   www.nytimes.com/2018/02/28/world/europe/circumcision-ban-iceland.html

10   www.israelnationalnews.com/Articles/Article.aspx/16413

11   www.theguardian.com/news/2015/jan/15/-sp-threat-to-france-jews

12   jcpa.org/article/the-jewish-community-in-germany-living-with-recognition-
     anti-semitism-and-symbolic-roles/

13   www.theguardian.com/world/2017/jan/12/rise-in-numbers-of-jews-leaving-
     europe-for-israel-is-not-an-exodus

14   www.jpost.com/Opinion/Prime-minister-Jeremy-Corbyn-543796

Can Europe Without Jews Be Europe?

Austrian Chancellor Sebastian Kurz stated in 2018, "Europe without Jews cannot be Europe."[1] His country currently holds the Presidency of the Council of the European Union until the end of this year. Austria is organizing a conference on antisemitism on November 20–21 2018 jointly with the European Jewish Congress in Vienna.[2]

Kurz's statement should be investigated in some detail. Since the Second World War, Jews have once again held very senior positions in a number of Western European countries. France, Austria and Switzerland have had Jewish Prime Ministers. Belgium has had a Jewish Deputy Prime Minister. There have been Jewish ministers in the UK, France, Ireland, Italy, Denmark and the Netherlands. The UK and France currently have Jewish ministers. In the UK, both the Conservative and Labour parties have had Jewish leaders while their party was in opposition. Is there however anything specifically Jewish about the way these people performed their duties?

One can play with models. If one theoretically assumes that all Jews will leave Europe, what of importance would happen to the continent? The jobs held by Jews would be taken by others. Similarly others might continue part of the Jews' businesses. New residents would live in the houses and apartments formerly occupied by Jews. The absence of some Jews might be felt for a few years. The German occupation of many European countries during the Second World War has shown that societies can continue to function almost painlessly without Jews. Then Jews were expelled rapidly. Nowadays their departure, unlikely to be total, would be gradual.

If one wants to analyze whether Europe without Jews will indeed still be Europe or not, one must investigate in other directions. A major traditional symbolic role of Jews has been as scapegoats in European societies. That is now shared with immigrants. If Jews were to leave, radical Muslims and extreme rightists would have to vent their violence exclusively on others.

Jews who live in European society make antisemitic verbal targeting easier. Yet there is proof that one does not need a Jewish presence to be antisemitic. Furthermore, many antisemitic stereotypes and lies are now projected on Israel. The names and meanings of Shylock and Rothschild are strongly embedded in European culture and will remain so long after the hypothetical departure of Europe's last Jew.

Another important symbolic role Jews play in Europe is as an indicator of the democratic health of a country. This is strongest in Germany. If all Jews were to leave that country it would mean that Germany's society and its culture would be in deep trouble. The presence of more than one hundred thousand Jews legitimizes German democracy.

In both 2015 and 2016, French Prime Minister Emanuel Valls—then still a socialist—said: "Without the French Jews France will not be France." His first statement came after the murder by a Muslim of four Jews in a Paris Jewish supermarket. By that time tens of thousands of Jews had already emigrated from the country.[3] This is a partial indicator of France's unsolvable antisemitism problem.

A *Jewish Chronicle* poll found that 40 percent of British Jews would seriously consider leaving the UK if Labour leader and terrorist sympathizer Jeremy Corbyn were to become prime minister.[4] Even if this were to happen, there is unlikely to be a massive exodus of British Jews. Yet thinking about leaving is already an indicator of ill-feeling.

Jews make up less than 0.2 percent of the population of Sweden, yet they are a major indicator of the shaky state of law in this ultraliberal country. Sweden is the only country in Europe where a Jewish community, the one in the town of Umea, decided to dissolve itself due to neo-Nazi threats.[5] Quite a few other examples of antisemitism can be cited as indicators of Sweden's poor state of law and order.

In the imaginary assumption that there will be no living Jews left in Europe, many dead Jews will remain. These are often better liked than the living ones. Jewish cemeteries will stay. There are more than a thousand in Poland alone.[6] In certain areas, ashes of burnt Jews are inextricable.

After the Holocaust, many synagogue buildings of destroyed communities were put to other uses. The same may happen with many existing Jewish buildings. Most streets named after Jews are unlikely to be renamed. Holocaust monuments will not necessarily be taken down. Visits to Auschwitz and other extermination camps can continue. One does not need Jews to commemorate Kristallnacht or International Holocaust Memorial Day annually.

There are European leaders besides Chancellor Kurz who use strong rhetoric against antisemitism. This may make some Jews feel good. Whether these statements mean anything in practice remains to be seen and requires detailed investigation.

Far more important are the results of the upcoming Vienna conference. A number of necessary recommendations can easily be defined. These include halting the immigration process of additional antisemites into Europe, the establishment of a uniform system of reporting antisemitic incidents in all EU countries, and the carrying out of a reliable study on the antisemitic experiences of Jews. The study conducted by the FRA, the European Agency for Fundamental Rights to be published cannot be accurate as the sample is not representative. Furthermore, antisemitism commissioners should be appointed in all EU countries, using the German example. In addition, the number of staff people working for the EU commissioner for antisemitism should be greatly increased. Many more recommendations can be made.

Chancellor Kurz's statement was undoubtedly well-meant. Yet, if and when the last Jew leaves Europe or dies, one relevant and convenient change would ensue: Europe's unsolvable battle against antisemitism could be abandoned.

The Jerusalem Post, November 15, 2018

1   kurier.at/politik/inland/kurz-europa-ohne-juden-ist-nicht-mehr-europa/400310580

2   Ibid.

3   www.lefigaro.fr/flash-actu/2016/01/10/97001-20160110FILWWW00025-valls-sans-les-juifs-de-france-la-france-ne-serait-pas-la-france.php

4   www.thejc.com/news/uk-news/nearly-40-per-cent-of-british-jews-would-seri-ously-consider-emigrating-if-corbyn-became-pm-1.469270

5   www.jta.org/2018/07/10/news-opinion/caught-between-jihadists-and-neo-nazis-swedish-jews-fear-for-their-future

6   jewish-heritage-europe.eu/2017/11/01/the-state-of-jewish-cemeteries-in-po-land-2017/

Europe on the Couch: Proposal for a New EU Psychology Agency

In view of the extensive confusion in the European Union (EU) it seems appropriate for the European parliament to establish a new office in the EU—the European Union Psychology Agency (EUPSYCH). The head of this body would be independent. EUPSYCH would represent the interests of the public by investigating absurd and irrational attitudes as well as major perceptual anomalies in the Union from a psychological viewpoint. Furthermore, the EU should legislate a requirement for all member countries to appoint a national psychologist tasked with specific focus on his particular country.

This idea did indeed start out as a parody. However the subject becomes more serious when one tries to view the EU response to the refugee inflow with some distance. The reactions to the Paris massacre have only strengthened the need for such an agency.

For decades, Germany's society was characterized by fear (Angst). It was thought partly to result from the feeling that there was something inherently warped in their nation's character, following the atrocities committed by their ancestors under Nazi rule. This Angst has now returned, awoken by the incongruous open-door policy of the German government toward the refugees.

A 2015 poll in Germany found that 87 percent of the population are worried about the rise of right wing parties. More than 75 percent expressed concern that the influence of Islam in Germany will be too strong, that the number of criminal acts will increase, and that the risk of terror in Germany will rise.[1]

In France, the various Islamic State terrorist acts have led to greatly increased levels of anxiety, shared to a lesser extent by the populations of other Western European countries. This fearfulness is not entirely rational. The Islamic State movement does not have the ability or means to undertake regular attacks of that size in France, or in any other European country for that matter. However heavy and horrific the death toll and that of the wounded is, the figure represents only 1:100,000 of France's total population. Yet the attacks have led many foreign tourists to cancel their bookings. There was far more logic involved when tourists cancelled their bookings in Sharm el Sheikh in Sinai due to the local situation. The rational and irrational aspects of fear are typical subjects for psychological investigation.

The idea that countries can be put on the couch is not new. This concept emerged, for example, at the end of the previous century when after decades of silence, the issue of Holocaust restitution again came to the fore. It led to soul-searching in many countries occupied by the Germans during the Second World War. It could be explained as a desire on the part of those nations involved, during a relative quiet period at the end of the twentieth century, to take stock of where they had morally failed in the past decades.

The psychologist leads the patient to observe his own behavior, so that he begins to see its irrationality. Similarly Europe 'on the couch' might observe the oddity of many of its actions and attitudes with more objectivity.

One often repeated statement which provides much fodder for psychologists is that Europe is an "economic giant, a political dwarf and a military worm." This expression was coined by the Belgian politician Mark Eyskens in 1991[2] and is not only an issue for political analysts. The maintenance of such a reality, and particularly the mindset which has enabled it, fall within the psychologist's domain of investigation. A far more pressing current matter for in-depth psychological evaluation is the way in which the leaders of an emotionally and mentally injured France now grandstand in a very incomplete effort toward a war against ISIS.[3] This too requires a form of analysis which goes beyond the political and the social.

The issue of European values should also be looked into. Safety of citizens versus human rights is but one theme among many for investigation. In

France, the need to profile members of the Muslim community, home to the country's most murderous ideological criminals, clashes with the national motto of "liberty, brotherhood and equality."

Social psychologists could explore the influence of interpersonal relationships on EU behavior. Germany has underplayed its power for many years within the German-French axis which controlled the EU The late German chancellor Helmut Schmidt warned that European resentment would result if Germany played a dominant role in the EU[4]

The psychological aspects of attitudes and behavior in Europe are so numerous that only a few examples can be given here. As Israel and the Jews take such a disproportionate place in the European public discourse this subject provides a wealth of initial subjects for investigation.

One prominent example is the fact that more than forty percent of the European population believe that Israel is conducting a war of extermination against the Palestinians. In Poland, the figure is much higher.[5] This delusion belongs in the realm of psychiatry. It should be treated as a mental disorder, as it is a perceptual aberration. Should all these Europeans be prescribed medication? It would be a boon for the pharmaceutical industry.

There is far too much to say about this issue than can be contained in one article, but one can mention some of EU members' significantly irrational moments to sharpen the point: Why has Belgium knowingly and recklessly ignored the development of a hotbed of extreme radical Muslims in the Brussels area? And of a very different but also irrational nature, why do The Netherlands remain the only Western country incapable of apologizing for its total disinterest of the suffering of its Jews in the Second World War?

Sweden is a prime candidate for the appointment of a national psychiatrist. Its Prime Minister Olof Palme compared Israel to Nazis.[6] Several of its social democrat foreign ministers, the late Anna Lindh, Laila Freivalds and currently Margot Wallström[7] suffer(ed) from negative obsessions concerning Israel. The same is true for the Moderate party foreign minister Carl Bildt. Under the social democrat mayor Ilmar Reepalu Malmö has become the European capital of antisemitism.[8] This can only be explained by defining these phenomena as a mental disorder not limited to Swedish social democrats.

Psychologists often claim that their profession is improving the world. The proposed EUPSYCH agency will give them much food for thought, and plenty of work to do.

The Jerusalem Post, December 2, 2015

1   http://www.welt.de/politik/deutschland/article148483375/Fluechtlingskrise-wovor-Deutsche-wirklich-Angst-haben.html

2   www.washingtonpost.com/wp-srv/inatl/longterm/balkans/stories/europe032699.htm

3   www.israelnationalnews.com/Articles/Article.aspx/17901

4   Helmut Schmidt, "Germany In, With and For Europe," *Social Europe*, August 12, 2015.

5   library.fes.de/pdf-files/do/07908-20110311.pdf.

6   Per Ahlmark, "Palme's Legacy 15 Years On," *Project Syndicate*, February 2001.

7   www.jpost.com/Israel-News/Politics-And-Diplomacy/Israel-condemns-hostile-Swedish-comments-linking-Paris-attacks-to-Israeli-Palestinian-conflict-434249

8   www.israelnationalnews.com/Articles/Article.aspx/16413#.Vk1voHYrK7R

Europe's Rule of Law
and the Jews

A key characteristic of democracy is the rule of the law. One cannot analyze the problems of such a complex subject easily in an area as big as the European Union (EU). As a useful shortcut, one can however focus one's assessment on a small community which has many interactions with the majority population and the state. Jews, who represent about 0.3 percent of the EU's population and in no country reach even one percent are an appropriate instrument for such an analysis.

A few extreme court cases or lack of them will expose a variety of problems of the rule of law in EU countries. For a start, there is the lawsuit brought in 2001 against Israeli Prime Minister Ariel Sharon in Belgium and two Israeli generals by family members of Palestinians murdered by Christian Lebanese militia in 1982 in the camps of Sabra and Shatilah. It was a political process of people who had already been investigated in Israel.

The Belgian procurer general did not want to prosecute, yet in a highly unusual decision the appeals court did not accept his position. The process finally dissolved to nothing because the Belgians overplayed their hand and wanted to prosecute under the same universal law also US president George Bush sr and two others. The American government thereupon threatened to move the NATO headquarters from Brussels. The Belgian parliament thereupon voted to change its laws of universal jurisdiction.

One scandalous judgment in Germany concerned three Palestinians who attempted to burn down a synagogue in the town of Wuppertal in 2014. In judging this, a German court decided that this was out of protest against Israel and could not be considered an antisemitic act. The perpetrators were given suspended sentences.[1]

In December 2017, three perpetrators threw a Molotov cocktail at a synagogue in Sweden's second largest city, Gothenburg. Some twenty Jewish youngsters in the building took shelter in its cellar during the attack.[2] A Swedish appeals court overturned a criminal tribunal ruling stating that one of the perpetrators, a Gaza-born Palestinian, would be deported at the end of his two year prison term. The court said that he should not be deported because the antisemitic nature of this attack could put him in danger from Israel.[3] The court apparently preferred the imagined interests of the perpetrator over those of his victims. If he stayed in Sweden he could commit other crimes.

An indirect result of the deficiencies of the rule of law in ultra-liberal Sweden was that the Jewish community of Umea was dissolved because of neo-Nazi threats. Nothing similar has occurred anywhere else in the EU in this century.[4]

Sweden's third largest city, Malmö, is considered by many experts as the capital of European antisemitism. The perpetrators of the many physical and verbal antisemitic acts are mostly, or perhaps even all, Muslims.[5] A record number of complaints about hate crimes in the city in 2010 and 2011 did not lead to any convictions.[6]

In the Netherlands, the failures of the rule of law are less extreme. In 2017, Israeli high schoolchildren visited the Dutch parliament. A Muslim municipal council member in The Hague, Abdoe Khoulani, called the students "Zionist terrorists in training" and "future child murderers and occupiers." A Dutch judge dismissed a court case against Khoulani, saying his remarks did not constitute incitement to hate.[7]

One court case in the United Kingdom is described in great detail by David Hirsch in his book *Contemporary Left Antisemitism*. It concerns the British Jewish academic activist Ronnie Fraser who in 2011 took his trade union, the University and College Union (UCU) to court for antisemitism. His argument was that a culture of institutional antisemitism has been created by the union, which meant antisemitic harassment against him. The tribunal judged that "there had been no antisemitism at all." It found against Fraser on everything: on technicalities, on legal argument and on every significant issue of substance and of fact. Hirsh details how a number of witnesses in favor of Fraser, were ignored and not mentioned in the court's judgement.[8]

In 2010, a British judge George Bathurst-Norman influenced a jury to clear a group of campaigners who had attacked and damaged a factory that made parts for Israeli war planes. In the criminal damage trial, he compared Israel to the Nazi regime.[9] The Office of Criminal Complaints later said that the judge was reprimanded for his words.[10]

The problems in France are again of a different nature. It took a long time before France recognized that the murder of Sarah Halimi in 2017 by her Muslim neighbor was a hate crime.[11]

This was all the more worrying because already in 2001 there was a huge outburst of antisemitic attacks in France mainly perpetrated by Muslim immigrants. For a long time both the press and public authorities hardly reported these cases.

The above few cases already demonstrate major legal failures concerning Jews in several European countries. They are indicative of shortcomings in the rule of law and indicative of these countries' democratic deficit.

The Jerusalem Post, November 3, 2018

1   www.jta.org/2017/01/15/news-opinion/world/german-court-affirms-ruling-that-said-synagogue-arson-isnt-anti-semitic; www.tagesspiegel.de/politik/antisemitismus-in-deutschland-wie-kann-ein-anschlag-auf-eine-synagoge-nicht-judenfeindlich-sein/19572812.html

2   www.thelocal.se/20180625/three-men-sentenced-over-attack-on-gothenburg-synagogue

3   www.telegraph.co.uk/news/2018/09/15/sweden-refuses-deport-palestinian-firebombed-synagogue-fear/

4   www.jta.org/2018/07/10/news-opinion/caught-between-jihadists-and-neo-nazis-swedish-jews-fear-for-their-future

5   www.jta.org/2012/09/24/life-religion/in-scandinavia-kipah-becomes-a-symbol-of-defiance-for-malmos-jews

6   www.jta.org/2013/01/09/news-opinion/world/in-malmo-record-number-of-hate-crimes-complaints-but-no-convictions

7   www.algemeiner.com/2018/07/26/dutch-muslim-parties-a-new-development-in-islamization/

8   David Hirsch, *Contemporary Left Antisemitism* (London and New York: Routledge, 2018) 154.

9   www.dailymail.co.uk/news/article-1297219/Judge-faces-anti-semitism-probe-speech-attacking-Israel-helps-free-arms-factory-protesters.html

10   www.bbc.com/news/uk-england-sussex-11493124

11   www.jpost.com/Diaspora/The-antisemitic-murder-France-is-trying-to-sweep-under-the-table-496803 www.timesofisrael.com/paris-muslim-accused-of-killing-jewish-woman-no-longer-charged-with-hate-crime

Open Letter to
the EU Ambassador to Israel

Dear Ambassador Emanuele Giaufret,

Welcome to Israel. As the European Union has often given doubtful advice to Israel, I take the liberty of making some suggestions on how your assignment here can be successful.

Please remember that you represent the greater part of a continent where antisemitism is ingrained in its culture for over a thousand years. The leading academic scholar of antisemitism in our generation, the late Robert Wistrich, has shown that almost all Europe's ideological currents during those centuries were infected with antisemitism.[1]

Please also be aware that in the past decades EU members have let in—without a selection process—millions of people from countries where most citizens are antisemitic. To make matters worse, in the past two years large numbers of more such people have been given the opportunity to immigrate to the EU.[2] The fact is that all Jews who have been killed in Western Europe for ideological reasons in the current century were murdered by Muslim immigrants or their descendants.[3]

Your predecessor, Mr. Ambassador, repeatedly kept telling Israel that "settlement construction." was a hindrance to peace. Sometimes he threatened us, for instance in 2014, "if Israel's settlement policies wrecked the current US-led peace efforts, then Israel would be held responsible for the failure of the negotiations."[4] He did not stress that the Palestinian Authority continuously pays high "salaries" to the families of murderers of Israeli civilians.[5] Not mentioning how big a hindrance to peace this is was one of many reasons why he frequently undermined the EU's credibility in Israel. He should have admitted publicly that the financing by European countries of the Palestinian Authority is indirectly giving a bonus to the murderers of Israelis.

I suggest also that you do not paint rosy pictures of a future peace. Your predecessor told us how beautiful the Middle East would look after a peace agreement is signed. He said, "Israel would be in a pole position to promote regional integration in the eastern Mediterranean"[6] The facts are that despite Israel's peace treaty with Egypt in 1978 and the one with Jordan in 1994 both countries appear in the list of major anti-Israel inciters and antisemitism promoters in a State Department report.[7, 8]

Earlier this year Palestinian murderers coming from the Temple Mount killed Israeli policemen. Israel thereupon took security measures. The Palestinians turned that into an opportunity for international Muslim incitement against Israel. It is not difficult to see that after Israel makes territorial concessions for a peace agreement with the Palestinians, nothing will prevent the Palestinians—if there is a two state agreement—from creating more unjustified international religious mayhem around the Temple Mount.

I would also suggest that you avoid giving advice which is so obviously bad. Your predecessor advised Israel to collaborate with the UNHRC investigation commission on the 2014 Gaza War, despite the fact that that body was biased against Israel from the outset.[9] Also please avoid making statements which lack of truth is transparent. That was the case with your predecessor's attempt to deny the discriminatory character of the EU's labelling of products from the West Bank. Israel's Foreign Ministry then accused the EU of ignoring more than 200 territorial conflicts around the world by singling out Israel as the only place requiring separate labels in the territories.[10]

It is indeed crucial for an EU Ambassador to be truthful and credible. In his departure speech Mr. Faaborg-Andersen said that Israel could learn from Europe about fighting terror.[11] There have been far more attempts at terror attacks in Israel than in Europe. Yet in none of the deadly attacks in Israel have as many people been killed as in those in Madrid in 2004, in London in 2005, in Paris in 2015 and in Nice in 2016. There is much information about

EU member countries' lack of ability to identify early the radicalization of Muslim individuals, their intention to join jihadi organizations or carry out terror attacks.

Your predecessor also said that "Antisemitism in Europe is a phenomenon we are combating—even more than Israel is."[12] The first step to do so in an orderly way is to have an accepted definition of what antisemitism is. The only working definition accepted by some in Europe was suddenly taken off the website from your Fundamental Rights Agency in 2013.[13] What would have been easier for the EU than to accept the 2016 definition of the International Holocaust Remembrance Alliance and become an associated member of the IHRA. All the above has helped create suspicion toward the EU even if there are many interesting aspects to EU-Israeli cooperation.

In light of the above, EU interference and comments regarding internal Israeli matters are not appreciated. People usually are open to advice from those who are supportive of them and not from those who have themselves made huge mistakes.

Mr. Ambassador, as you know well, the role of a EU diplomat is not only to represent his region. He also should report back to those who delegated him whether EU policies are conducive to better relations with the country in which he is stationed.

I wish you success in your endeavors.

The Jerusalem Post, September 13, 2017

1   www.israelnationalnews.com/Articles/Article.aspx/14217
2   www.bbc.com/news/world-europe-34131911
3   www.israelnationalnews.com/Articles/Article.aspx/20768
4   www.timesofisrael.com/eu-envoy-we-doesnt-understand-israels-jewish-state-demand/
5   spectator.org/251138-2/
6   www.haaretz.com/misc/haaretzcomsmartphoneapp/1.601978
7   www.thetower.org/5348-state-dept-report-anti-semitism-pervasive-in-iran-egypt-jordan-qatar/
8   www.state.gov/j/drl/rls/irf/2016/nea/268898.htm

9   www.jpost.com/Arab-Israeli-Conflict/Israel-calls-UN-Gaza-war-report-politically-motivated-and-morally-flawed-from-the-outset-406775

10 www.timesofisrael.com/eu-envoy-insists-settlement-labeling-purely-technical/

11 www.jpost.com/In-Jerusalem/Rock-Solid-Europe-Israel-ties-are-flourishing-says-outgoing-EU-envoy-504256

12 www.jpost.com/In-Jerusalem/Rock-Solid-Europe-Israel-ties-are-flourishing-says-outgoing-EU-envoy-504256

13 www.timesofisrael.com/eu-drops-its-working-definition-of-anti-semitism/

How European Jews Moved into Exile Without Relocating

After 1948, many Jews in the Western world gradually began to consider themselves as living in the diaspora rather than in *galut*, which translates as exile. The establishment of the State of Israel gave Jews abroad an increased self-confidence, and their self-perception changed accordingly. In addition, many Israeli institutions increasingly began to use the word *tfutsot* (diaspora) to describe Jews living outside the country. Like many of its predecessors, the current Israeli government has a ministry which has the term "diaspora" in its title.

In the new century, however, an increasing number of European Jews have moved—without relocating—from living in the Israeli diaspora to becoming Jews in exile. This change in perspective is a result of being the targets of violence and of feeling outsiders who, when they gather, must take security precautions which for others are unnecessary. There is also an increasing fear of expressing one's identity as one would wish, and it is often becoming impossible to freely state one's opinions.

Thus, these Jews are *de facto* in exile, even if their living conditions differ from those of the European Jews immediately following the Second World War. The Holocaust has taught many Jews that they were not considered part of the native population of their countries, no matter what passports they might hold. This was not because of what the German occupiers did to them, but rather due to the attitude and behavior of many of their co-nationals during that time.

In 2003, the late Israeli historian David Bankier eloquently described the

Polish reality, the country which had the largest pre-war Jewish population in Europe. When I interviewed him, Bankier said, "The Jews were never considered part of the fabric of Polish society. Their ancestors may have lived there for 900 or even 1,000 years, but, as they did not belong to the national majority, they remained foreigners. Most people did not see in the catastrophe befalling the Polish Jews a tragedy affecting the Polish nation. At best, they saw two parallel disasters caused by the Germans. One concerned the Polish nation, the other the Jews."[1]

Bankier also quoted an underground leader who claimed that it had been her duty to help save Jewish lives during the war. She added, however, that after the war, the Jews should leave Poland, because she wanted to live only among fellow Poles.

The Holocaust was a giant murderous challenge for all Jews in German-occupied countries. For assimilated Jews, however, it was also an intellectual challenge. Self-identification which included denying one's Jewishness was made irrelevant. A third party, the occupiers, now determined whether or not you were a Jew.

Once the State of Israel was established, the Jews of Western Europe gradually began to feel like other citizens. Antisemitism had largely become latent. All positions were open to Jews. In the Netherlands, for instance, certain official positions had been *de facto* closed to Jews before the war. These included appointments such as those of city mayors. Since the war, there have however been a number of Jewish mayors. In Amsterdam alone, there were four. The diplomatic service was also closed to Jews before the war. After the war there have been Jewish diplomats—one of them an Orthodox Jew.

In the 1950s, when I was a pupil at the Jewish high school in Amsterdam, the janitor would open the door when the doorbell rang without first checking who was standing outside. In the Jewish elementary school, during recess, we kids played in the street in front of the school. Today, when I walk through Amsterdam, I see kids in public schools playing freely in the schoolyard. There is no fear that somebody might attempt to hurt them. In stark contrast, children attending the Jewish schools nowadays do so in fortress-like buildings, and they are often told not to wear anything outside which identifies them as Jews.

In this new century, various Jewish leaders have recommended that Jews hide their identities in public places. In a 2003 radio interview for instance, then French Chief Rabbi Joseph Sitruk told French Jews to wear hats, rather than kippot, so as to avoid being attacked in the streets.[2]

One small example of how Jews are verbally attacked in the workplace for what Israel does, or allegedly does, was given by a Jewish hospital nurse from Amsterdam whom I interviewed. In view of the Dutch reality she requested to remain anonymous. She said: "Whenever the Dutch media wrote something about Israel, people would start a political discussion with me. They behaved as if I shaped Israeli politics. No one would ever say to someone with family in Italy: 'What crazy thing has Berlusconi done again?'"[3]

Even stating the truth proves to be problematic for Jewish leaders in some countries. In 2015, Roger Cukierman, the head of the umbrella body of French Jewish organizations, CRIF, said that all violence against the Jewish community was perpetrated by young Muslims, "even if they are a very small minority of the Muslim community."[4] Thereupon, French President François Hollande called for a 'reconciliation' meeting between Cukierman and a Muslim leader. The purpose of the meeting was essentially to obfuscate the truth.

We are still waiting for the first Jewish leader in Europe to state the truth - that the non-selective, mass immigration of large numbers of Muslims is the worst thing to happen to the European Jewish communities since the end of the Second World War. To be fair, one should add that this is partly the fault of the government authorities who let them in indiscriminately and were ill-prepared for their integration in society.

The reactions of many Jews to these developments show that their attitudes are becoming increasingly similar to the classic *galut* mentality. This became clear from a 2013 study conducted by the European Union Fundamental Rights Agency. It was undertaken in France, Belgium, Hungary, Denmark, Latvia, Italy, Sweden, and the United Kingdom. The study found that on average, 20 percent of the Jews in these countries said they always avoided wearing, carrying, or displaying things that might help people identify them as Jews in public.[5]

Of the countries included in the study, Sweden had the highest percentage of Jews who tried to avoid being identified, with 34 percent of those interviewed stating that they avoided such identification most of the time.[6] This cannot be explained solely by the frequent antisemitic incidents taking place in Malmö, which are mainly perpetrated by Muslims. The Jewish population in that city represents far less than 10 percent of Swedish Jewry.

In 2011, Islin Abrahamsen and Chava Savosnick conducted a qualitative study for the Norwegian Jewish community, regarding the experiences of Jewish children and young people with antisemitism in the country. Twenty-one young Norwegian Jews, of school age up to twenty-five years of age, were interviewed. The study found that young Jews often do not reveal their religious identity. Some have changed schools, or their parents have even changed residences because of the antisemitism they have experienced.[7]

While the hiding of one's Jewish identity may be the main indicator of this reborn *galut* mentality, there are many others.

While the *galut* phenomenon is quite established in Europe, it does exist in the United States as well. A typical example is the moot Jewish reaction to a variety of statements made by US President Barack Obama who regularly uses double standards against Israel.

As pressure on Jews abroad augments, the *galut* mentality among many Jews will intensify. It will become even clearer than today, that we should no longer speak about a Jewish diaspora, but about European Jews in exile.

The Jerusalem Post, July 5, 2015

1   Manfred Gerstenfeld, *Europe's Crumbling Myths: The Post-Holocaust Origins of To-day's Anti-Semitism* (Jerusalem: Jerusalem Center for Public Affairs, Yad Vashem, World Jewish Congress, 2003) 93–101.

2   Philip Carmel, "Proposals on yarmulkes, Yom Kippur given mixed reaction by French Jews," JTA, December 14, 2003.

3   Manfred Gerstenfeld, "Jewish and Cautious in Amsterdam," *Israel National News*, February 24, 2014.

4   "Propos sur les musulmans: Hollande réconcilie Cukierman et Boubakeur," *Le Parisien*, February 24, 2015.

5   "Discrimination and hate crime against Jews in EU Member States: experiences and perceptions of anti-Semitism," European Union Agency for Fundamental Rights, 2013, 36.

6   Ibid.

7   Stein Gudvangen, "Norske barn tør ikke stå fram som jøder," *Dagen*, June 6, 2012.

The Events of May 1968 and the Jews

In May 1968 huge demonstrations and strikes took place in France. An estimated eleven million people participated in the strikes. At the height of these developments the country came to a near standstill. This period was referred to as the "Events of May," even though the first event, an occupation of a building at the Nanterre branch of Paris University, occurred in March 1968. During the crisis then French President Charles de Gaulle even asked the military whether the army would be willing to intervene if the situation turned into a revolution.

Living in Paris at the time, I went several evenings to Boulevard Montmartre, a main street. From the corner of a side street I watched many young people shouting. There were probably far more hooligans among them than students. Opposite them, a few meters away stood the special French police, the CRS. The youth shouted: "CRS-SS."

After some time, the CRS were fed up and marched toward the protestors who fled. I moved away from the battlefield and walked up the side street. Tear gas, heavier than air, wafted from the underground Metro stations.

Among the leaders of the student uprising were a number of Jews. The best known was Daniel Cohn Bendit, nicknamed "Danni the Red." Scholar Yair Auron claims that personal or parental experiences in the Holocaust accounted for the move to the radical left of a number of Jewish youngsters in France. The parents of quite a few had immigrated from Eastern Europe.

Auron quotes a well-known joke about the leaders of the Trotskyite Communist Revolutionary League which played an important role in the strike. Why
did they not speak Yiddish among them when their movement's politbureau
met: because one of them was a Sefardi Jew. At the time Jewish radical leftists
were not yet consistently anti-Israel as is the case today. They were rather
ambivalent about the Jewish state, especially when it was in peril of being
wiped out. Here also the Holocaust experience as well as the fear of another
one played a role.[1]

The last position of my lengthy experience as a student leader was four
years as Chairman of the World Union of Jewish Students ending in 1967.
At that time international Jewish organizations still looked upon Jewish
students with near-benign neglect. This changed after 1968, partly as a result
of the "Events of May." In 2001, the UN World Conference against Racism
took place in Durban, South Africa. It was accompanied by a major NGO
conference. These gatherings turned into an anti-Israel hate-fest. Jewish
students were then in the forefront of defending Israel against the gathering
of antisemites.

The failed May 1968 "revolution" did not have a huge immediate impact.
It would take many people, including myself, decades to understand how
important the "Events of May" had been, together with other occurrences
which brought major changes to Western society at large.

One of the main results of societal change was the breakdown of authority. It affected governments, church leaders, student administrations,
teachers and parents. The "Events of May" were one of the major components
which led to this change. The impact of decolonization was another important
one among many others.

In the United States, the organization, Students for Democratic Society,
was an important influence in the mid-1960s. The expression "I am a human
being: Do not fold, spindle or mutilate" dates from that period. The unpopular
Vietnam War also contributed to many societal changes. In 1969, the Wood-
stock Festival came to symbolize this changed reality.

The greater openness of society was initially good for minorities, including the Jews. Their voices could now be heard more than in the past. This was
true especially at the end of the 1990s. It enabled an important new round
of Holocaust restitution in Europe accompanied by the revelation of many

additional data about those who had collaborated in Europe with the German Nazis. Switzerland was a prime example.

Partly due to the emergence of social media these changes overshot what was desirable. Greater freedom also means an increase in incitement. In the US, hate speech is widespread as the first article of the constitution makes the country a near-paradise for hate mongers. This is very relevant for Jews. Many American universities are currently at the forefront of the antisemitic trend focusing on Israel.

Jewish life is at its best in democratic societies where the rule of law is dominant. This is less and less the case in Europe. Several decades after the "Events of May" backpedaling on some civil liberties has become a necessity for the survival of liberal democracies. In Europe, massive immigration, which includes many who do not want to integrate, makes this even more necessary.

The Jerusalem Post, April 26, 2018

1   Yair Auron, *The Phenomenon of Jewish Radicals in France During the 1960s and 1970s*, Policy Forum, no. 19, Institute of World Jewish Congress, Jerusalem, 2000.

When Bevin Was a Supporter of Zionism

Interview with Ronnie Fraser

"In Zionist history, British Foreign Secretary Ernest Bevin was the most hated person in the immediate post-war years. This senior Labour politician had opposed removing the limiting of Jewish immigration to Palestine. It is however little known that Bevin was an important supporter of Zionism in the 1930s on the occasion of a hard fought parliamentary by-election in the Whitechapel area of London where 40 percent of the population were Jews."

Dr. Ronnie Fraser is the Director of the Academic Friends of Israel—a voluntary position—which campaigns against the academic boycott of Israel and antisemitism on campus. His doctoral thesis focuses on the attitude of the British Trade Union Movement (TUC) toward Israel over the years 1945–1982.

"In 1930, a minority Labour government headed by Ramsay MacDonald was in power. Lord Passfield (Sidney Webb), the Colonial Secretary, issued what became known as the Passfield White Paper on British Policy in Palestine on October 20, 1930. Its tone was anti-Jewish and it criticized Jewish institutions.

"One proposal of the White Paper required Jews to get permission from the British authorities before acquiring additional land in Palestine. Four days after the White Paper was issued Harry Gosling, the Labour MP of Whitechapel, died. In the 1929 elections he had obtained a 9,180 majority. It was then considered a safe Labour seat. Yet many Jewish constituents vehemently opposed the White Paper. Losing the seat in the following byelection would bring the Government down.

"The problems for Labour increased further when the Liberals put up a Jewish candidate for the seat, Barnett Janner, a leading member of the English Zionist Federation. The Labour Zionists of Poale Zion wondered whom to support. They considered however that the byelection enabled them to draw the attention of the Labour Party to the unfairness of the White Paper and largely undo its proposals.

"In 1928, Ben Gurion had sent Dov Hoz from Palestine to London as emissary of the trade union, Histadrut. Hoz encouraged the local branches of Poale Zion to campaign for the Labour party in the 1929 general election. Initially the Labour Party intended to put up a junior minister as their candidate for the Whitechapel by-election but withdrew him when Hoz informed Labour that Poale Zion could not support a member of the government which had issued the White Paper.

"Labour then asked Bevin, the General Secretary of the Transport and General Workers' Union (TGWU) to stand. He refused. The union thereafter proposed James Hall, another of its executives as candidate. Bevin knew that to retain the seat, the Jewish vote and the support of Poale Zion was needed. Hoz told Bevin that Poale Zion would not support the Labour candidate unless key conditions of the Passfield White Paper were undone.

"Bevin wrote to the government that he agreed with Poale Zion. After assurances he released a statement that the government had explicitly declared that they had no intention of altering the interpretation of the British Mandate in Palestine. Bevin furthermore told Hoz that all 26 MP's sponsored by the TGWU would vote against the government on the White Paper in the House of Commons. He was however unwilling to force the issue because the government would be defeated.

"Hall told Poale Zion that there were inferences in the White Paper which he could not reconcile with the Labour Party's past declarations and that he would vote in the House of Commons against changes in the party's policy on Palestine. The Labour Party also received many protest letters and telegrams against the White Paper from national and international trade union organizations.

"Due to Bevin's intervention and his undertaking to fight the White

Paper, Poale Zion decided to actively campaign on behalf of Hall. This decision to back the Labour candidate caused much criticism from fellow Zionists both in the UK and abroad. The *Jewish Chronicle* described Poale Zion's policy as a 'traitorous cause.'

"In Palestine, there was also much criticism from Histadrut members. The revisionists called Hoz a traitor for supporting a non-Jewish Labour candidate over a liberal Zionist Jew. They claimed that Hoz demonstrated that his loyalty to the working class was stronger than his commitment to Zionism. After Poale Zion's decision to support the Labour candidate, their election meeting in Whitechapel required police protection. Hall however retained the seat for Labour with a majority of only 1,099 votes.

"Barnett Janner would go on to become a Liberal MP and thereafter a Labour parliamentarian. He became a prominent British Jewish leader. Upon Janner's retirement in 1970, he was made a member of the House of Lords known as Baron Janner of the City Leicester."

"Two months later, MacDonald sent a letter to Chaim Weitzmann which effectively rescinded the White paper. That meant that Jewish immigration to Palestine could continue. Bevin went on to support the Jewish labour movement in Palestine throughout the 1930s and he remained friends with Hoz until the latter's death in a car crash in 1940. His relationship with the Zionists had prospered so much that by 1941, they regarded him as one of their friends in the British War Cabinet. Yet as Foreign Secretary he became a prime target of universal Zionist hate for abandoning the sympathetic stance of the Labour Party toward Zionism."

Israel National News, March 7, 2018

The Three Different Germanies

Contemporary Germany manifests itself in three ways: old Germany, new Germany, and 'mutant' Germany. Many events in Europe have aspects of relevance for Israel, Jews and/or understanding the impact of the Holocaust. In Germany this is more often the case than in other European countries.

The extreme violence in Hamburg by anarchists from a variety of countries before and during the 2017 G20 meeting of world leaders is a case in point. Already prior to the meeting rioters started fires, torched cars, shattered shop windows, and threw Molotov cocktails. More than 450 policemen were injured.[1]

One wonders whether the 20,000 policemen, who were later supported by additional forces, could not have prevented this violence by employing more forceful actions against the rioters. In Germany where the huge crimes of the Holocaust are often present in the conscious and probably even more so in the subconscious, it is preferred that citizens suffer from public disturbances rather than risk killing a rioter by mistake.

Strengthened by radically diverse experiences, Israel handles these matters differently. Six millions Jews were killed by Germans in the Second World War. The Israeli government prioritizes the security of its soldiers above that of those who attack them.

At first sight the German attitude toward rioters is not unique. During the autumn 2005 looting riots in France by immigrant youth from Muslim

179

countries, the government lost control for several days. Thugs burnt cars, shops and public buildings.[2] However, the reason the French government was careful in its actions against the hooligans differed from that of the Germans. If a rioter had been killed, additional mobs of youngsters might have joined the violence and looting. In Hamburg, however, even though there was sympathy for the hooligans in various left-wing circles,[3] the rioters had no significant back up forces.

The major immigration of refugees in recent years mainly from Muslim countries into Germany has 'Holocaust impact' and Jewish aspects as well. By bringing in to Germany more than a million, mainly Muslim refugees, Chancellor Angela Merkel tried to show the world that there is a new Germany. The message was clear: in contrast with the old Germany that murdered the Jewish minority, the new Germany welcomed a large number of another minority, Muslims.

There is however a catch. Many new immigrants came from countries where there is widespread extreme indoctrination of Jew-hatred. The new Germany thus facilitated the massive immigration of antisemites. That is not the only price paid. During 2015–2016 New Year's Eve celebrations, immigrants from Muslim countries sexually attacked hundreds of women in various German cities. The same also happened in a few other European cities.

One should thus examine the new Germany a bit more closely. The welcome in past decades for Russian Jewish immigrants is an indicator of a new Germany. So are the many Holocaust memorials around the country. Yet bringing in additional huge numbers of antisemites among the immigrants throws a shadow on this new Germany. The behavior of the most extreme Muslims may cause the emigration of some German Jews.

Some new versions of old Germany also remain. A small percentage of the population are neo-Nazis. These are not only classic antisemites concerning Jews, but they also hate Israel. Beyond that there is another important group which one might call "mutant Germany." These people have replaced the demonization of Jews with that of Israel.[4]

Seven studies between 2004 and 2015 published respectively by the University of Bielefeld and the Bertelsmann Foundation investigated the percentage of Germans who agreed that Israel acts toward the Palestinians like Nazis behaved toward the Jews. In the 2004 poll, 51 percent agreed.[5] By 2013, the percentage was 41 percent.[6] German media has played a key role in this demonization of Israel. More than 70 years since the Holocaust there are sufficient indications that contemporary German democracy still has huge dark spots.

The defining of three different Germanies is by nature a broad categorization. Yet as a tool it can be helpful to clarify—or at least ask well-defined questions about—many disparate events which occur in the country.

For instance, among Muslims there are segments which are close to the old Germany. Their most visible hatemongers march every year on Al Quds day in Berlin.[7] This demonstration is an invention of the Iranian Ayatollah regime aiming for the disappearance of Israel which can only be achieved through genocide.

Another example is a study by the British think tank Chatham House which shows that 51 percent of Germans want the country to stop accepting Muslim immigrants.[8] One can reasonably assume that the "old Germans" i.e neo-Nazis are part of those opposing immigration. However, it would be enlightening to have an opinion poll conducted which would show how many of the remainder are closer to the "new Germany" and who belong to "mutant Germany."

These are just two examples where the analytic tool of the three Germanies comes in handy. One does not risk much by predicting that there will be many other events in the ensuing years where using this classification will enable analysts to better understand them.

The Jerusalem Post, July 29, 2017

1   www.welt.de/regionales/hamburg/article166450093/Bei-G20-Krawallen-bisher-
      476-verletzte-Beamte.html
2   jcpa.org/article/the-autumn-2005-riots-in-france-part-i; jcpa.org/article/the-
      autumn-2005-riots-in-france-part-ii/
3   www.spiegel.de/kultur/gesellschaft/g20-ausschreitungen-in-hamburg-die-linke-
      muss-sich-entscheiden-a-1156717.html
4   www.welt.de/geschichte/article166649191/Antisemitismus-ist-niemals-links-
      falsch-gedacht.html

5   Aribert Heyder, Julia Iser, and Peter Schmidt, "Israelkritik oder Antisemitis-
     mus? Meinungsbildung zwischen Öffentlichkeit, Medien und Tabus," in Wilhelm
     Heitmeyer, ed., *Deutsche Zustände* (Frankfurt am Main: Suhrkamp, 2005) 144ff.
6   www.bertelsmann-stiftung.de/fileadmin/files/BSt/Publikationen/GrauePub-
     likationen/Studie_LW_Germany_and_Israel_today_2015.pdf. p.35
7   www.berliner-zeitung.de/berlin/zentralrat-der-juden--al-quds-demonstration-
     ist-schande-fuer-berlin---24308930
8   www.chathamhouse.org/expert/comment/what-do-europeans-think-about-
     muslim-immigration

German Government Promotes Antisemitism and Anti-Israelism

The German government's official policy is that it makes efforts to fight antisemitism. One example among many is provision of security services for Jewish institutions. Another is the appointment of a national antisemitism commissioner. It is also official policy that Germany is friendly toward Israel. One illustration of this is that a group of German ministers visit Israel from time to time to discuss possibilities of collaboration with their Israeli counterparts.

There are other aspects of German policy. These are direct and indirect acts of promoting antisemitism and anti-Israelism. These policy facets require analysis.

As far as promotion of antisemitism is concerned, since 2015 the German government has welcomed, without any selection, many immigrants from Muslim countries. Hundreds of thousands of these immigrants are antisemites. A study in Bavaria found that more than 50 percent of Iraqi, Syrian and Afghan immigrants agreed with the statement "Jews have too much influence in the world." Among Germans these figures are between 15 percent and 25 percent.[1] One might add to this that a nation whose grandfather generation murdered 6 million Jews should not welcome additional antisemites into their country. Justifying this with humanitarian reasons does not change the facts.

A major example of participation of Germany in ongoing incitement against Israel is its voting record at the General Assembly of the United Nations. The German daily, *Bild*, published that in recent years the General Assembly accepted more than 500 resolutions against Israel and not a single one against the Palestinian terror group, Hamas.

Bild gave some examples for the period 2014-2017. In 2014, of all resolutions directed against a specific country, 87 percent were against Israel. In 2016, the number was 77 percent. In 2017, 78 percent. In the United Nations Human Rights Council, more than half the resolutions were against Israel. The paper pointed out that Germany regularly sides with Israel's enemies. In November 2018, of 21 General Assembly resolutions against Israel, 16 were supported by Germany and on 4 it abstained.[2]

In the previous government, the leader of the socialist party, Foreign Minister Sigmar Gabriel, was a frequent anti-Israel inciter. Gabriel accused Israel of apartheid. It took several months before he apologized. When he spoke in January 2018 in Tel Aviv he falsely stated that he was a friend of Israel. He added that his country had a special commitment to Israel's security. In the meantime, he was responsible for a huge number of German votes against Israel in the United Nations, undermining its security.[3]

In the current government, Foreign Minister Heiko Maas, also a socialist, has often said that Auschwitz inspired him to go into politics.[4] Yet his ministry continues to support the demonization of Israel at the United Nations. The German votes against Israel in November 2018 took place under his responsibility.

Under Maas there has also been increased German support of UNRWA after the US pulled out. Rabbi Abraham Cooper, Associate Dean of the Simon Wiesenthal Center summarized the issue and Maas' role in it: "Following the US's move to pull support from the group that brainwashes kids on the many 'virtues' of martyrdom, German Secretary of State Heiko Maas announced a 'substantial' increase in funds from his country to UNRWA. With 100 million euros in aid money, Germany remains one of UNRWA's largest benefactors. Yes, support for the Palestinians' quest for a better future is right and important. But Hamas and Palestinian Authority curricula funded by UNRWA amount to textbook child abuse. Nobody I met with in Berlin could assure me that the German money did not directly benefit Hamas."[5]

In February 2019 under Maas' responsibility the German Foreign Ministry also sent representatives to the Islamic Republic of Iran's embassy in Berlin on the occasion of the celebration of the 40th anniversary of the revolution. This despite the fact that Iran frequently calls for the destruction of Israel.[6]

The reality is worse. German President Frank-Walter Steinmeier, also a socialist, "congratulated the Iranian Government cordially on the occasion of the 40th anniversary of the revolution, also in the name of my fellow country citizens." The daily *Tagesspiegel* wondered whether one had to remind Steinmeier that Iran is a sponsor of international terrorism, threatens Israel with destruction, denies the Holocaust, oppresses women, executes homosexuals and punishes religious conversions with death." It concluded: "The moral compass that should guide the words of a President of the German republic has in this case greatly failed."[7] To put the congratulation of the Iranian Government even more in perspective: when Donald Trump was elected as US president in November 2016, Steinmeier, then foreign minister, explicitly said that he did not congratulate him.[8]

The liberal party (FDP) which is in opposition at the beginning of 2019 asked the German government to change its policies at the UN. One of the party's parliamentarians, Frank Muller-Rosentritt, said that in one year 21 resolutions against Israel are decided while there is only one against Syria. He added that this 'disproportion shows that the enemies of Israel instrumentalize the UN to delegitimize the Jewish State.'[9]

The direct and indirect assistance to antisemites and anti-Israelis not only takes place at the national level, but also at the level of federal states. Establishing statistics on antisemitic crimes are their responsibility. The national antisemitism commissioner, Felix Klein, has stated that all the published statistics on this subject are misleading and that he intends to tackle this distortion. The many crimes against Jews in which the perpetrators cannot be identified are registered as being caused by extreme right wingers.

Klein stressed that the necessary change could only be achieved by convincing the interior ministers of the federal states to modify the way statistics are established. He stated that physical attacks on Jews by Muslims are far more numerous than what is recorded.[10] Jewish representatives have also often drawn attention to the many antisemitic incidents caused by Muslims which are poorly reflected in the statistics. If states do not correctly publish where to search for perpetrators, they are in effect assisting part of the antisemites.

The approval of schoolbooks is the responsibility of individual federal state governments. A 2019 study by two German professors, Samuel Salzborn, and Alexander Kurth, investigated antisemitism in German schools. Partly on the basis of an earlier study they found that with respect to textbooks, Israel is often presented as only negative and Palestinians as only positive in the fields of geography, history and politics. They concluded that Israel is only mentioned in the area of the conflict with the Palestinians. Israel's military actions and reactions to Palestinian terrorism are often presented as equally problematic as the terrorism itself.[11]

These are a few examples among many more. In view of Germany's horrible past and problematic present, an in-depth study should be conducted on how German national and state governments directly and indirectly promote antisemitism and anti-Israelism. Otherwise, Germany's double-faced approach will not be seen clearly.

Besa Center, March 3, 2019

1   www.hss.de/download/publications/Argu-Kompakt_2017-8_Asylsuchende.
    pdf; www.ajc.org/news/ajc-berlin-publishes-study-on-anti-semitism-among-
    refugees; ajcberlin.org/sites/default/files/ajc_studie_gefluechtete_und_anti-
    semitismus_2017.pdf

2   www.bild.de/politik/ausland/politik-ausland/deutschland-bei-der-uno-fdp-will-
    anti-israel-irrsinn-stoppen-59894948.bild.html

3   www.auswaertiges-amt.de/en/newsroom/news/gabriel-inss/1426618

4   www.timesofisrael.com/most-horrible-place-on-earth-german-foreign-minister-
    visits-auschwitz/

5   www.newsmax.com/abrahamcooper/germany-iran-unrwa-antisemitism/-
    2018/12/10/id/893886/

6   www.jpost.com/International/German-Foreign-Ministry-celebrates-Irans-
    Islamic-revolution-580612

7   www.tagesspiegel.de/politik/glueckwuensche-an-den-iran-wo-terror-beginnt-

endet-die-etikette/24024400.html

8   www.n-tv.de/politik/Steinmeier-gratuliert-Trump-nicht-article19045691.html
9   www.bild.de/politik/ausland/politik-ausland/deutschland-bei-der-uno-fdp-will-
     anti-israel-irrsinn-stoppen-59894948.bild.html
10   Ibid.
11   www.tu-berlin.de/fileadmin/i65/Dokumente/Antisemitismus-Schule.pdf

JEWISH COMMUNITIES

Jewish Masochism: from Abraham the Patriarch to Woody Allen

The largest Palestinian party, Hamas, which triumphed in the 2006 democratic elections, openly promotes genocide against Jews. It is explicitly stated in its official charter and repeated from time to time by its leaders. The second largest Palestinian party, Fatah, is only (sic) a racist party. Its leader, Palestinian President Mahmoud Abbas, has declared that no Israelis will live in a future Palestinian state.[1] The Palestinian Authority furthermore regularly glorifies murderers of Israelis.[2] Compared to those of other Arab states and entities, Palestinian levels of prejudice and criminality are probably somewhere in the middle. Polls indicate that should current elections be held, Hamas leader Haniyeh would easily win against Abbas.[3]

Despite all of the Palestinians' criminality, there is a significant number of Israelis who have little or no critique of them. Simultaneously, a certain number of these Israelis prefer to criticize the Israeli leadership for a variety of failures. However legitimate and significant these critiques might be, they pale in comparison to the moral degradation of the Palestinian nation, which voted Islamo-Nazis and glorifiers of murderers of civilians into political power.

This widespread masochist attitude among Israelis has deep roots in Jewish tradition. It begins with the founder of the Jewish people, Abraham. He pleads at length with God about how many righteous citizens of Sodom one would need to find in order that the evil city be saved. However, when God tells him to sacrifice his own son, Isaac, Abraham is willing to fulfill this divine order without any argument. God ultimately saves Isaac—but not because Abraham has asked him to do so.[4] That is the plain reading of the Bible text.

Besides this masochistic attitude, there is a second Jewish tradition which might be best described as the Mosaic one. Moses pleads for himself in addition to fighting for his people. When God tells him that he will not enter the Holy Land, Moses argues to convince God otherwise. It is in vain, but at least he tried.[5]

The Jewish masochistic tradition continues throughout the centuries. A variety of texts of the prophets also fit this approach. A Talmudic text even states it explicitly: "Rabbi Abahu says be always among the persecuted and not among the persecutors."[6]

Many Holocaust survivors would take exception to these words, which classically are seen as an expression of wisdom. The Holocaust generation is witness to how many Jewish doctors and humanitarians were murdered, and how many of the most brutal executioners survived and weren't even brought to justice.

An exegetic text of the Midrashic literature shows a similar attitude as the above Talmudic one: "Abel was the victim of Cain, Abel's offerings were accepted; Noah was persecuted by his contemporaries, Abraham by Nimrod, Isaac by the early Philistines, Jacob by Esau, Joseph by his brothers, Moses by Pharaoh, David by Saul, and Saul himself by the Philistines; and amongst all these the persecuted and not the persecutors were chosen by God."[7]

Similarly, some Jewish prayers have a strong masochistic content, which reaches its pinnacle in the prayers around the High Holidays. One such prayer is, "we have sinned more than any other nation." Taking into account global events such as the mass murders in the Arab world and in Africa, for instance, or the genocidal calls emerging from parts of Islam, the prayer's text is surrealistic.

A more extreme form of masochism is self-hate. Theodor Lessing, in pre-war Europe, coined the term as a title for his book.[8] A typical example of this self-loathing is evident from the politics of the Jewish Prime Minister of Austria, Bruno Kreisky. Only a Jew could plead the Austrians partly-free of their huge guilt during the war. His Jewish self-hate was made clear with statements such as, "If the Jews are a people, they are an ugly people."[9]

The Jewish masochist tradition also expresses itself in Jewish humor. The English make fun of the Irish, the Germans joke about the Poles and the Dutch laugh about the Belgians. Jews, however, often make jokes at their own expense. This is epitomized by a line from Woody Allen's film, *Annie Hall*. Alvy, the filmmaker's alter ego, says, "I am comparatively normal for a guy raised in Brooklyn."

In May 2014, the visit of then-president Shimon Peres to Norway yielded a far-going example of Israeli self-abasement. In Norway, antisemitism and anti-Israelism are rife. A poll showed that 38 percent of the population consider that Israel behaves like Nazis toward the Palestinians.[10] During the visit Peres said, "Norway is the pearl of humanity, built on human values, and seeks to keep people equal and free."[11]

This small selection illustrates a deeply rooted tradition which manifests itself to different extents across large parts of the Israeli political spectrum. The appeasers and peace movements who continue to push for further territorial concessions to the Palestinians are unable to learn anything from Ariel Sharon's disastrous decision to withdraw from Gaza. The masochism does not sit in their genes, however; children are not born masochist but get it from their education.

The masochistic tradition also sits, to a lesser extent, in many other places within Israeli society. Consecutive Israeli governments have not exposed the severity of official Palestinian criminality. Examples of Israeli masochism on this issue abound – and nothing is done about it. It is one of the main reasons why so many enemies of the Jews regularly enjoy a free anti-Semitic lunch.

It is essential that the fight against masochism becomes a central issue in Israeli society. This applies to the appeasers within Israel who choose to look away from the crimes of the enemy, and is equally valid concerning those Jews promoting anti-Israelism abroad.

The Jerusalem Post, July 20, 2015

1   "Abbas: 'Not a single Israeli' in future Palestinian state," *The Jerusalem Post*, July 30, 2013.
2   "Violence and terror," Palestinian Media Watch, 2015.

3   "Palestinian Public Opinion Poll No. 53," Palestinian Center for Policy and Survey Research, September 29, 2014.

4   Genesis 22.

5   Deuteronomy 3, 23–27.

6   T. Bavli, Bava Kama 93a.

7   Leviticus Rabba 27.

8   Reissued as Theodor Lessing, *Der jüdische Selbsthaß* (Berlin: Matthes & Seitz, 2004).

9   Robert S. Wistrich, *From Ambivalence to Betrayal: The Left, the Jews, and Israel* (Lincoln: University of Nebraska Press, 2012), 496.

10 "Antisemittisme i Norge? Den norske befolkningens holdninger til joder og andre minoriteter," Center for Studies of the Holocaust and Religious Minorities, 30 May 2012, www.hlsenteret.no/publikasjoner/antisemittismei-norge.

11 Lahav Harkov,"Norwegian royal family greets Peres with honor guard, cannons," *The Jerusalem Post*, May 12, 2013.

Is the Haggada Short on Sons?

One story in the Passover Haggada falls short of contemporary diaspora reality: that of the sons. Today this breakdown of Jews into four categories leaves out many individuals due to the post-modern fragmentation among the wide array of Jewish people abroad.

The Haggada's authors divided Jews into groups referred to as "Sons." The first was the "Wise Son." The second was the "Wicked Son," seen as the Jewish outsider who questioned the significance of Jewish religious customs for other Jews. The third was the "Simple Son." The fourth son was so ignorant that he didn't even know what to ask.

The last Rabbi of the Chabad movement Menachem Mendel Schneerson, who passed away in 1994, already felt that four categories were insufficient. He added a fifth son—the one who doesn't even show up to the Seder. Rabbi Richard Jacobs, President of the Union for Reform Judaism (URJ), has indicated the sorry state of what is currently the largest Jewish movement in the United States. At the organization's biennial meeting at the end of 2011 he said, "The fastest growing group in Jewish communal life is the lifelong unaffiliated and the lifelong uninspired." About the URJ Jacobs said, "Eighty percent of our children are leaving the synagogue by the end of 12th grade."

Following Rabbi Schneerson's lead, in post-modern diaspora societies one could indeed add a few more sons. The sixth could be the child of a mixed marriage who is brought up simultaneously in two different religious environments. He may even attend the Seder. One might call him the "Confused Son."

One could also add a seventh son—the one who expresses his Jewishness by attacking other Jews, or Israel. He may ask: why did God and the Jews oppress Pharoah and the Egyptians? One might call him the "Self-Hating Son." Such a son may represent those who believe "Let my people go" in modern times refers to so-called Israeli oppression of the Palestinians. In past centuries, some Jewish converts to Christianity showed an extraordinary hatred for Judaism. But they did not pretend that they were Jewish.

Today, many from this group of Jewish Israel-haters consider it an advantage to claim their Jewishness in order to make their incitement more effective. Many self-haters probably find the regular Seder too painful in view of the sufferings which eventually befell the Egyptians. They may feel the need to add sections emphasizing the evil perpetrated by the Jewish slaves on their Egyptian masters, and to demonstrate that the Egyptians really were the victims here.

There may even be an eighth "non-son," one who perhaps would like to be a stepson—the person who sometimes "feels Jewish," whether among Jews, or in general when Israel is attacked or antisemitism is mentioned. In the diaspora, the Seder ceremony is often also attended by non-Jews who are married to or friendly with Jewish family members, or simply interested in the Seder, one of the most broadly observed Jewish traditions today. This is also reflected in the number of suggestions for an interfaith Seder to be found in a Google search on the term. Seders also become increasingly popular among Jews for Jesus and other Christian groups that find parallels between the story of Exodus and Jesus.

This multiplication of sons and frequent revision of the traditional Haggada, rather than symbolizing Jewish fecundity, offers an illustration of post-modernity and its fragmentation of Jewish identity. Traditional Jewish identity has changed, broken down and splintered, especially in recent years. Leading American sociologist Steven Cohen says, "in the 1960s, there was still largely a consensus that being Jewish was a matter of obligations. Such norms can derive from God, parents, nostalgia, tradition, halacha [Jewish law], and/or belonging to the Jewish people. One could violate these, but then one felt guilty about it." Cohen observed that for most American Jews nowadays, Judaism is an "aesthetic understanding" and being Jewish has increasingly become a matter of individual choice.

What Cohen says is confirmed by a variety of studies, including those from the Pew Research Center. A 2013 study, titled "A Portrait of Jewish Americans," found that self-identification by Jews differs significantly from generation to generation. Ninety three percent of the generation born between 1914 and 1927 identify as Jews on the basis of religion, while the remaining 7 percent see themselves as Jews with no religion. However of the generation born after 1980 only 68 percent self-identify as Jews by religion, while 32 percent describe themselves as having no religion and self-identify as Jewish on the basis of ancestry, ethnicity or culture.

Rather than subject the Haggada to typical post-modern extrapolation and extension, we should best let this ancient text stand as is. The Haggada is an educational book, a historical narrative in which Jews relay to their children the story of the Exodus and becoming a free people. In preference to adding new sons, we should let the story of the Haggada lead us on the seder into a discussion of a viable sense of modern Jewish identity through shared consciousness and fate.

The Jerusalem Post, April 19, 2016

American Jewry's Challenges

Interview with Steven Bayme

"There are more than six million Jews in the United States. The numbers would be considerably higher, but over two million adults with one Jewish parent no longer self-define as Jews. To the extent one can speak of American Jewry collectively, it remains a strong, prosperous Jewish community that in many ways elicits the envy of other American ethnic and religious groupings.

"No society in Diaspora Jewish history has been as welcoming of Jewish participation as the United States. The Clinton Administration years marked the collapse of any remaining barriers to Jewish participation in virtually all sectors of American society. The Administration stopped counting how many Jews it employed."

Dr. Steven Bayme serves as the American Jewish Committee's Director of Contemporary Jewish Life. He currently holds the rank of Visiting Professor at Yeshivat Chovevei Torah. His published volumes include Understanding Jewish History: Texts and Commentary; Jewish Arguments and Counter-Arguments; and American Jewry's Comfort Level.

"Mixed marriage is the key barometer of assimilation. It is by no means the primary cause, which includes weak Jewish education and the over-whelming attractiveness of American cultural values and norms. Constructing a distinctive Jewish identity of necessity will entail considerable disso-nance with otherwise attractive American norms

"Non-affiliation and mixed marriage rates are at all-time highs. Within

198

Reform Judaism, over 80 percent of those who have married since 2000 have chosen non-Jewish spouses. While conversion to Judaism constitutes the single best outcome of mixed marriage, it has leveled off. The challenge of mixed marriage primarily affects the second and third generations. Mixed marrieds themselves rarely cease identifying as Jews. But successful transmission of Jewish identity to children and grandchildren remains a questionable proposition at best.

"The second challenge is maintaining and sustaining the US-Israel relationship. The cause of Israel remains broadly popular within America. However, support for Israel has been slipping among elites—academia, the media, and key ethnic and religious groupings. Most importantly, the cause of Israel has in the past been successful on a bipartisan basis. That bipartisanship today is at risk. If pro-Israel advocacy becomes identified primarily with Republicans, US-Israel relations are likely to suffer when Democrats return to power.

"A third challenge: American Jews had experienced a decline in antisemitism for decades. Recent years, however, have witnessed a spike in antisemitic activity. On the right, extremist groupings feel at greater liberty to express antisemitic views and even actions. On the left, anti-Zionism all too frequently morphs into antisemitism.

"American Jews are vigilant concerning antisemitism. If anything, the danger becomes one of crying wolf too frequently. We must distinguish between legitimate criticism and expressions of prejudice and bigotry. Much of what passes for vigorous criticism of Israel, especially in academia, is articulated by people who feel completely at ease and at home among Jews. For them, the State of Israel, tragically, has become Goliath rather than David.

"The BDS movement is the source of much noise on campus even if it attains no tangible victories. Pro-Israel students may often feel intimidated by loud and vocal demonstrations equating Israel with apartheid South Africa. Others may simply opt for silence. College education was meant to challenge one's thinking. The debate regarding Israel on campus, however, has become much too shrill and divisive, in turn causing considerable discomfort among the most committed American Jewish students.

"The number of Jews who have bought into BDS and other anti-Israeli arguments is relatively small. These provide a convenient cover for Israel's far more numerous gentile detractors. For most Jews on campus, the critical challenge with respect to Israel is one of indifference rather than hostility.

"As far as Jewish political behavior is concerned, since 1928 the general rule has been that Jews will vote for the more liberal candidate, provided he or she is not considered hostile to Israel. The unpopularity of President Donald Trump partly emanates from his more conservative politics and policies and partly from the self-image he projects. Jews will vote for the candidate who is considered more urbane, patrician, liberal, intellectual, and broadminded. Trump often projects the very antithesis of these characteristics.

"Notwithstanding continued debate among social scientists, the distancing from Israel is quite tangible in parts of American Jewry. One perceives it among the millennial generation due to assimilation. Distancing from matters of a Jewish nature generally connotes distancing from Israel. However, even among highly committed and active sectors of Jewish life, one may detect distancing. These Jews are working out positive Jewish identities. However, Israel remains a highly explosive, almost toxic topic of discussion for them.

"Reform Judaism remains the single largest denomination and claims the allegiances of over a third of adult American Jews. Conservative Judaism claims 18 percent, and Orthodoxy 10 percent. Those numbers represent denominational self-identification rather than formal affiliation with institutions and synagogues. Orthodoxy and the "nones" sectors are growing while the "middles" are shrinking. Yet it is those middles, active Conservative and Reform Jews, who serve as the architectural backbone of Jewish communal institutions.

"To date, the Reform movement has held its own numerically because it has proven itself most hospitable to mixed marrieds. Whether that can be sustained for the next generation is very much an open question as children and grandchildren of mixed marrieds marry out at even higher rates.

"Within Conservative Jewry, the shrinkage has become evident institutionally, with the closings of some synagogues and Solomon Schechter schools. To date, the network of institutions built over the course of the twentieth century have made American Jewry the single best organized and most resourceful community in Jewish history. Whether that will continue as numbers shrink and institutions forfeit some of their distinctiveness is very much a future challenge.

"The resurgence of Orthodoxy is one of the great success stories of American Jewry. Rather than submit to the tides of history, Orthodox leaders committed themselves to rebuilding their communities. They succeeded beyond expectations and will transform the face of American Jewry in the future. While Orthodoxy constitutes but 10 percent of adult Jews, 35 percent of children under five are raised Orthodox. If Israel advocacy becomes an Orthodox cause alone, the danger is that it will be far easier to dismiss pro-Israel voices as unrepresentative of the American Jewish community.

"Distinctions between Modern Orthodoxy and Ultra-Orthodoxy are nuanced and often blurred. The Ultra-Orthodox are becoming more modern in the sense that economic needs necessitate acquisition of secular education. Conversely, Modern Orthodoxy has drifted to the right in terms of greater religious observance, conservative politics, and limiting secular education primarily to utilitarian purposes. There are sectors within Modern Orthodoxy that have resisted this drift. Most have coalesced around new institutions and rabbinical seminaries; others have settled into a "Social Orthodoxy," which maintains high levels of observance without subscribing to all Orthodox beliefs and norms.

"The 1990 and 2000 National Jewish Population Studies and the 2013 Pew Report demonstrated that the story of Jewish renewal coexists alongside the story of assimilation. Our challenge for the future is strengthening the forces for renewal—and they occur within every sector of American Jewish life—while minimizing the forces of erosion and dissolution."

Israel National News, July 20, 2018

Jewish Religious Life in Dutch Provinces in the Early 1960s

In the early 1960s, organized Jewish religious life outside the main cities in the Netherlands only existed as part of the Nederlands Israelitisch Kerkgenootschap (NIK), the Ashkenazi community organization. This is a nominally Orthodox body, even though most of its members do not practice Orthodox Judaism. There were no Portuguese, liberal or non-affiliated Jewish communities outside of Amsterdam and The Hague.

The membership of what was then the chief rabbinate of Utrecht, which grouped all members of the NIK outside Amsterdam, The Hague and Rotterdam,[1] came to 3,891. It had declined by more than 8 percent over four years.[2] In each of the provinces of Northern Holland, Overijssel and Gelderland, the NIK had more than 700 members. In Utrecht and Northern Brabant, which included Zeeland, membership was around 550 and 500 respectively. In Limburg and Groningen it was about 200, in Drente over one hundred and in Friesland only sixty-two.[3]

The percentages of survivors in the various Jewish communities differed. The community of the town of Groningen was one of the worst hit. It numbered 3,500 Jews before the Second World War, while after the war it had only two hundred members. Enschede, where the Jewish council indirectly advised Jews to go into hiding and helped them do this, had 931 Jews in 1930 and 425 in 1951.[4]

The figures given here are only indicative because they were also influenced by people who moved from one community to another. In smaller communities there were even greater differences in the percentage of survivors. Most Jews of the tiny community in Enkhuizen survived. In 1930, it had twenty-five members, in 1951 there were twenty-three.[5] Most of the Jews in Haaksbergen also survived. In 1930, the Jewish community had thirty-seven members. In 1951, there were thirty-three members.[6] During the war, Friesland's Jewry was hit even harder than most other provinces. Yet more than half of the Jews of Sneek went into hiding and survived.[7] All the Jewish inhabitants of the town of Harlingen, which counted fifty-six Jews in 1930,[8] were, however, deported and murdered.

Immediately after the war, the Jewish community in Friesland's capital Leeuwarden still had 130 members,[9] though many survivors later left. In the beginning of the 1960s, Leeuwarden was the only remaining Jewish community in the province with forty-eight members in the town itself. There were also three families in Heerenveen, numbering thirteen people, one family in Scharsterbrug with five members, and one elderly lady in Sneek.[10]

Winschoten, on the German border in the province of Groningen, had been the provincial community where the Jewish presence was percentage-wise greatest before the war in the Netherlands. At one time, one thousand Jews lived there, which then represented 12 percent of the overall population. In the early 1960s, there were eleven Jews left in Winschoten and in 1964 the Jewish community was incorporated into Groningen. The town kept a Jewish presence because the well-known lemon sweets for Passover[11] were still made there under rabbinical supervision.[12]

The provincial chief rabbinate of Utrecht numbered fifty-two Jewish communities at the end of 1960. The largest were Utrecht with 412 members, Arnhem with 315, Enschede with 302, Haarlem with 279 and Bussum with 220. There were an additional eight communities with more than one hundred members. They were Almelo, Amersfoort, Deventer, Eindhoven, Groningen, Hilversum, Maastricht and Zwolle. The remaining thirty-nine communities each had less than one hundred members, out of which seventeen had less than twenty-five members.[13]

In the thirty years thereafter, the number of organized Ashkenazi Jews in the provinces would decline further in the geographic area of what has been called the Interprovincial Chief Rabbinate, IPOR since 1988. By 1991, membership was reduced by another fifty percent to about 2,000. The latest figure available is about fifteen hundred members in 2008.[14] The number of Jewish communities is twenty-seven.[15]

A Voyage Through the Provinces

In the early 1960s, I undertook a lengthy journalistic voyage in several Dutch provinces on behalf of the Dutch Jewish weekly, *Nieuw Israëlitisch Weekblad* (hereafter, *NIW*). It covered five of the eleven provinces: Groningen, Friesland, Drente, Overijssel and Utrecht. The series of seventeen articles was titled in Dutch, De vergeten mediene, which translates as "The forgotten Jews of the provinces." The title played on the name of Hartog Beem's book, *De verdwenen mediene* (*The Disappeared Jews of the Provinces*). In that book he reported on the characteristics of pre-war provincial Judaism that had largely disappeared.[16]

At the time, M.H. Gans was editor-in-chief of *NIW*. When I proposed this journalistic project, he saw its double importance. This series of articles was to describe—and therefore record for the future—Jewish life in some of the provinces as it was at the time. A second goal was to refer to the memories concerning the history of the Jewish communities visited. In autumn 2011, NIW would start with a somewhat similar series on Jewish communities.

A Vantage Point: Fifty Years Later

The early 1960s were a rather quiet period for Dutch Jewry. In the first ten years after the war, the re-emerging Jewish communities were under pressure. On the occasion of the memorial meeting in the town's New Church ten years after the Liberation, Amsterdam Chief Rabbi Aron Schuster said in 1955 "an anti-Semitic ideology [Nazism] has left its trails in the Netherlands even in circles where this had been inconceivable before." Present at that gathering were Queen Juliana, her husband Prince Bernhard and representatives of the churches and the government.

Rabbi Schuster is quoted as saying that the official government attitude toward the Dutch Jewish community was "as if we did not exist." Their position in Dutch society was largely normalized after an investigation by Senate

President Jan Anne Jonkman upon the request of Queen Juliana. Historian Joel Fishman wrote that this was a result of the Queen's reaction to the speech by Rabbi Schuster.[17]

What has changed in the fifty years since? Considering the outcomes upfront of this analysis makes it possible to gain a better perspective on the situation in the early 1960s. One major change is that, nowadays, the denominational composition of Jewish religious communities in Dutch provinces is pluralistic. In the 1960s, all communities belonged to the NIK, even if most of their members did not practice an Orthodox way of life. Since then, a number of non-Orthodox communities have been founded. One major difference is that in the non-Orthodox communities women can fulfill all religious functions.

Another important development is that the characteristics of religious functionaries of the NIK communities in the IPOR geographic region have changed. Most functionaries who were active in the early 1960s received their Jewish education at the Dutch Jewish Seminary. Today, many religious functionaries are adherents of the Chabad (Lubavitch) hasidic movement. The first Chabad rabbi in the Netherlands was Ies Vorst who served in the Amsterdam suburb Amstelveen from 1965.[18]

Third, Jewish rituals nowadays are far more under attack in the Netherlands than they were in the 1960s. The main contested subject so far has been ritual slaughter.[19] A major national debate on this issue took place in 2011. The Second Chamber of Parliament adopted a proposal for a law that would make kosher slaughter very difficult.[20] This proposal was rejected[21] in the Senate and the Dutch government presented a compromise solution which the Jewish community accepted, albeit with tensions within the NIK rabbinate.[22]

Male circumcision is also under fire.[23] There are occasional fears that government financial support for all religious schools, including Jewish ones, could be halted.[24] These developments have to be seen in two contexts. One is increasing secularization. The other is multiple attacks on Muslim and Jewish rituals in many Western European countries. Often the attacks focus on Muslims and this brings with it collateral damage for Jews.

Fourth, today Dutch provincial Jewry appears more in the public domain religiously, but also in other ways. Examples of such religious manifestations are the Chabad-initiated public lighting of the Hanukkah menorah in central places in a number of towns. These are often attended by the mayor and/or elected officials.

Fifth, there was a feeling in the NIK communities fifty years ago that they were fighting for their independent survival. This feeling still exists, the more so as membership in many Orthodox communities has shrunk much further since and many communities have merged with others or have increased cooperation between them. Yet several new Jewish communities have since started services. Some are Orthodox, such as Almere and Middelburg (Zeeland Jewish community). Most of the others are liberal, but there also Masorti (conservative) and other non-Orthodox communities.

Finally, today the future of the memory of dead Jews seems better assured in many ways than fifty years ago. There is now a widespread interest in keeping Holocaust memory alive. Yet, with other parts of the population, there is also Holocaust fatigue.[25]

A More Detailed Analysis

The main elements of Jewish religious community life to be analyzed are: synagogue services, the role of lay leaders, religious functionaries, Jewish education activities and those of youth movements.

Not all activities of a Jewish community have a religious character. Others are primarily social, cultural or Zionist. There are also often historical and memorial activities. Another relevant issue is the interaction of local Jews and their community and with society at large in the places they live.

Regarding religious activities, the main elements which enable a Jewish community to function are an active lay leadership and the local religious functionary. The remaining Jewish communities in the 1960s in Dutch provinces were mostly small. Thus, their functioning was often dependent on the leadership capabilities of one or two families or individuals. They formed the core of the community and often had to mobilize others to form a quorum (minyan) to hold religious services. A typical example was Deventer. Despite the departures of its core-members, it maintained some services until the 1980s. The Ashkenazi community there has since merged with Zutphen and Apeldoorn.

The synagogue building in Deventer in the Golstraat, which survived the Second World War, was sold afterwards and became a Christian Reformed Church. The building was too large for the decimated community. In the 1980s, the post-war synagogue in the Lange Bisschopstraat was also closed and later sold. Yet in 2011, a new egalitarian Jewish community was established under the name, Beth Shoshana. It holds services in the old synagogue in Golstraat which no longer serves as a church. In 2012, the synagogue received its first Torah scroll on loan from a community in Zurich.[26, 27]

Religious Functionaries

The religious functionary is a core official in the Jewish community. He is usually in charge of Judaic instruction, acts as the cantor who leads the prayer services and reads from the Torah. Often, he is also the community's secretary. As afore mentioned, with few exceptions, religious functionaries in the provincial communities in the early 1960s received their Jewish education before the Second World War at the Dutch Jewish Seminary. After the war there was great concern that no successors would be found for these functionaries when thy retired. In 1962, Gans wrote three articles about the "emergency situation" of Dutch Jewry for *NIW*. He mentioned that there was a mood of major concern about the future when the Central Commission, the council of the NIK, met. He wrote: "There are many reasons for that. It can almost be excluded that one can find in the future enough officials for education and cultural activities."[28]

It had also become clear that when these functionaries retired, there would hardly be any Dutch seminary-trained successors. Most post-war students at the seminary were part-timers. Their main aim was to acquire a Jewish education. They did not intend to develop a career as Jewish teachers or religious functionaries. Many of them eventually left for Israel.

Youngsters As Replacements

When the religious functionaries in provincial communities retired, they were often replaced by youngsters. Usually, but not always, these were university students whose aim was to serve for a few years only. In the early sixties, however, that was already the case in Groningen and Deventer.

In 1957, in Groningen, Joseef Vleeschhouwer was appointed as cantor, secretary and teacher. He also was involved with the Zionist youth organization Haboniem. Vleeschhouwer stayed on until 1962 when he left in order to complete his university studies.[29] In 1959, in Deventer, the religious functionary was a young part-timer, Uriel Moskowitz.[30] Both would later leave for Israel. They were to be followed by others who would become part-time teachers. This was also the case, for instance, in Bussum and some other communities. Only later, a number of permanent Jewish functionaries—many of them Chabad followers—would start occupying these positions. That is largely the case today.

For the High Holidays, people were frequently brought in from elsewhere, often from Amsterdam, to assist the local religious functionary in leading prayer services, or to lead them entirely. This was the case, for instance, in Leeuwarden, Zutphen, Maastricht, Oss and Deventer in 1961.[31] Sometimes an additional person came from elsewhere to blow the shofar (ram's horn).

Jewish Education

Educating Jewish children was an important activity. If there was a local religious functionary, he would teach them. In some places where there was no local Jewish community, teachers from the nearest community gave courses. For instance, religious functionary, Vojtech Schick, from Enschede taught in nearby Goor.[32] Moskovits from Deventer also taught the Jewish children in Holten and Zutphen.[33] In other places traveling teachers, provided by the Central Education Commission (COC), gave Judaic instruction. At the time, eleven such teachers taught 180 students spread over forty Dutch municipalities. These teachers from time to time also tried to maintain contact with parents of the students.[34]

To get an idea of the trajectory of a religious functionary, one can view the career of Leonard Frank Israels. Before the war he had been cantor, teacher and ritual slaughterer in, Zaltbommel, Veghel and Roermond, respectively. After the war, he became cantor and teacher at the Jewish community in Almelo. This was a part-time function. He also taught on behalf of the COC in Apeldoorn, Emmen, Hardenberg, Nieuw Amsterdam and Steenwijk. His wife gave lessons, without being paid, in Almelo and Nijverdal.[35]

In some communities all activities were undertaken by volunteers. In Hengelo, the religious functionary was murdered in the war. After 1945 no one was appointed to replace him. In the early sixties, there was still a minyan every Friday evening. A board member volunteered to lead the services and read from the Torah. He also prepared boys for their bar mitzvah, visited the sick and took care of the organization of the services.[36]

In the small Jewish community of Haaksbergen services were still held on Jewish holidays, provided these did not coincide too often with market days. They were led by the head of the community. Sometimes he would leave for Amsterdam for the holidays, in which case holiday services would not take place. On Yom Kippur (Day of Atonement), he was assisted by a person from Almelo.[37]

Among the Jewish holidays, the Passover Seder (when the text of the Haggadah is read accompanied by a festive meal) held a very prominent place. Many communities had a joint Seder or made arrangements for people to attend the Seder in private homes.[38] In some communities, Israel's Independence Day, Yom Haatzmaut, was celebrated annually with a synagogue service.[39]

Other Efforts

Another effort to reach out to Jews concerned the Central Contact Commission (CCC) of the NIK. For instance, in 1960, on its behalf, A. Kuyt established contacts with local Jews in more than one hundred Dutch municipalities. They aimed at "bringing dispersed Jews closer to Judaism and in particular, to make those who lived in isolation aware of the fact that they belonged to the greater Jewish community, i.e., the NIK."[40] The CCC also organized regional meetings in various places.[41]

Arrangements had to be made for special groups. The first army rabbi, Lion Slagter, was appointed in 1956. It was a part-time function as he remained the religious functionary in Arnhem. A student rabbi was also appointed. The first was A.S. Goudsmit in 1964. In some towns there were Jewish inmates in prisons who were visited regularly by someone on behalf of the Jewish community. In 1960, efforts were made to come to a final arrangement with the Ministry of Justice to supply jail inmates with kosher food, in particular for Passover and before and after Yom Kippur.[42]

Chief Rabbi Berlinger

Rabbi Elieser Berlinger had come to the Netherlands from Sweden in 1954. He became Chief Rabbi of the Utrecht rabbinate in 1956.[43] The small number of Jews in many provinces had created a situation where they could no longer maintain a chief rabbi of their own. Centralization was thus necessary. Rabbi Berlinger fulfilled a major role in the religious life of provincial Jewry. For small Dutch communities at the time, his visits, accompanied by his wife, were a major event.

On most Saturdays of the year, he visited communities that had a service with a minyan. At the time, there were still thirteen communities in his rabbinate's area that held such services every week. A few others held services from time to time.[44] Rabbi Berlinger visited other communities on weekdays, for instance during the Purim and Hanukkah holidays.[45] In some of the bigger communities he gave regular Jewish courses. That was the case in Enschede every four weeks[46] and in Groningen every three weeks.[47] When there was no alternative available people occasionally joined him on his frequent train travel to benefit from his lessons.[48]

Rabbi Berlinger had many responsibilities in the field of education and also in supervising teachers of Judaic instruction. He often had to answer queries and once said: "The inhabitants of small towns need to know more about Judaism than those of the bigger cities because the latter can always ask somebody for information." He added, "People need someone who can be of help to them with their personal problems. Many people only want to discuss them with their rabbi." He also mentioned halakhic (Jewish law) questions, of which a substantial number concerned cemeteries. This was, for instance, the case when remains of Jews, who during the war had been buried in a general cemetery, were transferred to Jewish cemeteries. Other problems that came up were what to do when municipalities wanted to empty Jewish cemeteries because their towns were expanding.[49]

In some communities, human remains in Jewish cemeteries were dug up and moved to other Jewish cemeteries or separate parts of general cemeteries. This was the case when the state of a Jewish cemetery was such that it could not be maintained properly.[50]

The chief rabbinate of Utrecht has since become the inter-provincial chief rabbinate. This formalized the reality of interprovincial cooperation which de facto had existed since the nomination of Rabbi Berlinger as chief rabbi of Utrecht. Rabbi Berlinger's successor, Chief Rabbi Binyomin Jacobs, resides in Amersfoort, the community where he was formerly the religious leader. This changing primacy of Utrecht and Amersfoort as residence of the chief rabbi was already an issue in the nineteenth century.

Typical of Rabbi Berlinger's views was a remark he made at a very heated annual assembly of the Dutch Zionist Organization (NZB). He said that he could never have carried out his work if he was as stern about the failures of people as was common in the Zionist organization.[51] Many years later, Rabbi Jacobs who initially had assisted Rabbi Berlinger said that the latter's approach was to seek out the Jews. He was unyielding for himself but wanted to be flexible for other Jews.[52]

Other Aspects

Some communities had minhagim (religious customs) in their services that were slightly different from the common ones in Dutch Orthodoxy. These involved only minor issues. Yet a community that upholds its minhagim, however marginal, also maintains part of its specific identity through them. For example, in Utrecht, except for Rosh Hashana (Jewish New Year) and Yom Kippur, the selichot prayers were said aloud sentence after sentence. Elsewhere only the first and last lines were said aloud.[53] In Groningen, after the reading from the Torah scroll was completed, it was rolled up by the same person who had been given the honor of lifting it. This differed from the common Dutch practice in which the two honors were given separately to different individuals.[54]

Before the war, there had been organizations in many communities called Chevres which dealt with specific issues. These disappeared after the war. For instance, in Zwolle Reisjies Chogmo organized Jewish courses every evening for adults. Teref Chouliem paid the costs of food and the kosher cook in a local hospital. Ngeits Chajiem was a Jewish youth movement. Hadras Koudesj dealt with sacramental clothing. Misjenes Zekeiniem supported the elderly, Gemiloes Chasodiem buried men and Nosjiem Rachmonijous buried women. Bikoer Chouliem visited sick people. After the war, all these activities were taken over by the Jewish community of Zwolle.[55]

In some communities, a local paper was published, such as Kol haKehilla in Deventer.[56] The Enschede paper, Chiddoesj, distributed 150 copies weekly. The subscription cost four guilders per year.[57] In Enschede there was still a synagogue choir after the war, but it could not be maintained.[58]

Kosher Food

In the early 1960s, there were still some kosher butchers in provincial towns, i.e., Samson in Enschede and the Utrechtse Vleeshouwerij in Utrecht. In Almelo, chickens were slaughtered once a week.[59] In Deventer, which could not obtain a ritual slaughterer to come regularly, those who kept kosher bought, as a group, a number of chickens and called in a ritual slaughterer who slaughtered them all at once. They kept the chickens in a deep freeze in order to prolong the time it could be stored.[60] Today, there is only one kosher butcher left in the whole of the Netherlands, Marcus in Amsterdam.

In these matters, there had been further decline after the war. In Leeuwarden after the war, there was still kosher slaughter and kosher bread was being baked.[61]

Youth, Student and Sport Movements

Jewish youth movements also played an important role in keeping Jewish communities together. The youngsters usually met in local synagogue facilities.[62] Not all of them were part of Jewish religious life. Haboniem, the largest youth movement at the time was Zionist, socialist and not religious. In the early sixties, outside of the major towns, it had branches in Groningen, Het Gooi, Arnhem, Hengelo, Zwolle, Utrecht, Haarlem and Oss.

Bnei Akiva, affiliated with the Mizrachi movement and Poale Agudat Yisrael affiliated Hasjalsjelet strengthened Jewish religious life in the provincial towns they were active in. Bnei Akiva had branches in Deventer, Eindhoven, Maastricht and Winterswijk.[63] Hasjalsjelet had branches in Almelo and Utrecht.[64] The Left Socialist movement, Hashomer Hatzair, only had branches in Amsterdam and Rotterdam.[65]

Children in small communities who lived far from the nearest location with a youth movement had few, if any, other Jewish children of their own age to play and interact with. That was the case in Leeuwarden where the closest Jewish youth movement was located more than an hour away by train.[66]

The youth movement meetings were mainly led by volunteer youth leaders (madrichim). They often came from the three bigger Jewish communities in the west of the country. An important role was also provided by the movements' summer and winter camps where provincial Jewish youngsters came in contact with youngsters from the same age groups in the larger communities. The role of these movements and the impact they have made on their members' lives merit a detailed study.[67]

The Dutch Zionist Student Movement (NZSO) had branches outside of Amsterdam in Leiden, Utrecht and Groningen. The presence of these students often increased Jewish life in local communities. The sport organization Maccabi had some activities outside of the big cities, for instance in Eindhoven[68] and Enschede.[69]

Marginal Communities

There were also religious Jews in places where no services could take place. One example was Almelo, an independent Jewish community with a Judaic instruction teacher. It held regular Sabbath services but had no minyan, other than when there was a bar mitzvah, or a special occasion. On the High Holidays and some other holidays there were enough people to hold services with a minyan. Without a regular minyan, the reading of the Torah on the Sabbath could not be done from a scroll—handwritten by a specialized scribe—but had to done from a printed text.

In order to pray for a yahrzeit (anniversary of the death of a parent or sibling) one had to find a day when ten men would be willing to come to the synagogue. The fact that Almelo had its own Judaic teacher meant that some of the twenty-two children got up to three hours of Judaic instruction per week instead of one hour, if they were taught by a teacher from the COC.[70]

Another marginal community, Stadskanaal, in the province of Groningen, still held some services in the 1960s. On Yom Kippur they held joint services with Emmen, the only Jewish community in the province of Drente. These services alternated between the two towns. To maintain Jewish communal life in Stadskanaal, members met on Sabbath afternoon for coffee.[71]

At the time, there were still three Jewish families living in Veenendaal, all of whom were Orthodox. They belonged to the Jewish community in Utrecht. For the Jewish holidays, they invited people from elsewhere to stay with them so that they could have a service with a minyan.[72] In Oldenzaal, the last remaining Jew was learning mishnayot (talmudic texts) regularly by himself in order to maintain the tradition of the local Jewish community.[73]

Synagogue Buildings

Many pre-war synagogue buildings survived the German occupation. A significant number were sold or destroyed in the years after the war. There were 158 synagogues in the Netherlands at the beginning of the Second World War. By 2008, twenty-six of those were still in use by Jewish community members and sixty-seven had been destroyed. The others had a variety of uses. Some were churches or shops. In The Hague and Tiel, former synagogues were converted to mosques.

In some communities where synagogue buildings had not survived, new synagogues were installed. Haarlem is one example. A second one is Apeldoorn where a new synagogue was inaugurated in 1960.[74] In 1994, the Zeeland Orthodox community started regular synagogue services in the restored synagogue of Middelburg. In Almere, a town built in a newly dried polder, there are Ashkenazi Orthodox, liberal and Conservative communities.[75]

Jewish religious life in the 1960s had a largely private character. Jewish communities usually kept a low public profile. With memories of the Holocaust still strong, many thought that no good could come from high visibility. Yet some Jewish communities had a different approach. In 1954, in Deventer, the paper Kol Hakehilla was celebrating its fifth year of circulation, and an exhibition of Judaica was organized in the art center De Muntentoren. Two thousand people visited the exhibition. In 1958, when Israel celebrated its tenth year of statehood, there was a week-long Israel exhibition with emphasis on Israeli stamps, in which two thousand visitors attended. The Israeli dance group, Inbal, appeared during that week. The publicity gave that Jewish community a much higher profile than elsewhere. The religious functionary of the Deventer Jewish community was often invited by Protestant pastors to tell their confirmation candidates about Judaism. At the memorial ceremony in 1960 for the liberation of the Netherlands, the Roman Catholic and Protestant pastors spoke in Deventer's Great Church along with the Jewish religious functionary.[76]

In Haaksbergen, where the Jewish community was very small, its head had public status and in view of his function he was invited to ceremonies such as the installation of a new Roman Catholic pastor.[77]

In Winschoten at the time, the interest in Jewish matters expressed itself very differently. The comedy Potasch en Perlemoer, in which Jews had a major role, drew a full house for three days. Also, Amsterdam Jewish comic, Max Tailleur, could count on a large audience.[78]

Lighting the Hanukkah Menorah in Public

The Chabad movement has brought the lighting of the Hanukkah menorah into the public domain in many countries, including the Netherlands. Chief Rabbi Jacobs said in June 2012 that he was already booked for all eight evenings of the Hanukkah holiday six months ahead. He added: "On some evenings I will even light the menorah twice publicly [in different locations]."[79] At the end of 2011, Rabbi Jacobs and other Dutch rabbis presented a menorah as a gift for the Dutch parliament to the chairpersons of the Senate and the Second Chamber.[80]

Jacobs also mentioned that in a Jewish-owned hotel in the town of Maastricht, Christmas trees stood on the roof. He made a remark about that to the owner. He later said, "Since then we light the menorah every year. I know about people who passed there and in that way once again got in touch with their Judaism."[81]

Of a different nature was the recognition of the role Jews had played in local history. This author's article on the Jewish community of Leeuwarden appeared in 1962. On that occasion the municipality published an advertisement in the Nieuw Israëlietisch Weekblad (NIW) in which it said that the Jewish community had held an important role in the development of the town as a center of trade. It added, "Also today the municipality of Leeuwarden appreciates the share of the Jewish community in the economic and cultural life of the capital of Friesland."[82]

Streets were named after Jews in many towns. In other towns, a street or square was named after Israel. For example, in Winschoten there is an "Israel" square.[83] Also there has been twinning of Dutch and Israeli towns. In 1963 this was initiated between the community of Opsterland in Friesland and the Israeli town Ra'anana.[84] Another such twinning exists between Delft and Kfar Saba in Israel. There are several more examples.[85]

Prospects

As mentioned before, there was a feeling in the Jewish communities at the time that they were fighting to maintain their existence. When the chairman of the Jewish community in Groningen left the town around 1960, he donated two silver candlesticks to his community. He did so under the condition that twenty-five years later they would be sent to Hadar Am, a community in Israel where a number of immigrants from Groningen lived. He added that if the Groningen Jewish community dissolved before that date, the candlesticks should be sent to Israel at that time.[86]

One of the post-war pillars of the Jewish community in Zwolle was the local butcher, Leo Marcus. When I visited him in the early 1960s, he said, "What we do here on Shabbat is playing synagogue." When Marcus turned eighty in 1981, he was quoted as saying, "Provincial Jewry is doomed to die."[87]

Already in the 1960s, this was a widespread feeling. Rabbi Berlinger said publicly that he wanted to leave for Israel with all the members of the communities he was responsible for. In 1974 he said, "If a Jewish community has shrunk because of emigration to Israel I consider that a big success. Dutch Jewry has a great future in Israel."[88] In 2012, Chief Rabbi Jacobs said, "I see myself as a life guard of Dutch Jewry. It is the saving of drowning persons. The [overall] potential remains small."[89]

Other Community Building Elements

Not all elements which constituted Jewish life in the provinces were religious. There were also social connections. An important role was played by the Jewish Social Organization (JMW). It was active throughout the country and was often the sole Jewish connection for Jews who were not members of any Jewish organization.[90]

In 1960, the old age home, Beth Zikna, was inaugurated in Arnhem. It existed until 1998.[91] There was also an old age home in Enschede from 1962 until the 1980s.[92]

Before the war, the sole Jewish psychiatric hospital in Europe was Apeldoornse Bos. After the war, Jewish psychiatric patients were spread out over many non-Jewish hospitals in the Netherlands. Yet, as a sign of Jewish renewal in 1960, the Sinai Clinic was opened in Amersfoort. In recent years it has moved to Amstelveen. More recently, the first Jewish hospice in Europe opened in Amsterdam. In the 1960s, there was still a national Jewish convalescent home in Den Dolder. It closed in 1972.[93]

Zionist Activities

After the war, leaders of the Dutch Zionist Organization (NZB) wanted to conquer the Jewish communities. What happened instead was that in the first post-war years the religious communities grew stronger while the Zionist organization gradually got weaker.

Zionist activities remained however. In the 1960s, this was expressed in part through meetings of local NZB groups. Even in a small community such as Leeuwarden, the NZB periodically organized lectures.[94] In other places, the Jewish community and the NZB sometimes organized joint meetings. This was the case in Tilburg.[95]

The *tarbut* (culture) department of the NZB arranged Hebrew lessons in many towns. It also organized winter seminars, usually at the conference venue De Pietersberg in Oosterbeek.[96] At the end of 1961, however, there was so much demand that the gathering had to be moved to a hotel in Noordwijk aan Zee.[97]

Another Zionist activity was the presence of volunteer commissioners of the Joods Nationaal Fonds (Jewish National Fund, JNF) in many communities. Even in towns with tiny Jewish populations that did not have any religious activities such as Borne[98] or Goor, there was a JNF commissioner. Three times a year, visits were made to local Jews, usually by youngsters, for contributions.

The donors were offered a small jar of honey for the Jewish New Year, almonds for the new year of the trees, and a little bouquet of flowers for the

Shavuot (Whitsun) holiday. In some places such as Haarlem, the JNF also organized separate activities such as a Purim evening with artists.[99]

The Dutch branch of the Women's International Zionist Organization, (WIZO) was only established after the war. It increasingly played a significant role in provincial community life and still does. Its role went beyond the classic activities of WIZO. For instance, an exhibition on Jewish life in Zwolle was organized by the local branch.

Often the local NZB[100] and WIZO branches were co-organizers of activities, for instance in Enschede.[101] Elsewhere, they were joint organizers together with local Jewish communities. In Deventer, the WIZO and NZB organized joint meetings, yet the dominant force were the ladies of WIZO.[102] Even in a small community such as Apeldoorn there were meetings.[103]

There were also specific links to Israel. In Hengelo, two visits by an Israeli handball team from Rehovot became major post-war events for the Jewish community there. Each time they came, the Israeli players stayed with community members. Once they stayed for three weeks. There were eighteen Israeli players and staff members hosted by the community which only had sixty-three members including children.

The first game took place in 1954, at which twenty thousand people were present. One of the members of the community said, "In one of the areas of the stadium, mainly Jews were sitting. Tears stained their cheeks." When one of the members of the community visited Israel, half of the Israeli team waited for him at the airport.[104]

Cultural and Entertainment Activities

There were also cultural and entertainment activities such as theater groups in Borculo[105] and in Zwolle. Jewish organizations organized festivities. For instance, the Jewish cultural organization in Zutphen announced that at its annual festivity the evening's program would be a dance orchestra.[106] Even in a small community such as Emmen, an evening with theater and dancing was organized by the local Jewish cultural organization.[107]

For many years, the Jewish theater organization of Deventer held its annual event around Christmas. In 1961, part of the program consisted of a recitation by the Jewish declamatory actress Enny Mols-de Leeuwe.[108] The

JOC Noord Brabant organized its festivities for the entire province.[109] In Enschede, there was "Tegia," which in 1961 held a cabaret with thirty participants and a big ball in the local theater.[110] Twice a year, it arranged a family evening for members. It also organized a ballroom dance course.[111]

In Zwolle, there was a separate entertainment organization which organized an annual car rally[112] and a tea evening for the Simchat Torah holiday.[113]

Sometimes a combination of organizations planned festivities such as the Jewish communities in Het Gooi, Utrecht and Amersfoort together with the NZB and the WIZO. In 1962, many artists performed and 350 people attended.[114]

In some towns, industries owned by Jews played an important role. These have mainly merged or disappeared. Several of my articles in the *NIW* were sponsored by local industries, such as the textile factories of the Levie Brothers in Groningen, Menko in Enschede, Spanjaard in Borne and de Jong & Van Dam in Hengelo. The Organon entity survives as part of a far bigger American pharmaceutical corporation. It was a division of the former Dutch meat packer and pharmaceutical industry Zwanenberg Organon in Oss.

Yet in the 1960s, the small Dutch Jewish community in Enschede could claim that it had the only modern equipped matzo bakery on the continent, the N.V. Paaschbroodfabriek Hollandia. However, at that time, the Dutch demand for matzos was already down to three percent of the total annual production of the company's matzos and crackers and was supervised only part of the year.[115]

Remembering the Jews Who Died: A Major Issue

The philosopher Ludwig Wittgenstein has posited that death is not part of life. Yet in the context of this analysis, the remembrance of Jews who died has to be included. Major changes as to how Jews are memorialized in the Netherlands have taken place in the past fifty years.

In the early 1960s, memorials for the victims of the Holocaust were mainly located in Jewish locations such as synagogues and cemeteries. In Deventer, for instance, there was a memorial in the synagogue for the 400 Jews murdered during the war.[116] In Veendam, there was a monument at the Jewish cemetery.[117]

At the time, there were only a few towns with monuments for murdered Jews in the public domain. In the small town of Gorredijk such a memorial was already established in 1956.[118] Zierikzee was another place with an early memorial in the public domain.[119] In Oss, a memorial was established in 1960 in memory of the 300 dead from Oss, most of whom were Jews.[120] Most Holocaust memorials in Dutch cities were however established much later.

This reality has been described by the historian Frank van Vree in broader terms. He wrote that in the 1960s, "for the first time space was created for the Jewish perspective and that of other victim groups. This space then became concretely visible in the shape of monuments, films and documents, restitution and the introduction of the theme in education, scholarship and art."[121]

In Groningen, for instance, a monument in the public domain was inaugurated in 1977.[122] In Leeuwarden, the monument for murdered Jews was unveiled in 1987.[123] A monument at the Prins Bernhardlaan in Veendam was unveiled in 2002.[124] In Winschoten, in the 1960s, there was a memorial at the Jewish cemetery. The memorial in the public domain was unveiled in 2005.[125] In 1998, a memorial tablet was unveiled at the house where former rabbis lived at one time.[126]

When the synagogue in Deventer was sold in 1987, the memorial for the murdered Jews was moved to the municipality building. Since 1985 in that town, on the bank of the IJssel River, there is a monument in remembrance of Etty Hillesum, whose war-time diary became known internationally. There is yet another monument for murdered Jews on the corner of the Papenstraat and the Ankersteeg.[127]

In 2010, six stone bags were placed as memorials in various locations in Leiden.[128] In 2011, in the former Jewish orphanage there, a memorial tablet was unveiled, inscribed with the names of Jewish inhabitants who were murdered.[129]

The massive wave of books about the history of Jewish communities was just starting in the 1960s. There have also been other important developments concerning remembrance and the writing of history. There are now books on Jewish war monuments in various provinces.[130] Many books have been written in the past fifty years on the history of Jews in various Dutch towns. Others are works in progress. Many books on the Holocaust are still being published. One of the most important was written by Guus Luijters and

Aline Pennewaard titled, *In Memoriam*, which lists the names of the children murdered by the German occupiers during the war.

In some towns, school classes maintain local monuments to murdered Jews and clean the surroundings. This is usually done by the seventh or eighth grade classes of elementary schools. A ceremony is generally held once a year next to the monument where the children have the opportunity to read poems or other texts. For example, such a ceremony was held in Assen on October 4, 2011.[131]

Another newer development is the stolpersteine, the "stumbling stones" (small cobblestone size memorial to individual victims of Nazism), introduced by German sculptor, Gunter Demnig, in 1997. Ten years later, the first stolpersteine in the Netherlands were laid down in Borne in remembrance of murdered members of the local Spanjaard family.[132] There are now stolpersteine in many communities.[133] Maassluis has a virtual memorial for the Jews murdered there.[134]

It should also be mentioned that many municipalities maintain Jewish cemeteries at their expense.[135] Thus the future of deceased Jews in the Netherlands seems to be assured, at least as far as their remembrance is concerned.[136]

To conclude, the latest demographic study shows that the number of Jews in the Netherlands has not shrunk over the decades.[137] If we look back fifty years, however, the denominational composition of organized religious Jewry has greatly changed. And what is even more important, the same is true for the overall position of organized religion in the Netherlands, as well as in Dutch Jewry. Organized religion still plays a core role in Dutch Jewry, but at the same time, it only attracts a relatively small minority of the Jewish population.

Based on lecture at Conference on Religious Cultures of Dutch Jewry, November 2011.

I am very grateful to Bart Wallet for his many comments and to Wendy Cohen-Wierda for her assistance in the research.

1   Also the small Jewish community of Leiden, which is close to The Hague, did not belong to the chief rabbinate of Utrecht.

2   "Het opperrabbinaat Utrecht in 1960," *NIW*, July 14, 1961.

3   Ibid.

4   www.jhm.nl/cultuur-en-geschiedenis/nederland/overijssel/enschede

5   www.jhm.nl/cultuur-en-geschiedenis/nederland/noord-holland/enkhuizen

6   www.jhm.nl/cultuur-en-geschiedenis/nederland/overijssel/haaksbergen

7   www.jhm.nl/cultuur-en-geschiedenis/nederland/friesland/sneek

8   www.jhm.nl/cultuur-en-geschiedenis/nederland/friesland/harlingen

9   M. Gerstenfeld, "De vergeten mediene. De Joodse Gemeente Leeuwarden," *NIW*, January 26, 1962.

10 Ibid.

11 Known in Dutch as "Citroenballetjes."

12 M. Gerstenfeld, "De vergeten mediene. De Joodse Gemeente Groningen III," *NIW*, October 26, 1962.

13 M. Kopuit, "Cijfers spreken boekdelen," *NIW*, September 22, 1961.

14 Information from the NIK secretariat.

15 www.ipor.nl/?id=kehillot

16 H. Beem, *De verdwenen mediene. Mijmeringen over het vroegere joodse leven in de provincie* (Amstelveen: Amphora Books, 1982).

17 J. Fishman, "Een keerpunt in de naoorlogse geschiedenis van de Nederlandse joden. De toespraak van opperrabbijn Schuster in de Nieuwe Kerk (1955)," in *Wie niet weg is, is gezien. Joods Nederland na 1945*, ed. H. Berg and B. Wallet (Zwolle: Waanders, 2010), 118–29.

18 H.L. Hartog, "Joods Amstelveen vroeger en nu," *Amstel Mare* (1999), as quoted in P. van Trigt, "Een religieuze crisis?" in Berg and Wallet, *Wie niet weg is, is gezien*, 189–200.

19 The history of Jewish ritual slaughter in the Netherlands is described in B. Wallet, "Ritual Slaughter, Religious Plurality and the Secularization of Dutch Society (1919–2011)," *Sacrifice in Modernity: Community, Ritual, Identity*, ed. A.M. Korte, J. Duyndam, M. Poorthuis (Leiden: Brill, 2016); and B. Wallet, "Ritueel slachten en godsdienstvrijheid in een seculiere samenleving," *Religie & Samenleving* 7(2) (September 2012), n.p.

20 "Kamer achter verbod onverdoofd slachten," *De Telegraaf*, June 28, 2011.

21 "Senaat verwerpt verbod rituele slacht," *de Volkskrant*, June 19, 2012.

22 M. Swirc, "Eindelijk handtekening," *NIW*, June 8, 2012.

23 M. Gerstenfeld, "Angst voor Moslims heeft grote gevolgen voor Joden," *Nederlands Dagblad*, December 7, 2011.

24 M. Gerstenfeld, interview with Henri Markens, "Integreren en de eigen identiteit bewaren," in *Het Verval* (Amsterdam: Uitgeverij Van Praag, 2010).

25 M. Gerstenfeld, "Dode Joden versus levende Joden," Joodse Omroep, April 19, 2012. www.joodseomroep.nl/:artikel/dode+joden+versus+levende+joden.html

26 "Joodse gemeente Deventer krijgt Thorahrol uit Zurich," *Reformatorisch Dagblad*, October 31, 2011.

27 Since this article was written Beth Shoshana was forced to leave the Golstraat building. Its services are now held in the nearby town of Raalte.

28 M.H. Gans, "Noodtoestand van het Nederlandse Jodendom," *NIW*, May 18, 1962.

29 "Joodse gemeentes zoeken voorgangers," *NIW*, February 16, 1962.

30 M. Gerstenfeld, "De vergeten mediene. De Joodse Gemeente Deventer," *NIW*, December 15, 1961.

31 *NIW,* September 29, October 6, 13 and 27, 1961.

32 M. Gerstenfeld, "De vergeten mediene. De Joodse Gemeente Enschede," *NIW*, August 11, 1961.

33 Gerstenfeld, "De Joodse Gemeente Deventer."

34 M. Kopuit, "Cijfers spreken boekdelen."

35 M. Gerstenfeld , "De vergeten mediene. De Joodse Gemeente Almelo," *NIW*, October 20, 1961.

36 M. Gerstenfeld, "De vergeten mediene. De Joodse Gemeente Hengelo," *NIW*, November 10, 1961.

37 M. Gerstenfeld, "De vergeten mediene. De Joodse Gemeente Haaksbergen," *NIW*, December 1, 1961.

38 M. Gerstenfeld, "De vergeten mediene. De Joodse Gemeente Zwolle," *NIW*, May 18, 1962.

39 Gerstenfeld, "De Joodse Gemeente Enschede."

40 M. Kopuit, "Cijfers spreken boekdelen."

41 Bijeenkomst C.C.C., *NIW*, February 9, 1962.

42 Ibid.

43 M. Gerstenfeld, interview with Chief Rabbi E. Berlinger, *NIW*, August 11, 1961.

44 For instance, visit to Heerlen and visit to Tilburg, on two consecutive Saturdays. "Nieuws van kehillot en organisaties," *NIW*, March 11, 1960.

45 Gerstenfeld, interview with Chief Rabbi E. Berlinger.

46 Gerstenfeld, "De Joodse Gemeente Enschede."

47 M. Gerstenfeld, "De vergeten mediene. De Joodse Gemeente Groningen," *NIW*, September 14, 1962.

48 Gerstenfeld, interview with Chief Rabbi E. Berlinger.

49 Ibid.

50 "Cijfers spreken boekdelen, grepen uit het jaaroverzicht van de P.C.," *NIW*, September 22, 1961.

51 M. Kopuit, "Algemene vergadering NZB, Eenheid niet te herstellen," *NIW*, March 30, 1962.

52 S. Whitlau, "Een rabbijn heeft altijd dienst," *NIW*, June 15, 2012.

53 M. Gerstenfeld, "De vergeten mediene. De Joodse Gemeente Utrecht," *NIW*, July 13, 1962.

54 Gerstenfeld, "De Joodse Gemeente Groningen."

55 Gerstenfeld, "De Joodse Gemeente Zwolle."

56 Gerstenfeld, "De Joodse Gemeente Deventer."

57 Gerstenfeld, "De Joodse Gemeente Enschede."

58 Ibid.

59 Gerstenfeld , "De Joodse Gemeente Almelo."

60 Gerstenfeld, "De Joodse Gemeente Deventer."

61 Gerstenfeld, "De Joodse Gemeente Leeuwarden."

62 "Chadasjot, haBoniem beHolland," *NIW*, November 17, 1961.

63 "Chadasjot Bné Akiva," *NIW*, November 17, 1961.

64 "Chadasjot Hasjalsjelet," *NIW*, November 17, 1961.

65 "Chadasjot Hasjomer Hatsair," *NIW*, December 15, 1961.

66 Gerstenfeld, "De Joodse Gemeente Leeuwarden."

67 About Hasjalsjelet see Sh. Emanuel, Kamnu we-nitoded. Pirke zichronot mipeilut chinoechiet besheerit ha-pleita be-Holland [We Rose and Were Encouraged. Memories of Educational Activity among the Refugees in Holland] (Sha'alvim 2008). The book *Veerkracht, de (her)oprichting van de Joodse jeugdbewegingen in Nederland 1945–1965* (Amsterdam 2019) by Manfred Gerstenfeld and Wendy Cohen-Wierda provides much information on the Jewish youth movements in the post-war years.

68 "Nieuws van kehillot en organisaties," *NIW*, April 13, 1962.

69 Gerstenfeld, "De Joodse Gemeente Enschede."

70 M. Gerstenfeld, "De vergeten mediene. De Joodse Gemeente Twente," *NIW*, October 20, 1961.

71 M. Gerstenfeld, "De vergeten mediene, De Joodse Gemeente Groningen II," *NIW*, October 5, 1962.

72 M. Gerstenfeld, "De vergeten mediene. De Joodse Gemeente Utrecht II," *NIW*, August 3, 1962.

73 M. Gerstenfeld, "De vergeten mediene. De Joodse Gemeente Enschede II," *NIW*, August 25, 1961.

74 www.jhm.nl/cultuur-en-geschiedenis/nederland/gelderland/apeldoorn

75 K. Rijken, "Leve de Mediene: Almere," *NIW*, June 22, 2012. www.nik.nl/2010/01/almere/; www.verbond.eu/index.cfm?pid=CU-page-7E4F8932-1F29-0BD1-72854D8011354359 (Liberaal Joodse gemeente Flevoland) rabbijn Marianne van Praag www.masorti.nl/MasortiAlmere/index.htm

76 Gerstenfeld, "De Joodse Gemeente Deventer."

77 M.Gerstenfeld, "De Joodse Gemeente Haaksbergen," *NIW*, December 1, 1961.

78 Gerstenfeld, "De Joodse Gemeente Groningen III."

79 S. Whitlau "Een rabbijn heeft altijd dienst."

80 "Rabbis present Menorah to Dutch Parliament," December 21, 2011. https://crownheights.info/chanukah/40075/rabbis-present-menorah-to-dutch-parliament/

81 Ibid.

82 Advertisement in *NIW*, January 26, 1962.

83 www.jhm.nl/cultuur-en-geschiedenis/nederland/groningen/winschoten

84 www.stedenbanden.nl/detail_city.phtml?know_id=383&username=gast@stedenbanden.nl&password=9999&publish=Y&username=gast@stedenbanden.nl&password=9999&groups=STEDENBANDEN

85 www.stichtingdelft-kfarsaba.nl/home.html

86 Gerstenfeld, "De Joodse Gemeente Groningen."

87 I. Cornelissen, *Joods levensbeeld als Joods tijdsbeeld, Ter gelegenheid van de tachtigste verjaardag van Leo Marcus* (Zwolle, 1981) 25.

88 B. Wallet and H. Berg, "65 jaar joods Nederland," in Berg and Wallet, *Wie niet weg is, is gezien*, 7.

89 Whitlau, "Een rabbijn heeft altijd dienst."

90 I. Lipschits, *Tsedaka, Een halve Eeuw Joods Maatschappelijk Werk in Nederland* (Zutphen: Walburg Pers, 1997).

91 www.jhm.nl/cultuur-en-geschiedenis/nederland/gelderland/arnhem

92 www.jhm.nl/cultuur-en-geschiedenis/nederland/overijssel/enschede

93 Lipschits, *Tsedaka*, 308.

94 Gerstenfeld, "De Joodse Gemeente Leeuwarden."

95 "Nieuws van kehillot en organisaties," *NIW*, February 2, 1962.

96 See advertisement *NIW*, December 1, 1961.

97 "Winter seminarium thans in Noordwijk," *NIW*, December 22, 1961.

98 M. Gerstenfeld, "De vergeten mediene. De Joodse Gemeente Borne," *NIW*, December 1, 1961.

99 "Nieuws van kehillot en organisaties," *NIW*, March 9, 1962.

100 "Nieuws van kehillot en organisaties Dordrecht," *NIW*, March 30, 1962.

101 Gerstenfeld, "De Joodse Gemeente Enschede."

102 Gerstenfeld, "De Joodse Gemeente Deventer."

103 "Nieuws van kehillot en organisaties," *NIW*, February 23, 1962.

104 M. Gerstenfeld, "De vergeten mediene. De Joodse Gemeente Hengelo," *NIW*, November 10, 1961.

105 "Nieuws van kehillot en organisaties Borculo," *NIW*, March 30, 1962.

106 *NIW*, 29 September 1961.

107 "Nieuws van kehillot en organisaties," *NIW*, March 16, 1962.

108 "Niews van kehillot en organisaties Deventer," *NIW*, November 17, 1961.

109 *NIW*, 20 October 1961.

110 See advertisement, *NIW*, January 5, 1962.

111 Gerstenfeld, "De Joodse Gemeente Enschede."

112 "Nieuws van kehillot en organisaties Zwolle," *NIW*, April 15, 1962.

113 Gerstenfeld, "De Joodse Gemeente Zwolle."

114 "Poeriem in Het Gooi," *NIW*, March 23, 1962.

115 M. Gerstenfeld, "De vergeten mediene, de fabricage van matses door de Hollandia Paaschbroodfabriek," *NIW*, August 11, 1961.

116 Gerstenfeld, "De Joodse Gemeente Deventer."

117 Gerstenfeld, "De Joodse Gemeente Groningen II."

118 www.4en5mei.nl/oorlogsmonumenten/monumenten_zoeken/oorlogsmonument/2098/gorredijk%2C-%27joods-monument%27

119 www.4en5mei.nl/herinneren/oorlogsmonumenten/monumenten_zoeken/oorlogsmonument/3070

120 "Nieuws van kehillot en organisaties," *NIW*, May 13, 1960.

121 F. van Vree, "Iedere dag en elk uur. De Jodenvervolging en de dynamiek van de herinnering in Nederland," in Berg and Wallet, *Wie niet weg is, is gezien*, 70.

122 www.4en5mei.nl/oorlogsmonumenten/zoeken/monument-detail/_rp_main_elementId/1_11268

123 www.4en5mei.nl/herinneren/oorlogsmonumenten/monumenten_zoeken/oorlogsmonument/362

124 www.4en5mei.nl/herinneren/oorlogsmonumenten/monumenten_zoeken/oorlogsmonument/1286

125 www.4en5mei.nl/herinneren/oorlogsmonumenten/monumenten_zoeken/oorlogsmonument/2394

126 www.jhm.nl/cultuur-en-geschiedenis/nederland/groningen/winschoten

127 www.jhm.nl/cultuur-en-geschiedenis/nederland/overijssel/deventer

128 N. Nederlof, "Monumenten voor Leidse oorlogsslachtoffers," *Leiden Lokaal*, March 12, 2010.

129 C. Knoester, "Onthulling plaquette namen omgekomen inwoners Joods Weeshuis," Sleutelstad.nl, March 11, 2011.

130 H. Hamburger and J.C. Regtien, *Joodse oorlogsmonumenten in de provincie Overijssel* (Bedum: Profiel, 2002).

131 Herdenking Joods Monument, MoiAssen, www.moiassen.com/indd.php?p=read HYPERLINK "http://www.moiassen.com/indd.

132 www.stolpersteine-borne.nl/de_familie_spanjaard-2.htm

133 "Stolpersteine (herdenkingssteentjes) in Hillegersberg geplaatst," Rotterdam World Port World City, May 4, 2011. www.rotterdam.nl/www_rotterdam_nl_stolpersteineherdenkingssteentjesinhillegersberg_geplaatst

134 www.joodsmaassluis.com/ nl.wikipedia.org/wiki/Joodse_begraafplaats_ (Zierikzee) stenenarchief.org/stenen_project/den_ham/Den_Ham_list.php

135 www.jhm.nl/cultuur-en-geschiedenis/nederland/overijssel/ommen

136 M. Gerstenfeld, "Holocaust herdacht én verdoezeld in Nederland," *Reformatorisch Dagblad*, May 12, 2012.

137 H. van Solinge and C. van Praag, *De Joden in Nederland anno 2009 continuïteit en verandering* (Diemen: AMB, 2010).

GREAT PEOPLE GONE

Simon Wiesenthal

Simon Wiesenthal z.l. is one of the most fascinating post-war European Jewry personalities. I am glad that Beit Lohamei Hagetaot in Israel houses the Digital Memorial dedicated to him. I want to express my appreciation for Herman Braaf who has taken this initiative.

Willy Lindwer, a well-known Emmy award winning Dutch moviemaker crafted a compelling documentary about Wiesenthal. It was made on the occasion of Wiesenthal's 85th birthday and is entitled *Freedom Is Not a Gift from Heaven*. Lindwer's documentary was the Dutch nominee for the international Emmy award for Best Documentary in 1994.

In the documentary, Wiesenthal talks about his life, recounts his youth in the Ukraine, his experiences during the war in various concentration camps and his liberation by American soldiers. A ten-minute preview of the film can be seen on YouTube.[1]

Wiesenthal is known as the Nazi hunter. There was far greater importance to his activism than people realize. For each Nazi caught, another thousand became frightened. The multiplier effect of Wiesenthal's actions was thus enormous.

I want to address a few other aspects of Wiesenthal's actions which are less known internationally. In 1968, Wiesenthal wrote an article about East Germany's news service which was far more anti-Israeli than that of other communist countries. He found that some texts in the East German press and propaganda literally corresponded to remarks in former Nazi newspapers. It became evident that these articles had been written by the same people who had written antisemitic articles in Hitler's Germany.[2]

After the war Wiesenthal lived in Vienna. A confrontation with the most powerful Jew in that town, Chancellor Bruno Kreisky, was unavoidable. The number of Jews in Austria is tiny. They barely represent one-tenth of a percent of the population. Yet Kreisky, became the best-known post-war Chancellor of Austria. Kreisky was a self-hating Jew. He said, "If the Jews are a people, they are an ugly people."[3]

The greatest academic scholar of antisemitism of our time, the late Robert Wistrich, wrote that Kreisky maintained a strange silence concerning the Holocaust and grossly underplayed the role of antisemitism in the 1930s.

These two diametrically opposed Viennese Jews, Wiesenthal very positive about his Judaism, Kreisky very negative, inevitably clashed. Kreisky, leader of the socialist party, appointed four ex-Nazis in his first cabinet. Wiesenthal found that then Minister of Agriculture, Öllinger, had been a lieutenant in the SS during the Nazi regime. Öllinger thereupon resigned. Kreisky's response was that everyone had the right to make political mistakes in their youth. Kreisky told the Dutch weekly *Vrij Nederland* that Wiesenthal was a Jewish fascist. Wiesenthal responded that Austria was the only country in Europe that still had former Nazis in its government. It became a major verbal battle.[4]

Some 15 years ago, I published a book of interviews titled *American Jewry's Challenge*. One of those interviewed was Rabbi Marvin Hier, founder and dean of the Simon Wiesenthal Center in Los Angeles. He told me: "In the mid–1960s, I led my first mission to Holocaust sites, including Auschwitz and Treblinka. I stopped in Vienna on that trip, and met Simon Wiesenthal. I greatly respected him. As an architect, he had never imagined he would one day chase war criminals. He was untrained to be an investigator and an unlikely FBI agent, yet he started a movement. We have a letter from him to the US Army, dated May 9, 1945, in which he volunteers to help seek out the perpetrators of murderous crimes against the Jewish people. His work yielded results when—within a short time—he submitted his first list of war criminals. After meeting Wiesenthal a number of times, I wondered whether he would be amenable to having an institution named after him."

Hier added that in Los Angeles he met Roland Arnall—an important Jewish communal leader who said "we should both fly to Vienna immediately to discuss it with Simon Wiesenthal." I called Wiesenthal and said we wanted to create an institution in the United States that would be active in the battle against antisemitism. We intended to use the Holocaust as a reminder to the world of what happens when antisemitism runs rampant . . . We made it clear to Wiesenthal that the center would be named after him, but it would be an independent institution and he would not be involved in its management."[5]

It is one of the Center's executives, the director of its Israel office, Efraim Zuroff, who tirelessly continues Wiesenthal's work to this day. The Simon Wiesenthal Center is regularly quoted worldwide. As a result of this Center's many activities, Simon Wiesenthal's name is mentioned nowadays more regularly in international media than probably any other Jew who was active in the decades after the Holocaust.

One often wonders how Jews after the Shoah had the enormous resilience to take up their lives and rebuild families and make a success of their work. But there were people who went beyond this. Simon Wiesenthal was one of the most remarkable. The Jewish people should be grateful for what he did. May his memory be blessed.

Text read out, prepared on the occasion of the inauguration of the digital memorial dedicated to Simon Wiesenthal, Beit Lohamei Hagetaot, February 5, 2019.

1   https://www.youtube.com/watch?v=EWkYxFXESfQ
2   J.H. Brinks, "Political Anti-Fascism in the German Democratic Republic," *Journal of Contemporary History*, 32, 2, 1997, 207-217.
3   Robert S. Wistrich, *From Ambivalence to Betrayal: The Left, the Jews, and Israel* (Lincoln: University of Nebraska Press, 2012) 496.
4   Robert S. Wistrich, *A Lethal Obsession: Anti-Semitism from Antiquity to the Global Jihad* (New York: Random House, 2010) 221ff.
5   Manfred Gerstenfeld, *American Jewrys's Challenge* (New York: Rowman & Littlefield, 2005) 184.

Per Ahlmark

Per Ahlmark (January 15, 1939–June 8, 2018) was one of the greatest friends of Israel in years, when very few European leaders—let alone Scandinavian ones—were willing to identify with the country. This Swedish politician and writer was a member of the Swedish Parliament from 1967–1978 on behalf of the Liberal People's Party. He led the party from 1975–1978. Ahlmark was the Swedish Minister of Labor and Deputy Prime Minister from 1976 to 1978. Ahlmark was a poet and essayist. He was a columnist for the daily *Dagens Nyheter*. He was the founder of the Swedish Committee Against Antisemitism.

The American Jewish Committee (AJC) instituted in 2004 the Jan Karski Award in memory of this exceptionally brave Polish resistance fighter. The first recipient of this award was Ahlmark. When presenting the award, the Executive Director of the AJC, David Harris said: "No one I know comes closer to embodying the spirit, the courage and the commitment of Jan Karski than our honoree today."

Harris added that Ahlmark had "devoted his life, his every waking moment to the very same values that defined Jan Karski." He mentioned on that occasion that Ahlmark had visited Israel 70 times. When Israel was under assault by missile attacks from Saddam Hussein's Iraq, in the first Gulf War during 1990–91, Ahlmark flew to the country and stayed for weeks. He said that Israel was the only place in the world where he wanted to be.

Ahlmark was also active in the campaign for Soviet Jewry and many other pro-Israeli and pro-Jewish issues. One of his functions was as co-Chair of the NGO UN Watch.

In his 2004 Swedish book, of which the title translates as "It's the Democracy, Stupid!" Ahlmark showed that he understood already then how antisemitism and anti-Zionism were linked. He wrote: "Anti-Zionism today has become very similar to antisemitism. Anti-Zionists accept the right of other peoples to national feelings and defensible state. But they reject the right of the Jewish people to have its national consciousness expressed in the state of Israel and to make that state secure. Thus, they are not judging Israel with the values used to judge other countries. Such discrimination against Jews is called antisemitism."[1]

Interview with Per Ahlmark

I interviewed Ahlmark in 2004 when he came to Israel to attend a conference at Yad Vashem. This interview was published here for the first time.

A few decades ago, three socialist prime ministers initiated the major propaganda campaign which gradually led to the current anti-Israel climate in Europe. These were Olaf Palme of Sweden, Andreas Papandreou of Greece and Bruno Kreisky of Austria."

Per Ahlmark, a former Swedish Deputy Prime Minister, and former leader of the Liberal Party, explains how the anti-Israel mood in Sweden grew: "In July 1982, the Social Democrat leader Olaf Palme, then in opposition, compared the treatment of the Palestinians in the Lebanese War to that of the Jews in the Holocaust. He put the Israelis side by side with the Nazis. This was the absolute low in relations between Israel and Sweden. A few months later Palme became Prime Minister, as his party won the elections.

"When Palme made his statement, I was in Israel and went to see Shimon Peres. He said angrily: 'This is idiotic. I'll bring it up in the Socialist International. Where are our gas chambers, our concentration camps? This is perverse.' I published in Sweden what he had said."

From Erlander to Palme

Ahlmark traces the development of his country's attitudes toward Israel: "Sweden has been ruled by the Social Democrats for most of the past 60 years. In the first decades after the War it was pro-Israel. Tage Erlander, the historic leader of the Social Democrats, admired it. During the Six Day War, he said that he was very scared of what could happen. When Israel won the war he felt relieved. It took however, only half a year before people started romanticizing the Palestinians. Since then we have seen in Sweden increasing comparisons between Israelis and Nazis.

"The Yom Kippur War in 1973 brought with it increasing oil prices and fear of shortages. In 1976, Palme's Social Democrats were defeated. The new government was formed by a coalition of the Conservative, Center and Liberal parties in which I became Deputy Prime Minister. Shortly thereafter the Security Council—of which Sweden was a member—discussed whether Arafat should be invited to the United Nations. My election platform supported Israel and opposed antisemitism and terrorism. I was against the invitation of Arafat unless he would denounce terrorism and accept Israel's right to exist.

"Palme, then leader of the Social Democrat opposition, strongly supported Arafat's invitation. The Center party didn't care about Israel or Jewish problems and the Conservatives gave up as well. Only the Liberal party voted against the invitation and thus lost. This happened at a luncheon where our two coalition partners made it clear that they would support the previous government's position. It was the first time that there was a public break on foreign policy in a Swedish Government."

Covering Up Europe's Guilt

"A new anti-Israeli peak was reached during the Lebanese War in 1982. It released a number of barely hidden anti-Semitic feelings. Michael Melchior, then Chief Rabbi of Norway, took the initiative for an international hearing in Oslo against antisemitism. Its Chairman was Elie Wiesel. The attendants warned that a new antisemitism was developing in Europe. There, the Norwegian psychiatrist, Professor Leo Ettinger, an Auschwitz survivor, said that the way the Norwegian media had written about the Lebanese War indicated a wish to cover up for European guilt.

"After Palme compared Israel to the Nazis, we organized a petition signed by many people demanding he apologize for his antisemitic remarks. The Prime Minister at the time, Thorbjorn Falldin, didn't care much about the matter. He was the leader of the Center party, the former Agrarian party, and was not very interested in foreign policy or Israel. He however, never made statements resembling Palme's. Our coalition partners tried to be even-handed, a rather foolish attitude considering the nature of the conflict.

"Over the decades the Social Democratic party's attitude toward Israel has become increasingly worse. Many of its parliamentarians claim that Israel is a brutal colonizer. Israel still has friends in the party. These however feel oppressed and are not active on Israeli issues. Palme already blocked the career opportunities of the pro-Israelis."

Palme: A Friend of Dictators

"Palme's attitude became worse after he met Arafat in Algiers in 1974. He had not read the PLO program which proclaimed Israel's destruction and said: 'my feeling is that this man wants peace.' Nor did Palme comment about the PLO's murder of the Jewish athletes at Munich.

"Sweden's attitude toward Israel would have worsened anyhow, in line with the changed European Union position on the Middle East. Palme however, anticipated this process very early and aggressively and turned anti-Israelism into part of his political platform. He always praised Arab countries when visiting them. Palme also embraced Castro and was frequently positive toward dictatorships.

"Palme radically changed a number of basic foreign policies of Sweden. He had been a strong critic of the United States in Vietnam, of the Soviets in Czechoslovakia, and of Pinochet in Chile. This created his false image as an adversary of dictatorships. Palme was however, friendly with several dictators and there were many tyrannies he did not criticize. He told Swedes not to censure the Soviet Union and developed the country's neutral foreign policy. Palme was a very divisive figure in the democratic world."

Palme's Influence Still Major

When asked how Palme rhymed this with Socialism, Ahlmark replies: "He was a typical opportunist. Many in the party distrusted him as he came from an upper-class family. He thus wanted to appear more Socialist than the real ones."

Ahlmark mentions that Palme's impact lasts until today. "In 2003, many European socialists were in favor of the war in Iraq when it started. British Prime Minister Tony Blair is the most prominent one. I am not sure however, that there is one significant figure in the Swedish Social Democratic party who supports it.

"Goran Persson, the current Swedish Prime Minister and Social Democrat leader, tried to be moderate in his criticism of the United States. He discovered that this is impossible and has thus accepted the wave of anti-Americanism in his party. In the first Gulf War in 1990, still a few Social Democrats came out in its favor. The Iraqi conquest of Kuwait was in breach of everything they believed in."

Persson: A More Supportive Policy

"The Social Democrats were defeated in 1990 again and were in opposition until 1993. The next Prime Minister, Carl Bildt, was a successful Conservative party leader, a reliable anti-Communist with a good knowledge of foreign policy. He had opposed Palme's flirtation with the Communists but didn't understand Jewish issues and never condemned antisemitism.

"When Göran Persson became Prime Minister, he told me that he wanted to return to a policy more supportive of Israel. On one of his first official visits, he came to Israel in order to change the atmosphere between the two countries. He started to make positive remarks about Israel and then took the initiative for the Stockholm International Forum on the Holocaust, which convened in January 2000. This was a very positive step. This Conference was successful, and the Stockholm Declaration condemning the trivialization of the Holocaust was an important statement.

"Persson's party didn't follow his lead in a more positive attitude toward Israel. He also to a certain extent destroyed his image when he was President of the EU a year later. When the racist forces expressed their blatant anti-semitism at the United Nations Anti-Racism Conference in Durban in 2001, Persson did not react. He remained silent when the Muslim states not only trivialized the Holocaust but also inverted it, accusing Jews and Israelis of causing a new one."

The Wrong People in Key Positions

Ahlmark adds: "As far as Swedish-Israeli relations are concerned, often the wrong people are in key positions. This goes far beyond Palme. In 2002, when the biased condemnations of the United Nations Human Rights Commission against Israel reached their extreme, the Swedish ambassador at the UN in Geneva was Johan Molander. At a time when already a third of all the Commission's resolutions condemned Israel, he asked for more condemnations. Molander was also very active in removing the United States from membership of that Commission."

Ahlmark sits on the board of UN Watch, a body founded in 1991 by Morris Abrams, a leader of the American Jewish Committee. He had been Reagan's human rights ambassador and was very upset by the UN's discrimination against Israel. Once Molander was invited for a lunch with the board of UN Watch, whereafter all participants said that they had never met such an arrogant ambassador from a democratic country.

Persson's Lack of Courage

Ahlmark thinks that Persson, if he could, would make positive statements about Israel. "He doesn't because he leads an anti-Israeli party and lacks courage. He is a broken man who might have resigned already were it not that his expected successor, foreign minister Anna Lindh, was murdered.

"While Sweden has a pro-Israel prime minister in Persson, it had in Anna Lindh probably the most anti-Israeli foreign minister ever. She belonged to the 1968 generation, which tends to be very anti-Israeli. In meetings of EU foreign ministers, she often wanted stronger condemnations of Israel than the already negative consensus.

"While Lindh had a good understanding for the Kosovo problem for instance, she did not comprehend that terrorism is so ugly that all democrats, including the Swedish Social Democrats, should fight against it. She never understood that Israel is fighting for its survival and cannot afford to lose any war. Such a defeat would mean its end."

Two Political Murders

Ahlmark points out that Sweden has had to deal with the murder of two politicians in the last 20 years, and that the Swedish police have been incompetent in both cases. "Palme was murdered in February 1986. He had escaped his bodyguards, not wanting them constantly around him. There had not been a political assassination in Sweden since democracy began more than 100 years ago. Thus he didn't think he was taking a risk."

Ahlmark says that Sweden is unable to learn from its own experiences. "Anna Lindh had no police protection despite her stance in favor of Sweden joining the Euro monetary zone, on which there was a referendum four days after her murder. The day before the referendum, she would have been one of the main debaters in favor of joining which was the minority position.

"There are Swedes however who have shown an ability to learn from what happens elsewhere. Suicide bombings and Al-Qaeda's actions have taught them lessons. Many non-Socialists however are still full of illusions, and not only the Social Democrats. The latter have difficulties imagining the cruelties of totalitarian regimes and their leaders. Something similar might have happened without Palme, but the movement of flirtation with the totalitarians is identified with him. He jump-started it and became its prominent leader."

A Socialist Archbishop

As to Swedish foreign minister Leila Freyvalds, who came to Israel in order to criticize the Israeli government, Ahlmark remarks that she does not have the same extreme attitudes as her predecessor, Lindh. "Persson wanted a woman in the position. Freyvalds was a fairly good justice minister but has little experience in foreign policy. These disparate reasons made her a good candidate for foreign minister. Swedish prime ministers often want weak cabinet ministers, and in particular for foreign affairs. Then they can decide much of their foreign policy themselves. Freyvalds is a typical fellow traveler. If her EU colleagues would become more understanding toward Israel, she would also do so.

"Another unfortunate situation is that the Archbishop of the Lutheran Church nowadays is very anti-Israeli. K.G. Hammar was very active in the Socialist and Communist movements in 1968. One wonders whether an Archbishop should really be an activist for Socialist causes, making enemies in many areas. He claims that Israel is to blame for the Middle East crisis and that sanctions should be taken against it.

"There is much opposition against him concerning his anti-Israeli remarks. There are however, several other bishops who are extremely anti-Israel. One of them, who always makes negative remarks about Israel, was praising the cultural revolution in China."

Exaggerating Bad News for Israel

"In the media also, one finds several wrong people in the right places. There is a tendency among many news reporters to exaggerate the bad news for Israel and mitigate bad news for the Palestinians. The Middle East desk at the very prestigious national news agency, Teris Telegram Bureau (T.T.), is headed by Hjatir. Twenty or 25 years ago when he was still a Communist, he was also a denier of the Holocaust. The Swedish Committee Against Antisemitism in the 1990s asked Hjatir whether he distanced himself from his previous statements. He said: "No." He does not explicitly claim today that the Holocaust never occurred because that is impossible for someone who works for T.T.

"This person, who is relatively unknown, sits at a place where he has the power to decide what news to distribute. He can delete positive elements for Israel, as well as information on the multiple murders and corruption of the Palestinians. Many local papers take their news from T.T., thus in a way Hjatir influences what the population reads.

"As far as the media is concerned, in general the news journalists are more anti-Israeli than the leading editorial writers. One exception is the largest paper, *Aftonbladet*. This afternoon tabloid now has an anti-Israeli former priest as its editor-in-chief. She makes Israel the scapegoat and is supported in this by other editors.

"*Svenska Dagbladet*, a leading morning paper, leans toward a pro-Palestinian line on its news pages. Its editorial page however, is balanced. As far as the other major morning paper, *Dagens Nyheter*, is concerned, I am one of its columnists so I shouldn't comment."

An Excess of Marxist Journalists

In Ahlmark's view, the recruitment system of journalists enables many Marxist views to permeate into society. In Sweden, there are opinion polls of journalists. In 1968, three percent of them were positive toward Communism, similar to the votes the Communist party got in the 1968 election. By 1989, the year the Soviet system collapsed, about 30 percent of the journalists had sympathies for Communist or Marxist ideas. Thus a major gap between public opinion and the media one has been created.

"These people were not removed after the Soviet Union collapsed. They are being promoted normally. Sometimes they moderate their opinions a bit, but they still have sympathies for radical causes. This is the main explanation of why Swedish public opinion has evolved in leftist directions.

"Thus it didn't matter much when in Camp David 2, Israeli Prime Minister Ehud Barak made fargoing concessions to cede the West Bank, Gaza and recognize a Palestinian state with a central part of Jerusalem as its capital. Arafat said no and started a war. The conclusion of reasonable people is that Arafat is not only a crook but a terrorist, and the Palestinians are to blame for the bloodshed which has followed in the last few years. Politics and the media however are not rational."

A Silent Minority

Ahlmark stresses that he considers it his duty to publish information on the major dangers of terrorism to Western civilization. "Even at the paper I write for, many people do not understand the risk terrorism embodies. As I feel at home in Israel, this makes me suspect for many people. It also turns me into a columnist who says things rarely mentioned by others.

"When I write columns in favor of the United States, I am an exception. Afterwards, I am often stopped in the streets, on buses, in the Underground, and people say: 'Thank you for what you wrote today.' These are ordinary people who do not publish, but are glad that somebody writes what they think. There is a sizeable silent minority, which is fairly big, but is not heard in public."

In August 2004, at an International Conference of Yad Vashem, Ahlmark spoke about antisemitism, anti-Americanism and anti-Zionism. He mentioned the European rhetoric claims, which say the Europeans do not go to war but to the negotiating tables. He defined their position as: "We do not exhaust our resources by spending hundreds of billions of Euros on weapons and soldiers. Now the rest of the planet should learn from us how to live together without terrorizing each other."

Ahlmark went on saying: "As a Swede, I have heard this boasting all my life. We have not been at war for two centuries; it proves that Sweden is sort of a moral superpower. Now this type of bragging has become part of the EU ideology. We are now the moral continent. In a way we now experience the Swedenization of European attitudes to other regions."

He then criticized Western Europe severely, saying that it forgets that without the US army, it would not have been liberated in 1945, and without the Marshall Plan, it would not have taken off economically, adding: "Without the policy of containment under the American umbrella, the Red Army would probably have strangled the dream of freedom in East and Central Europe for maybe another century."

Israel's Democracy: A Miracle

Ahlmark adds that he also expresses clearly his criticisms of Israel. These concern mainly two areas. The first is the usefulness of the settlements. The other is the establishment of a Palestinian state. He wrote the first book in Sweden in favor of a Palestinian state because he considered that Palestinian nationalism had to be satisfied. Ahlmark said that such a state could only come into being if it was democratic and lived in peace with Israel. "Democracies never go to war with each other. It is Israel's tragedy that it is the only democracy in the Middle East. Had there been many Arab democratic states, there would have been no wars.

"Despite my critical remarks on Israel, I'm still regarded as a pro-Israeli fanatic in Sweden. I consider it a miracle that Israelis have built a democracy under constant threat of annihilation. It has never happened in any other country. My criticism of Israel is however considered by many as an alibi; something that in their eyes I say in order to pretend to be balanced."

At the Yad Vashem Conference, Ahlmark said that he was born in 1939 at the beginning of the Holocaust. He did not meet a Jew until he was 18 years old, which was still possible in Sweden in the 1940s and 1950s. When he came on his first visit to Israel, he started to understand that antisemites of different centuries have always aimed to destroy the center of Jewish existence.

In 1983, Ahlmark became the founder of the SKMA, the Swedish Committee Against Antisemitism. He observes: "This body initiated Holocaust education in schools. In schools attended by many Muslim children, teaching the Holocaust is sometimes very difficult or impossible. The number of Muslims in Sweden is on the rise, and it by far exceeds the Jews among the nine million inhabitants of the country."

Antisemitism: Mainly on the Left

"Antisemitic incidents in Sweden are partly caused by Muslims. In that community there are also individuals with sympathies for radical Middle Eastern movements. They are also almost always anti-American. The far right is small, and one could cope with them if they were the only other problem.

"The main challenge in Sweden is on the left side of the political spectrum. The former Communist party received about eleven percent support in the last election. The Social Democrats need their voting support for their minority cabinet. Another party supporting the coalition government is the Green party, which got 6 percent of the votes.

"The founder of the Green party Per Gahrton has been campaigning against Israel for at least thirty years. He was also a supporter of Ahmed Rami's Radio Islam, a Swedish pro-Nazi radio station. Once one becomes so critical of Israel, one starts to use anti-Semitic language. Different values and norms are applied against Israel than against any other country in the world. This is discriminatory. Saying that all people have the right to have a state and a national feeling, except the Jewish people, is anti-Semitic. With this definition one sees that among Communists, Greens and Social Democrats—in particular in the news organizations—one finds leftist antisemites and racists."

Intimidating Jews

"Violence against Jews is rare. On Israel's Independence Day, we held a demonstration against antisemitism and for Israel. There was a counter demonstration by Muslims who shouted threats and destroyed our banners. Several hundreds of people marched on our side. Most of them were Holocaust survivors. When they heard what the Muslims were shouting, they had associations of other times and pogroms. There were less demonstrators on the other side but they were violent. The police protection was deficient.

"Nowadays, solidarity meetings for Israel are held in synagogues where there is security. We discuss whether we should hold them in a public square in the center of Stockholm, but then consider we will be disturbed. A shouting match is not the way to celebrate Israel's independence, but if we have a solemn surrounding in the synagogue we don't reach anyone beyond the Jews."

Ahlmark says that Swedish Jews are intimidated. "Young Jews do often not want to carry a Star of David or a kippa. Those who speak on television on behalf of Israel ask themselves whether they will also be physically attacked as happens in other European countries. If somebody wears a kippa and goes into the subway in the evening, which is basically a safe place, and finds himself in a carriage with a number of Muslims, he wonders what will they do.

"When Jews were attacked in Goteborg, the Chairman of the Jewish community made public statements about the sort of fear they instill in Jews. Or even in those who identify with the Jewish community. A process of intimidation has thus crept into democratic Sweden.

"Primary responsibility for this situation lies with Prime Minister Persson. He speaks out against the violence but should do so in a much more energetic way. He should go to pro-Israeli meetings, criticize the police when they do not protect these enough, and say explicitly that he is shocked by what is happening."

Manipulating Media Panels

Ahlmark mentions that bias manifests itself also in another way. He is often asked by television or radio stations to take part in debates about Israel or the Middle East. "I always inquire first whether anyone on the panel has Nazi sympathies, is a known antisemite or has been an active Communist without publicly distancing himself from it. If so, I do not participate. Often the invitees are three people against me while I am alone. In such situations, they want me as an alibi. I reply then: 'Either one-one, or two-two,' otherwise my opponents will get the floor again and again. Actually, I have to refuse most offers.

"Others who television or radio invite are supporters of Ahmed Rami. Radio Islam has been closed and Rami has been sent to prison a number of times, however the station still exists on the internet. I cannot be with those people in a room because that way I give them legitimization."

With some nostalgia, Ahlmark thinks back to the days when he was leading his party into the elections of 1976. "Even when I wasn't asked a question, I raised in meetings Israel's right to exist in peace without terrorism. We won the elections. Today, theoretically if I wanted to do so, I would probably be faced with protests and need major police protection."

Besa Center, June 25, 2018

---

1   Per Ahlmark, *Det ar demokratin, dumbom!* (Stockholm: Timbro, 2004) 307.

Dan Vittorio Segre

Perhaps only out of Italian Jewry and at rare intervals can such colorful personalities emerge like Professor Dan Vittorio Segre, who passed away at the age of 91 in 2014. Segre grew up in an assimilated and fascist Italian environment, but fled to Palestine after racist laws were enacted in his country of birth in 1938. He almost did not make it, as he was accidentally nearly shot dead by his father at the tender age of five.

Segre marched forward from a soldier in the Jewish Brigade of the British Army to officer in the fledgling Israeli Defense Forces, became an ambassador of Israel, and was suspected and later cleared of treason because of his contacts with a Russian diplomat. He then went on to become an academic at Oxford and a professor of political science at Haifa University, Stanford, MIT and Bocconi University in Milan. Segre, already at an advanced age, founded the Department of Mediterranean Studies at the University of Lugano, Switzerland, of which he became the first Director. He was for decades a journalist for major French and Italian papers such as *Le Figaro*, *Corriere della Sera* and *Il Giornale*. All the above represents but a very incomplete curriculum vitae.

His three-part autobiography only covers a small selection of what he lived through. The first part, *Memoirs of a Fortunate Jew*, was translated into many languages. It is beautifully written and full of incredible stories. One small example illustrates the breadth of his personal journey: in the Second World War the British did not provide pork for meals to their Jewish Brigade to which Segre belonged. The Jewish soldiers then went on strike, as they were denied "equal rights." They asked and succeeded in being given bacon for breakfast like all others. Segre would later become Modern Orthodox and remained so his whole life.

Whenever Segre would sit at the Friday night table at our home, the other guests, whether they had known him for years or had just met him, were amazed and fascinated by what he told. In some way, he embodied serendipity itself. Segre indeed enabled others to continuously make "accidental" surprising discoveries. One of these, among many, was when he told me, quite casually, that he had been the very last person in Palestine to talk to Enzo Sereni, the leader of the Palestinian Jewish parachutists who went to their deaths in the Second World War.

In his last years, when he was suffering from many health problems, he related stories about his treatments by a French miracle doctor, Cohen, who alleviated many of his painful symptoms. Despite this, Segre regretted that he could not get well enough to go horseback riding again. He had been riding since he was a child. It is difficult to imagine that in pre-Israel Palestine, Segre, together with another future Israeli ambassador, went regularly to the major British army base in Sarafand to go horseback riding.

As he lived through so many adventures, no obituary can encompass more than a fraction of them, so it is probably best to tell some personal memories. Segre told me that after he had been cleared of treason charges, Prime Minister Golda Meir offered him any diplomatic post he would want. He told her that he wanted to leave the diplomatic service. With the help of the internationally renowned philosopher Josef Agassi, who had been a soldier under his command in Israel's War of Independence, Segre entered into St. Anthony's at Oxford. One of the lessons Agassi taught Segre was that before he started to research a project, he should write whatever he thought that the conclusions would be. That would help him to focus on the research to be done, even if the final conclusions were radically different from what he had initially written. Later, when I hesitated about the quality of my PhD thesis to be presented, Segre introduced me to Agassi and said, "if you can answer his criticisms, nobody can destroy your thesis."

Segre and I were jointly involved in promoting an ambitious project which never got off the ground, although not for lack of trying. Each of us had different contacts among the top management of Silvio Berlusconi's business interests. One day, Segre told me that he had been informed by one of his contacts that the Italian government considered Berlusconi to be too powerful, since he controlled three Italian television channels, as many as the Italian public broadcasting system. The government wanted to take away one of Berlusconi's channels under the pretense that these channels broadcast nothing but entertainment. I suggested that Segre and I would carry out interviews with the best brains in the world within various fields and that these interviews would be broadcast late at night by Berlusconi's TV channels. This would have a double advantage. With such a prestigious program, no longer could anyone claim that there was only entertainment on the channels. In addition, not much advertising revenue would be lost on such programming at late evening hours. Our contacts liked the proposal very much and set up a meeting for the two of us with Berlusconi. One day before the meeting was to take place, the Italian police came to see Berlusconi in order to investigate major corruption charges. Our meeting was cancelled. Berlusconi decided to go into politics, which would protect him from the Justice Department officials. It was both the beginning of Berlusconi's path to becoming the Prime Minister of Italy, and the end of our project which would have been extremely interesting to implement.

In 1994, I interviewed Segre for my post-Oslo agreements book *Israel's New Future*. Rereading the text twenty years later it shows his extraordinary insight. To quote one paragraph: "Europe does not seem to have renounced some aspects of its Shylock policy. It wants from Israel a pound of flesh in territorial concessions without paying attention to the damage these may cause to the whole body as far as the defense capabilities of Israel are concerned. To insist on unilateral concessions after the Yugoslav experience would look comic if it was not so tragic."

In the last years of his life, Segre carried on as if he had no health problems. He spent much of his time in his new apartment in Jerusalem. He brought with him an excellent Italian cook, who had previously wasted her great skills on the assembly line of the Fiat car company in Turin. On his balcony, Segre entertained his friends with fine meals and stories as if he were decades younger.

Despite all his experiences, Segre remained a modest man. He did not think of himself as much of an academic, even though some of the universities he taught at were among the most prestigious in the world.

Any obituary can provide but a mere glimpse into the fascinating life of such a unique personality as Segre. May his memory be blessed.

The Jerusalem Post, October 6, 2014

Robert Wistrich

Professor Robert Wistrich was the leading historian of antisemitism, and published important books in other fields of history as well. The combination of his intellectual depth and prolific authorship made him a leader in many aspects of the antisemitism field. His presence was most important in an area where the number of scholars has unfortunately not caught up with the recent explosion of hatred and its mutations, from despising the Jewish religion and the Jewish people to the defamation of the Jewish State.

Robert was a spokesman and a representative of the Jewish people, roles to which he stayed fully committed. The many projects he led included a joint exhibition of the Simon Wiesenthal Center and UNESCO on "Book, People, Land. The 3,500 Year Relationship of the Jewish People With the Holy Land." A very different matter was his membership of the International Catholic-Jewish Historical Commission—established in 1999—which reassessed Pope Pius XII's role in the Second World War. Robert did not let pressure from Church sources affect his integrity, which eventually contributed to the premature suspension of the Commission's work.

When one writes the obituary of such an outstanding intellectual, his biography and many human qualities are only one aspect of his personality. Important others can be seen by focusing on some of his great analytical work.

Decades ago, I read a publication of the World Union of Jewish Students. Among the many articles written by the student authors was one which stood out by far above the rest. That was how I came across Robert's name for the first time.

Antisemitism studies became a field of research thanks to French scholar, Léon Poliakov (1910–1997), who wrote much of the fundamental works in the field. However, it required the development of a high-level institute to cover the field in greater scope, and Robert was instrumental in this endeavor. He held the Neuberger chair for Modern European and Jewish history at the Hebrew University of Jerusalem. When Robert took over as head of the university's Vidal Sassoon International Center in 2002, he transformed it into a place which published a broad array of antisemitism scholarship, covering many countries and subjects.

Robert was not only a very skillful writer but also a sophisticated speaker. Born of Polish Jewish parents in the Soviet Union, English was not his mother tongue, but one among the languages he mastered. This and his encyclopedic knowledge allowed him to gain deep insight into various cultures.

It is impossible to review all of Robert's works unless one writes a lengthy essay—so I will focus on some of his more recent publications. His magnum opus, *A Lethal Obsession*, subtitled *Anti-Semitism from Antiquity to the Global Jihad*, was released in 2010. Its individual chapters can be read as self-standing essays.

In this book, Robert devoted an entire chapter to "Jews against Zion." He covered the history of Jewish self-haters, beginning with the apostates in Christian Spain after the massacres of the Jews in 1391. He referred to a statement already quoted by the turn of the nineteenth century Viennese playwright, Arthur Schnitzler: "Antisemitism did not succeed until the Jews began to sponsor it." Extreme masochistic trends, including psychological self-flagellation, which regularly occur amongst Jews, probably exceed those of other cultures. Robert's analysis, for example, of the post-war Austrian Jewish chancellor, Bruno Kreisky, a socialist whitewasher of former Nazis, was lethal.

Many scholars look away from the widespread antisemitism emanating from Muslim states and from parts of the Muslim population in Western countries. Despite the backlash, Robert remained outspoken when his post-9/11 essay on Muslim antisemitism, originally published in English, was updated and republished in German in 2011. Therein, Robert claimed that the hardcore antisemitism in the Arab and Muslim world is comparable only to that of Nazi Germany. Expressing such an opinion was far more than an academic judgment. It was an act of courage. Much more gentle criticism about extreme ugly phenomena in Muslim societies was already being labeled as Islamophobia. Such criticism is constantly stifled not only by Muslims but also by many "politically correct" Westerners. Robert explicitly stated that Muslim hatred for Israel and Jews is "an eliminatory antisemitism with a genocidal dimension."

From Ambivalence to Betrayal. The Left, the Jews, and Israel was released in 2012. The book includes the chapter, "Great Britain: A Suitable Case for Treatment?" Robert had gone to school in the UK, where the British literary classics on the curriculum, he had to read, were almost all antisemitic in nature. Robert's analysis started with Chaucer's *Canterbury Tales* from the late fourteenth century and Christopher Marlowe's *The Jew of Malta* from the end of the sixteenth century. He came out unequivocally against the whitewashing of the antisemitism of Shakespeare's *The Merchant of Venice*.

Probably more so than anyone else, Robert has proven that antisemitism is not only inherent in European history but that it is an integral part of European culture. I once persuaded him to lecture at the Jerusalem Center for Public Affairs about the long tradition of intellectual antisemitism. He illustrated how each change in the social environment brings about a mutation of antisemitism. In Europe, Catholic antisemitism laid down the ideological infrastructure from which much of the demonizing of the Jews, Judaism and the Jewish people developed. From Martin Luther and Protestantism, the Enlightenment, including Voltaire, the great German idealist philosophers, the early French socialists, to Karl Marx—many intellectuals and innovative movements gave their own "contribution" to antisemitism.

Robert was a passionate and tireless fighter for his ideas. A comrade-in-arms against the many ugly enemies of the Jewish people, and a man of principle, I had the privilege of last speaking with him—a lengthy, and as always, stimulating and pleasant conversation—during the 2015 Global Forum for Combatting Antisemitism, a few days before his passing. His sense of purpose remained unabated until the very end. Like all great intellectuals, he will live on through the legacy of his profound work and original thought.

The Jerusalem Post, May 21, 2015

Indonesian President Wahid, Israel and the Jews

Interview with C. Holland Taylor

C. Holland Taylor is a retired American businessman who has lived in Indonesia since 1999 and was a close friend of President Wahid.

"His Excellency Kyai Haji Abdurahhaman Wahid served as president of Indonesia from 1999–2001. He is the only Indonesian president who visited Israel and did so a number of times. President Wahid was deeply aware of the cultural, historical, intellectual and spiritual dimensions of Judaism, as well as the intimate religious and linguistic connections between Judaism/Islam and Hebrew/Arabic.

"President Wahid—popularly known as "Gus Dur"—was a humanitarian and viewed others primarily through the lens of love, compassion and respect. He regarded Jews and Judaism as an integral and profoundly legitimate "thread" within the fabric of human existence, whose contributions to humanity have been immense. That's why he agreed to sponsor the 2007 Bali Holocaust Conference with our friends from the Simon Wiesenthal Center and accepted the organization's Medal of Valor at an award ceremony the following year in Los Angeles.

"Gus Dur had a number of Jewish friends. One of these was an Iraqi Jew named Ramin, with whom he worked at an import/export business in downtown Baghdad during the 1960s. Gus Dur studied the Kabbalah with Ramin in some depth. He also studied with a Sunni Sufi Shaykh who was later tortured and murdered by the Baathist regime in Bagdad. Together with Ramin, Gus Dur witnessed the public execution of nine Iraqi Jews who were falsely accused of spying for Israel.

"From Gus Dur's perspective, the treatment of the nine Iraqi Jews and the Sufi Shaykh was identical. They were all victims of extreme brutality and injustice. In that context, ethnicity and religion were irrelevant to Gus Dur, except insofar as what made the Sunni Shaykh and Iraqi Jews targets of a vicious regime. To Gus Dur, their humanity and suffering were paramount.

"After his stay in Iraq during the 1960s, Gus Dur's next intensive engagement with Jews and Judaism—beyond his extensive reading of Jewish literature—most likely occurred during his term as chairman of the Nahdlatul Ulama (NU) Executive Board from 1984 to 1999. This Indonesian charitable organization is the world's largest Muslim movement, with over 50 million members.

"During his chairmanship of NU Gus Dur traveled extensively and developed many international contacts, including with the American Jewish Committee. Following his term as Indonesia's fourth president, Gus Dur maintained these contacts and continued to visit both the United States and Israel.

"He regarded Israel as having a legitimate right to exist, and believed that Jews have a right to dwell in their historic homeland. Gus Dur once said to me: 'You know why the conflict between Israel and its neighbors has never found a peaceful resolution? It's because Arabs refuse to accept Israel's right to exist.'

"During his first week in office as President of Indonesia, Gus Dur publicly called for establishing diplomatic relations with Israel. He said: 'Indonesia has diplomatic relations with China, a communist—and thus atheist—country. Why shouldn't we have normal relations with Israel, whose people and government believe in God, as we do?'

"Gus Dur believed that the demonization of Jews, Judaism and Israel were manifestations of a profound psychological and emotional illness that afflicts a large percentage of human beings, and works to the detriment of humanity at large. He wished to normalize relations with Israel through his straightforward words and actions.

"I do not know the full range of Gus Dur's contacts with Israel, although they were extensive. For example, he received an honorary award from Netanya College, where he served on an advisory board with Mikhail Gorbachev and prominent Israeli figures. He also had a close relationship with Prince Hassan bin Talal, King Hussein of Jordan's younger brother. This relationship was connected to certain positive dynamics between Israel and Jordan.

"Before his death, Gus Dur said to me: 'The fact that we are friends with Jews and Israel does not mean that we wish to take Israel's side against its neighbors. We are also friends to Palestinians and Arabs. And the fact that we are friends with Shimon Peres does not mean that we should be equally close to any and all Israeli politicians. We defend Jews and Israel as a matter of principle, on the basis of our shared humanity, but we should never allow ourselves to be used inappropriately by anyone in Israel who might wish to do so.'

"President Wahid was a towering figure, widely regarded as a saint. This strongly colored the majority of Indonesians' views and acceptance of his conduct in regard to Jews and Israel. Nowadays, the spiritual wing of the NU and the related political party PKB generally recollect and accept President Wahid's attitudes toward Israel. A number of leading figures consciously share his attitude. They view people of other faiths in light of our common humanity; have no animosity towards Jews; and regard the conflict between Israel and its neighbors as territorial in origin, unrelated to the essential teachings of religion, except insofar as either side chooses to ignore these universal principles, which all religions share in common."

Israel National News, 5 april 2018

Daniel Elazar's Heritage: Five Years After

At the end of December 2004 was Daniel Elazar's fifth yahrzeit. We stood at his grave on Har Hamenuhot, the family members and a few close friends. There were words in Dan's honor and remarks about how we remembered him. That is the case with most of those who are no longer with us. Their family recalls them and so do a few good friends.

Dan, in the last months of his life, needed all his forces to fight against his illness. At some moments however he thought about the future without him and wondered what would become of his life work. We discussed frequently his many fields of activities and he suggested who could continue some of them. He expressed doubts whether all the colleagues would do so.

Five years after his death, Dan is very much with us at the Jerusalem Center for Public Affairs (JCPA). His oil painting in the library, with remarkable likeness, watches when there are lectures and reminds us of how much effort he, the JCPA's founding president and chairman, had put in establishing the center. Many of our lecturers, in particular but not exclusively from the United States, spontaneously mention in their presentations how they met Dan and what impact he has had on their personal development.

We hear about scholars who continue his work at Bar Ilan University and elsewhere. His name and work comes up in projects we at the JCPA do, in articles in the *Jewish Political Studies Review* and in many other ways. His widow Harriet told me that even now she is still regularly contacted by journalists abroad who want to interview Dan, or by scholars who seek his advice, not knowing that he passed away.

Publications and Conferences

There is much more to tell. Several publications on his work are in progress. In 2002, a big conference in his memory was held, jointly by Bar Ilan university and the JCPA. A book with the text of the lectures held there will be published. It is not only those who were close to him who have seen the light he has spread. In another few weeks Rowman and Littlefield will publish the fourth and last book of the JCPA's PEW project, which deals with Judaism in the American public square. It deals with the changing attitudes of prominent American Jews after the mega events in the 21st century. This book concludes the largest research project Dan ever initiated.

It was Dan also who started the sessions on contemporary Jewish studies and public affairs at the World Congress of Jewish Studies. Every four years the JCPA ran a program there under his leadership devoted to the changing situation of the Jewish people. At the fourteenth Congress in the beginning of August 2005 we will again continue the tradition he started. There is so much interest that we will for the first time have two days of lectures rather than one. Several of the sessions will be devoted to the analysis and further development of Dan's research.

The JCPA

All this together already amounts to an impressive list concerning the work of a scholar who is no longer with us. This is much more than a few students of an academic teacher who continue part of his research and take it further. Most living scholars would be very happy if they were told that there would be such an interest in their work five years after their death.

Yet I have only covered a very limited part of what there is to be said. In his last months Dan from time to time wondered whether the JCPA would survive. Who watches the center today sees how all indicators show a continuous growth. We have many more activities than ever. Our speakers range from the deputy Prime Minister to the chief of staff, to the country's prime political commentators, to the leaders of the Jewish world and top academics from all over the globe.

We have many more attendants at these lectures than we ever had. Foreign ambassadors, the senior representatives of the foreign press and Israeli experts from many disciplines. We have also more foreign student interns from more countries than ever. We would get many more if we only could accommodate them.

The publications of the JCPA reach millions of readers per year. Mainly through emailing and the website, to a lesser extent now through hard copies. In addition to our classic publications *Jerusalem Viewpoints* and the *Jewish Political Studies Review* we have many new ones introduced by our President, Ambassador Dore Gold and others, the Daily Alert, Issue Briefs, Campus Watch, the NGO Monitor, Post Holocaust and Anti-Semitism and soon to come Changing Jewish Communities. All this was built on the solid infrastructure Dan constructed with so much effort, helped by our now retired Director General Zvi Marom and the loyal staff which stays with us.

Dan always wanted the Center to deal with the cutting edge public affairs issues confronting the Jewish people and Israel. I am sure he would have been very happy that the center no longer focuses only on Israel and the United States but also gives much more attention to the Arab world and Europe.

Any academic would be proud if he left behind him a living legacy of this size, impact and variety. Yet what I have described until now far from sums up the importance of Dan's work and the interest in it.

The Online Library

Perhaps the major indicator of the great interest in Dan's work are the many visits to the Daniel Elazar online library which can be found on the JCPA website. In Spring 2001, with the generous foresight of the JCPA's longstanding friend, Bill Berman, Mark Amiel took 240 of the most important and accessible articles in electronic format and put them on the website. This offers full text versions of Daniel Elazar's writings as a lasting memorial to the ideas he pioneered.

They cover a broad range of topics divided into ten major categories: American political culture, federalism, the idea of Covenant, the Jewish political tradition including Biblical Studies, Jewish political thought, Jewish community studies, Israel Diaspora relations, Israel – it's constitution, government and politics, Israel and the Middle East, and finally religion and society.

It is now three and a half years since the library was established. Almost any living academic who regularly produces new research material would be happy if he had several hundred visitors to his website every month. If there were a few months where he would have a few thousands visitors, he would probably feel elated.

The Daniel Elazar online library attracts far more interest. The average monthly number of page views is about 30,000. This would not be impressive if he had been a pop star but for a scholar it is gigantic.

Broad Interest

What is even more impressive is how broadly the interest in his work is spread. Among the more popular articles are, Jacob and Esau and the Emergence of the Jewish People, the World History Curriculum in Federal Studies, the Constitution of the State of Israel which is part of our section on Constitution, Government and Politics, Are there really Jews in China? This article like the much read one on the Jewish community in Costa Rica is among Jewish community studies.

Yet another article with many readers: Frontiers and Founding, which is part of the American Political Culture section, Religion in Israel: A Consensus for Jewish Tradition. The most popular topics in the website index are Israel, Religion and Society, Federal Systems, Israel Constitution, Government and Politics, as well as the American political tradition.

I think that I have answered the question as to Dan's lasting influence as a teacher already in the first part of what I said. But from the visits to the website, the evidence is overwhelming. It brings the proof how Dan's work continues to guide large numbers of people all over the world.

Daniel Elazar was both a profoundly committed Jew and a Renaissance person. He was a champion of the Sephardi tradition. He was a political scientist who was the world's academic leader in federal studies. He initiated the new field of Jewish political studies and developed Jewish community studies. He started many publications. We can only wonder how much there could have been had he not left us far too young.

I hope in these few minutes to have shown you how the influence of Dan's work lives on in a great variety of ways. Through this interest in his thought and work, his memory has become a blessing for many. All the signs are that in future this will be even more the case.

Lecture at Jerusalem Center for Public Affairs, January 23, 2005.

BOOK REVIEWS

Serving Israeli Prime Ministers

This book review was published in *Jewish Political Studies Review*
vol. 22, nr. 3/4 (Fall 2010).

Title: The Prime Ministers. An Intimate Narrative on Israeli Leadership
Author: Yehuda Avner
Publisher: The Toby Press, Jerusalem
Publication year: 2010
Language: English
Pages: 715

For most of his career as an Israeli Foreign Ministry staff member, Ambassador (ret.) Yehuda Avner was assigned to the Prime Minister's Office carrying out sensitive tasks. Avner served as speechwriter and secretary to Prime Ministers Levi Eshkol and Golda Meir. Later he was an adviser to Prime Ministers Yitzhak Rabin, Menachem Begin, and Shimon Peres. Thereafter Avner represented Israel as ambassador to Great Britain and nonresident ambassador to Ireland, followed by an assignment as ambassador to Australia.

The book's title, *The Prime Ministers*, illustrates the most important part of its content. It relates many events that took place in the Prime Minister's Office in which Avner participated or observed firsthand. The major added value of this fascinating book is the author's insights and personal appreciation of some of the key people who helped shape Israel's history. His judgments of people, however, can be subjective, and the reader should take this into account.

Avner states that he is a great admirer of Begin. This not only involves the way he handled the crucial peace agreement with Egypt but also his overall approach to policymaking in a sovereign Jewish state. Avner stresses Begin's uniqueness, placing his contributions and decisions in the context of the history of the Jewish people.

The author also introduces arguments aimed at improving the way in which many in contemporary Israeli society view the late Yitzhak Rabin. Rehabilitating the man is a far more difficult task. Rabin campaigned in the 1992 elections on a platform that eschewed negotiations with the Palestine Liberation Organization (PLO). Heads of government in many countries have betrayed important election promises shortly after being elected. If, however, such an act results in a major failure, such as the 1993 Oslo Agreements, history's judgment must be harsh, even if such a person possessed many other virtues. Had Rabin not been murdered—which makes many reluctant to criticize him—his responsibility for the consequences of his actions would have been the subject of closer scrutiny.

One of Rabin's great successes was his handling of the aftermath of the hijacking of the Air France plane to Entebbe in 1976, which led to the courageous freeing of the Israeli hostages on Ugandan soil. Avner describes then-foreign minister Shimon Peres's initial ineffectiveness and rhetorical showing off. Indeed, the brief period the author served under Peres was rather an unhappy one.

One can only give a few examples from this rich reservoir of inside knowledge. The conventional wisdom is that the European socialist leaders' dislike for Israeli governments is linked to the Likud Party's rise to power. Avner, however, disproves this by recalling how European socialist governments let Israel down when they refused to permit the refueling of American planes bringing weapons during the Yom Kippur War. Golda Meir of the Labor Party was then Israel's prime minister.

At the conclusion of the war, Meir asked West German chancellor Willy Brandt to call a meeting of the Socialist International. All socialist leaders, whether in government or in the opposition, attended, and Meir sharply rebuked them. When the chairman of the meeting asked whether anybody wanted the floor, nobody did. Then a voice behind Golda said: "Of course they won't talk. They can't talk. Their throats are choked with oil."

The misbehavior of many European socialist politicians toward Israel sometimes crossed the border of antisemitism, disguised as anti-Israelism. To a certain extent they were part of a reemerging, ideologically criminal current of thought in Europe. The many examples of such behavior include the late Austrian Prime Minister Bruno Kreisky, the late Swedish Prime Minister Olof Palme, and the late Greek Prime Minister Andreas Papandreou, the former Danish socialist leader Mogens Lykketoft, Norwegian Prime Minister Jens Stoltenberg, and Spanish Prime Minister José Luis Rodríguez Zapatero.

Avner relates another story that yields insight into today's situation. During a White House dinner hosted by President Jimmy Carter, Chief Justice Arthur Goldberg took Avner aside. He told him that Carter considered Begin's "Greater Israel" policies a danger to the United States and that ultimately the powers might try to impose a settlement on Israel. Avner responded that there was a 1975 letter from President Ford assuring Rabin that America would not impose a settlement on Israel. Goldberg said that such letters were not binding commitments. This raises the question of what value any other commitment by a US administration should have or, alternatively, how long it will retain its value.

Any reader interested in Israel's history, the workings of its highest political echelon, and how its policy is made will find this book a source of valuable information and precious insights.

Between Rabin and Arafat

This book review was published in *Jewish Political Studies Review* vol. 27, no. 3/4 (Fall 2016).

Title: Bayn Rabin Le-Arafat: Yoman Medini, 1993–1994 (Between Rabin and Arafat: Political Diary 1993–1994)
Author: Jacques Neriah
Publisher: Jerusalem Center for Public Affairs, Jerusalem
Publication year: 2016
Language: Hebrew
Pages: 399

Jacques Neriah was the political advisor of Prime Minister Yitzhak Rabin from August 1992 to June 1994. During part of that period, he maintained a diary, which has now been published. Neriah was not involved in the Israeli-Palestinian negotiations that took place in Oslo. Yet the book gives new insights into many issues during that period, including events and politics, as well as an additional understanding of Rabin's personality. For instance, during those two years, Rabin never asked Neriah how he or his children were; nor did he ever tell Neriah anything about his own family.

Neriah also writes about how Rabin keeps certain issues totally to himself while on others, he selectively informs some of those who are around him. In order to get a better picture, his staff had to exchange information between each other.

Rabin knew about the negotiations with the Palestinians in Oslo. At the beginning he didn't give them much chance. It was only one month before signing that he took a serious interest in them. He asked indirectly for clarifications from Abu Mazen about the procedures to be followed. As Rabin did not know Arabic, Neriah translated many texts for him. One of these included the answer received from Abu Mazen. It assured Rabin that negotiations with the Palestinians would take place in two stages.

Before he had a first meeting with Arafat, Rabin was told that Arafat's English was poor and that he preferred to have an interpreter present. Rabin then asked Neriah to join him as he wanted to be sure that the interpreter translated correctly what Arafat said in Arabic.

The American government at the time wished to push for an agreement with Syrian President Hafez Assad—the father of the current Syrian President Bashir Assad. Assad showed interest, but indicated that full Israeli withdrawal from the Golan was required. America put pressure on Rabin to follow the Syrian peace negotiations route. Yet, Rabin was well aware that simultaneously negotiating with the Palestinians and with Syria was impossible in Israel's political reality at the time. He told the Americans that any withdrawal from the Golan would have to be ratified by a referendum among the Israeli people. Today we can be happy that the Golan is under Israel's control, rather than that of ISIS.

Neriah is loyal toward Rabin but not uncritical. He comments negatively on the way he approached the American establishment. Rabin was convinced that he would succeed in his aims by talking to then President Clinton and his Administration. He neglected Congress. That enabled the Likud to establish a lobby in Congress against Rabin's policies.

Regarding American Jewry, Rabin was suspicious of AIPAC. Yet, he was very open about his intentions with the heads of the Presidents Conference of American Jewry. Rabin also neglected other large parts of the American Jewish leadership, which became one of the bulwarks of the noisy opposition against the Israeli agreements with the PLO. He also opposed strengthening the American branch of the Israeli Labor Party.

What motivated Rabin in his negotiations with the Palestinians was that he did not want Israel to add large numbers of Palestinians to its population. He thought that a final agreement with the Palestinians could be reached without the establishment of a Palestinian state. Ehud Barak, at the time Israel's Chief of Staff, had many objections concerning Israel's security in the wake of a possible agreement with the Palestinians. Even though Rabin saw security as a top priority, he overruled Barak's concerns.

Regarding the relationship between Rabin and Peres Neriah is clearly on his boss's side. His judgment seems fair. In October 1993, Neriah traveled with Peres and his entourage to Cairo to meet the Palestinians. He notes that Peres was the opposite of Rabin in many ways. Rabin was usually silent during flights, while Peres was at ease. He spoke with journalists and the military personnel accompanying him and even joked with the flight attendant. He exuded openness in every way.

Also, the preparatory meeting in his office the day before, where Peres led the discussion, was professional. First the points for the Cairo meeting were discussed one after another. Thereafter there were a number of informal points which were to be raised in the meeting with the Palestinians. Peres let all those present express themselves freely. He also gave the impression that he was willing to be convinced by arguments. There was no feeling—as was characteristic in discussions with Rabin—that he competed with those present concerning knowledge.

The book is full of revelations. One can only mention here a few more. In December 1993, Neriah was sent to Morocco to meet then King Hassan II and get his support for Israel's peace negotiations with the Palestinians. One subject discussed there was the issue of international forces. The Moroccan king said that he had been pressured to allow an international force to be placed in the Sahara. He strongly refused this, saying that the responsibility of defending Morocco's borders was only his. Hassan was also highly critical of the Palestinian aims to turn Jerusalem into the capital of a Palestinian State. He stressed that Jerusalem was an issue of the Islamic world at large, and not of the Palestinians.

The Egyptians did not have a high opinion of Arafat. Egypt's ambassador to Israel, Mohammed Bassiouni, told Neriah that the Egyptian President Hosni Mubarak had said to Arafat that if he continued to take increasingly extreme positions in his negotiations with Israel, he would lose everything.

Mubarak told Arafat that he should listen carefully to Rabin because he would not find a better partner for negotiations. Arafat would be well advised to take what Israel was willing to give him and keep his mouth shut. Mubarak's adviser, Osama Al-Baz even called Arafat a "convenience store owner from a small village."

Neriah has written his observations in real time. That often gives one the feeling as if one is retroactively present at some of the scenes. He for instance describes in great detail how some time after the signing of the agreement on the lawn of the White House, Rabin and Arafat met in Cairo. Before Rabin and Arafat entered the room, the members of both delegations were already present. A minute passed in complete silence. Then finally Shimon Sheves, the director general of Rabin's ministry, broke the silence. He said: "We cannot sit here and say nothing." He went over to the Palestinans and shook the hand of each of them.

During the meeting Rabin introduced the members of the Israeli delegation with their titles. Yet when he got to Neriah, he said instead that he was from Lebanon. A discussion followed with those Palestinian delegates who also had lived in Lebanon. From Neriah's descriptions, one senses the atmosphere of the meeting. Mostly, it is polite and relatively constructive. During the meeting, however, Rabin told off Chanan Ashrawi after she irritated him by raising the same subject repeatedly.

Before the meeting Rabin had already been told that for the Palestinians, very often, content is not as important as symbols. For instance, Arafat desperately wanted Palestinian policemen posted on the bridges over the Jordan. What they would do there was far less important to him.

Neriah remarks that the West supplied Iran and Iraq with technologies that could be used for military purposes. Russia, however, never enabled the civil technologies it transferred to Muslim countries to be applied to the military.

Some Israelis and Europeans still think that if only Rabin had been in power instead of Netanyahu, European-Israeli relations would have been much easier. However, Neriah writes, "Rabin was disgusted by the European institutions which used to condemn Israel automatically and even discriminate against it in comparison to their attitude towards Arab countries." His staff members knew in advance that every European issue which would be raised for discussion would receive a critical reaction from him."

Neriah illustrates with a specific case how Rabin viewed the Europeans. He had a meeting scheduled with the new Secretary General of the Italian Socialist Party. Neriah told Rabin that the guest was waiting outside. Rabin reacted almost angrily: "Who needs this?" Neriah pointed out that it was the first time that this Italian socialist was visiting Israel, and that it was perhaps worthwhile to invest in him. Rabin became angry saying: "What for? Europe today is worthless. It is only about economics and nothing else."

Rabin believed that Europe was two-faced. It was willing to close its eyes when a business deal was at stake. This could be with a government which suppressed human rights, or even one that tried to obtain weapons for mass destruction. At the same time, Europe preached morality to Israel about its attitudes toward the Palestinians.

Neriah explains that Rabin had a particularly negative opinion of the French. France was the first European country whose foreign minister received Arafat, and it had supplied the nuclear reactor to Iraq, which the Begin government destroyed. Rabin viewed Russia with similar suspicion. Like Europe, the Russians were far too involved in the region, and much too inclined towards the Arabs, to play a balanced role in regional politics.

Neriah also mentions the well-known problems of the Israeli political reality. One of these is that various Israeli politicians—at that time from the Labour Party—talked to the Palestinians without Rabin's authorization. They made promises to convince Rabin to accept any concessions they made, if the Palestinians agreed to them. Finally, Neriah was sent to Arafat to tell him that whatever Rabin had not personally agreed to was worthless. This trip made Peres furious with Neriah, yet Peres was one of those who conducted talks with the Palestinians without Rabin's agreement.

Sometimes meetings would take place between Israeli and Palestinian delegations, and even though it was known that nothing would be achieved there, those present had to go through the motions.

Another aspect of the Israeli reality is that while an Israeli delegation was in the United States, many of its members complained about not being invited to specific dinners, meetings, and so on. This led to a lot of intrigue. There is intrigue on the Palestinian side as well. Neriah and his colleagues were surprised when members of Palestinian delegations made critical remarks to them about other Palestinian delegates.

From the book, which includes a foreword by retired ambassador Freddy Eytan, it also becomes plain that the apparent closeness between Peres and Rabin in the years before the latter was murdered, was a myth created by Peres. Nothing in the book indicates that their relationship was friendly in Rabin's last years.

Rabin emerges from the book as a strong analyst with the ability to make decisions. It confirms that he was a person of integrity. Yet, as known, politics was not his strong side. This was true concerning the situation in his own party as well as in dealing with the United States' political scene.

These are just a few of the many nuggets this book contains. Translations in foreign languages could do much good. They could help people understand how inflexible the current positions of Palestinians are, which former US president Barack Obama has made such an effort to look away from.

Israeli Diplomat's Wife in Cairo

This book review was published in *Jewish Political Studies Review* vol. 27, no. 1/2 (Spring 2015).

Title: La Maison du Pacha: Souvenirs d'une Israélienne au Caire (The Pasha's House: Memories of an Israeli Woman in Cairo)
Author: Michelle Mazel
Publisher: Éditions Elkana, Jerusalem
Publication year: 2014
Language: French
Pages: 250

In the early 1980s, several articles by an unknown writer named Michelle Mazel appeared in *The Jerusalem Post*. She is the wife of retired Israeli diplomat Zvi Mazel, who at the time was the counselor at the Israel embassy in Cairo. These articles on her impressions of Egypt were the subject of public attention because of her keen observations and readable style.

Mrs. Mazel continues to write both fiction and non-fiction. Her book, *The Pasha's House*, further develops the themes of her earlier articles. The book covers a wide range of issues that the Mazels dealt with during their stay in Cairo when the Israel embassy opened in 1980 until 1983, and later, from 1996–2001, when Zvi Mazel served as Israel's Ambassador to Cairo. His assignment ended several days before the mass murders of 9/11. According to the author, they were celebrated in Cairo with "explosions of joy."

Michelle Mazel notes a particular feature that characterizes life in Egypt. She relates an anecdote in which an Egyptian salesman comes to Madrid and explains the meaning of the Arabic word "bukra" (literally, tomorrow) to his Spanish host. The word may also mean "if Allah wills it." The Egyptian continues: "It is a bit like 'mañana' in Spanish, but without the urgency of that word." Just as the word "mañana" may imply "never" in Spanish, one can only imagine what possibly may be less urgent than that.

The house of the Pasha, which gave the book its title, was the residence of the ambassador from the time of Israel's first ambassador to Egypt, Eliyahu Ben Elissar, until the Mazels left Cairo. A villa built by a former minister in the Cairo suburb of Maadi, its large gardens enabled the Mazels to entertain many other diplomats and members of the local elite, as well as visiting and local Israelis. The small Jewish community was also invited during the Jewish holidays.

Most of the events related in the book took place during the terms of President Muhammad Hosni Mubarak, who succeeded President Muhammad Anwar Sadat, after he was assassinated in 1981. An object of criticism during his tenure, perhaps today, Mubarak's leadership would be remembered by many Egyptians more positively.

Throughout the book, the author describes the differences between the two periods of their stay in Cairo. In the 1980s, the peace treaty between Israel and Egypt was still fresh and the atmosphere hopeful. To be sure, not all Egyptians were friendly or even polite to Israeli diplomats. Nevertheless, Mazel was hired as a French teacher at the American School in Maadi, where children from around the world were enrolled, including those from countries extremely hostile toward or even officially at war with Israel.

Many Egyptian friends and other contacts that dated from her first stay in Cairo avoided her when she returned in 1996 as the wife of the ambassador. Apparently, they were afraid that the Egyptian secret service would interrogate them after meeting with her and, certainly, after visiting her at the ambassador's residence. For example, the author could not find a private tutor to help her improve her Arabic. Those who had agreed to teach her always found an excuse to cancel the session before the first lesson, even after she had agreed to pay their exorbitant fees. Furthermore, when the Mazels accepted invitations to stay with Egyptian friends, their hosts were embarrassed by their neighbors or confronted by the intelligence services.

Mazel devotes an entire chapter to the Egyptian press. It could have been entitled the "Egyptian Hate-Israel Press." The author, however, is an acute observer, not a radical critic. She points out that Egypt's three major newspapers—*Al Ahram, Al Gomhuria* and *Al Akhbar*—are owned by the government, which did not deter them from vicious attacks against Israel, despite the peace treaty.

Rumors prevalent in Egyptian society or mentions of Israel in the press frequently were accompanied by new versions of classic antisemitic tropes that subsequently were spread by the media. The only time a correction appeared was after a sustained protest by Ambassador Zvi Mazel. *Al Ahram* had published that Israeli soldiers had injected Palestinian children with the AIDS virus. According to the author, sixty newspapers throughout the Arab world copied these lies and did not refute them, even though *Al Ahram* did so. She lists similar cases of antisemitism. For example, in 1999, another newspaper stated that Israel sold contaminated blood to Arab countries. The Egyptian Minister of Health subsequently announced that Egypt no longer would buy blood from Israel and that there was no reason for public concern. And, in 2001, a senior columnist in *Al Akhbar* praised Hitler. Shortly afterward, he received an award from the Egyptian press.

The media, however, not only were engaged in spreading antisemitism but also invented some of the more absurd lies. For instance, an editorial in *Al Ahram* claimed that "the Israeli attacks against the Arabs seem to intensify during April. Some analysts explain this phenomenon due to the depressive sentiments felt by the diaspora since the Jews were thrown out of Egypt on Easter, which was the 15th of April." An editorial in *Al Gomhuria* argued that history shows that Judaism was born after Christianity and Islam. The author also mentions a professor at the University of Suez who contended that the Al-Aqsa Mosque in Jerusalem was built a thousand years before Solomon's Temple.

The antisemitism in the media and the general atmosphere made it nearly impossible for Egyptians to form independent opinions on Israel. Michelle Mazel's observations must be understood in this context. For example, she relates that many succulent mangoes grew in the garden of the ambassador's residence and she wanted to give them to the Egyptian soldiers who guarded the grounds of the villa. Several Egyptians warned her against it because if a soldier would get sick, she would be accused of poisoning him.

The book contains much material on security precautions. In the years after the Mazel's first tour of duty, a terrorist murdered two official Israeli representatives in Egypt. Therefore, security precautions continuously became stricter. Neither Israeli nor Egyptian authorities wanted to take risks. They rarely allowed the ambassador to go anywhere on foot, although they did not pay much attention to his wife. An exception was Yom Kippur, when Zvi Mazel was permitted to walk to the slightly renovated synagogue in Maadi. After the outburst of the Second Palestinian Intifada in 2000, even that short walk had to be cancelled. The Mazels had celebrated the Bar Mitzvah of their son, Yossi, in that synagogue during their stay in the 1980s. American Ambassador Daniel Kurtzer, then posted in Cairo, led part of the service.

The book also includes some facts that are not generally known. For example, the author mentions that there has been intensive agricultural cooperation between the two countries for many years and that Israel has helped Egypt considerably. The book concludes with a few pages about contemporary Egypt by Zvi Mazel, an expert political commentator on Arab affairs.

On the whole, *The Pasha's House* is well-written, highly readable and interesting for those who have little knowledge of Egypt as well as for those who are well-acquainted with the country. Mazel presents many aspects of Egypt, which other authors either do not consider important or scrupulously avoid. In conclusion, there appears to be little room for optimism.

The Dutch
a la Carte Jews

This book review was published on February 11, 2018
at *Israel National News*.

**Title: Ontroerende onzin. De Joodse identiteit in het Nederland van nu
(Moving Nonsense. Jewish Identity in the Contemporary Netherlands)**
Author: Ronit Palache
Publisher: Prometheus, Amsterdam
Publication year: 2016
Language: Dutch
Pages: 311

Every week the Dutch Jewish weekly, *NIW*, publishes a short interview with
a little-known Dutch Jew. The paper's editor, Esther Voet, carries out the
interviews asking five questions: the interviewees' youth, their beliefs, their
attitude toward Israel, the interviewees' worries as well as their dreams.

This project was started by the journalist, Ronit Palache. In her time, the
interviews did not follow a recurrent scheme. One hundred and twenty five
of her interviews are published in a book whose Dutch title translates as:
Moving Nonsense. Jewish Identity in the Contemporary Netherlands.[1]

The internationally known sociologist, Abraham de Swaan, wrote the
book's Foreword.

Jewish identity in the Netherlands varies greatly. A 2009 demographic study on Dutch Jews[2] started from a database of close to 53,000 Jews in the Netherlands. Four percent of these did not consider themselves as Jews while 32 percent saw themselves "not so much as Jews but as somebody of Jewish origin." Another 7 percent said: "I see myself sometimes as a Jew depending on the situation." The remainder, approximately 57 percent or 30,000 people, self-defined as Jews.[3]

Dutch Jewish organizations altogether have about 10,000 members at most. The largest Jewish organization remains the nominally Orthodox Ashkenazi community (NIK). Its membership has declined to about 5,000. Those members who keep both a kosher household and the Shabbat laws are in the minority.

Palache writes about her book: "The external world sees Jews as a uniform group. I want to show the non-Jewish world that there are so many ways of living one's Jewishness. In addition, I hope that the Jewish community uses this book to look more critically at itself."[4]

The interviews can be read as individual illustrations of the data found by the demographers. One of the few somewhat known interviewees is Hadassa Hirschfeld, a former Deputy Director of CIDI (Center for Information and Documentation on Israel). She defines her Jewish identity as "Judaism a la carte."[5]

In view of the small number of Jews keeping the main Jewish ritual laws, almost the entire Dutch Jewish community can be defined as a collection of "a la carte Jews." Many adhere to different elements of the "Jewish menu." Hirschfeld reveals that she was once ultra-orthodox. Now she remarks: "I have a liberal heart in an Orthodox soul."

Palache has said elsewhere that a prominent non-Jewish journalist told her that he expected a number of collective themes to emerge throughout the book. Among these were: "To be religious or not, the war, antisemitism, Israel, people with a Jewish father [but not a Jewish mother], ambivalence, sticking together, quarrelling and so on." All these motifs and several others indeed appear in the interviews.

As with various other interviewees, the Holocaust appears in Hirschfeld's interview in a major way. She says: "I divide the world into people where I could go into hiding and those where this would not be possible." Another interviewee, says: "My mother never spoke about religion or traditions, only about the war."[6]

Antisemitism in the Netherlands, like elsewhere in Europe has greatly increased in the current century. Before it was not properly monitored. Several interviewees however mention incidents from their youth. One says that in addition to other antisemitic experiences a teacher told her that Hitler should have killed all the Jews.[7] Another says; "I knew that I was Jewish when I was scolded by young boys from the neighborhood."[8] Yet another says: "They said at the school and in the army: 'hi, lousy Jew.'"[9]

In 2014, there was a huge outburst of antisemitism in Western Europe after the "Gaza war." The "where can I hide issue" became more exposed when David Serphos, the former director of the NIHS Ashkenazi community in Amsterdam, wrote, "I don't dare to trust the authorities after the mayor of The Hague, and now even of Amsterdam do not interfere when Jews and Judaism are threatened. Often I spoke jocularly with friends about reliable addresses to go into hiding [like in the Second World War] if it would ever be necessary. In recent times I look far more seriously to that very short list."[10] He left out a further relevant observation: which people would betray him when they knew where he was hiding?

Relations of Jews and non-Jews manifest themselves in various ways. One interviewee says that she frequently suffered from the jealousy of non-Jews: "They were always jealous about what we had even though this wasn't excessive because I do not come from a wealthy family. With the emphasis on 'you' they said: 'You go on holidays, you have a car.'" She added:"'Also my boyfriend at that time participated in this. It meant the end of our relationship.'"[11]

Another important issue is what a la carte Jewish menu items will get passed on to their children. The Friday night meal is a recurrent theme. It often includes chicken and chicken soup. Yet will the interviewees' children marry Jewish? Quite a few of them do not consider this important "as long as they are happy." If they do not marry Jewish, their Judaism will in most cases become even more diluted.

This book shows that one can define Judaism as a tree with many branches. All interviewees are connected to some of its branches. However, what binds these people together is far less clear. Some claim that humor plays a role, others consider that one talks differently among Jews than with non-Jews. They speak about "feelings." These they cannot define.

Palache has indeed provided raw material for Jewish community leaders to reflect on how they can strengthen the Judaism of this heterogeneous and to some extent confused collection of Jews. It is also a treasure trove for sociologists and psychologists. In the meantime, the *NIW* continues to publish additional interviews with a la carte Jews. At the end of December 2017, an interviewee who married out says that when she and her husband became serious in their relationship she questioned him: "'Are you sure? Our children will be Jewish and antisemitism thus will also affect your children.' I wanted him to realize this."[12]

It would be interesting if similar interviews with local Jews were also published in other European countries. It would provide better understanding of their Jewish communities. It would also allow a comparison between Jewish communities in different countries. Palache has shown how to do this. Others might use her experience.

1   Ronit Palache, *Ontroerende onzin. De Joodse identiteit in het Nederland van nu* (Amsterdam: Prometheus, 2016).

1   Hanna van Solinge en Carlo van Praag, *De Joden in Nederland anno 2009. Continuïteit en verandering* (Diemen: AMB, 2010).

2   Ibid., 60.

3   www.niw.nl/het-mensch-boek-555/

4   *Ontroerende onzin*, 140.

5   Ibid., 138.

6   Ibid., 177.

7   Ibid., 77.

8   Ibid., 272.

9   www.jpost.com/Opinion/European-Parliament-More-words-replace-an-anti-Semitism-task-force-386199

10 *Ontroerende onzin*, 113.

11 Esther Voet. "Het gaat over jouw kinderen." Interview with Naomi Vereggen-Dessaur, *NIW*, December 22, 2017.

Ajax, Holland and the War

This book review was published in *Jewish Political Studies Review* vol. 21, no. 3/4, Fall 2009.

Title: Ajax, Holland vehamilhama (Ajax, Holland and the War)
Author: Simon Kuper
Publisher: Maariv, Tel Aviv
Publication year: 2008
Language: Hebrew
Pages: 240

Ajax, a leading Amsterdam soccer team, was Dutch champion many times and winner of the European Club Championship on several occasions. However, discussion of the soccer club and game in Simon Kuper's book is, for the most part, a means by which to tell the story of the Jews in Dutch society before, during, and after the Holocaust. This is a clever marketing exercise. A book with a title focusing only on the Holocaust in the Netherlands would probably have attracted far fewer readers.

Kuper, the book's Jewish author, was born to South African parents and moved to the Netherlands when he was six. Afterwards, he lived in the UK and worked for the *Financial Times*. He now resides in France. The book was originally published in Dutch in 2000. In 2003, an extended version was published in English, the source for the current Hebrew text.

While at the heart of the book are Ajax and the Netherlands, it also addresses some other countries and the attitude in their soccer world to Nazism and the Jews. One of its most telling illustrations is a picture of the British team lifting their arms in the Hitler salute at an international game against Germany which took place in Berlin in 1938.

Jews presently constitute less than two percent of Amsterdam's population, compared to ten percent before the Holocaust. Before the Second World War, Jewish soccer players belonged predominantly to lower league clubs which had many other Jews as members. At Ajax, a first league club whose members came predominantly from the middle class, Jews were seen mainly on the tribunes. One notable exception was the Jewish national team player Eddie Hamel, who died in a concentration camp.

In the 21st century, the mythical image of the Dutch people as rescuers of the Jews in the Second World War has been deconstructed, even if many Israelis still believe in it. The diary of Anne Frank in hiding remains a major icon of the Netherlands. It is often conveniently forgotten how she was betrayed, arrested, transported, and guarded in a transit camp by Dutchmen before she was sent to Auschwitz and later to Bergen-Belsen where she died. Kuper's book further undermines the Dutch war mythology.

In the post-war period, Ajax became identified with Jews in a number of ways. There were few Jewish players, but two of them, the "half-Jews" Bennie Muller and Sjaak Swart, were prominent members of the Dutch national team. After his family's bitter war experiences, Swart (who had a Jewish father) refused to speak explicitly about his identity. When Kuper asked him where his father had played soccer he mentioned a long-forgotten lower league club which was predominantly Jewish. Kuper saw it as a sign that Swart meant to tell him implicitly, "you and I are Jewish and we both know it."

After the war, a group of Jewish supporters met on the stadium's tribunes, most of them unaffiliated with the organized Jewish community. They had lost many relatives during the Holocaust, and Ajax became a meeting point for them to be in Jewish company and create a substitute family feeling. Several also frequented a Jewish-owned non-kosher sandwich shop in the center of Amsterdam, in part for the same purpose. Jaap van Praag, the chairman during the glorious period of the 1970s, had a Jewish father who had been in hiding during the war. In April 2008, the Jewish insurance executive Uri Coronel became the club's chairman.

Ajax gained high "Jewish" visibility mainly due to a group of fanatic non-Jewish supporters who started to call themselves "Jews." They also brought Israeli flags to the games. During games against Ajax, the supporters of the main Rotterdam team, Feijenoord, started to sing antisemitic songs, a habit which was later taken over by many other Dutch clubs. The best known texts are "Jews you have to kill" and "Hamas, Hamas, Jews to the gas." There were also hissing sounds symbolizing the gas in the gas chambers.

The Ajax supporters in turn sung "Bomb Rotterdam," as a reminder of the lethal German bombardment of the town, which led to the Netherlands' rapid surrender to the invading German army in May 1940. At a championship celebration at the end of the 1990s, one Feijenoord player even shouted an antisemitic slogan several times into the microphone.

Even in the present, these and many other hate songs are a major problem of Dutch soccer, along with fights between supporters. Because the clubs' umbrella body, the Royal Netherlands Football Association, and the Dutch authorities for many years did nothing to stop the extreme hate songs, they have gradually spread into wider Dutch society. These hate songs in the public domain are the one area in which the Netherlands is an antisemitic world leader.

I experienced this on a visit to Amsterdam a few years ago. Whilst travelling on an Amsterdam electric tramway four dark skinned teenagers, probably Dutch Moroccans, entered the tram. A few minutes later one of them started to sing "Jews you must kill, but that is forbidden" as part of his repertoire. It was not meant against me, because he was sitting way behind; at best he could see my back, and I was not wearing a kippa. There were more than a hundred people in the tram. Nobody said a word, either because they did not care, or because they were afraid of the youngsters.

Binyomin Jacobs, the chief rabbi of part of the Netherlands, is easily recognizable as a Jew because of the way he dresses. He told this author that he once boarded a train, together with a non-Jew, aboard where many Feijenoord supporters were present. When they saw them they sang "Jews to the gas." Jacobs says that "you can treat such an incident as hooliganism, but if one of these idiots had attacked us, many others would probably have followed."

The negligent attitude toward such realities is part of a broader structural flaw in the mentality of many Dutchmen, which Kuper exposes throughout his book. People are largely indifferent toward a great variety of manifestations of intolerance in Dutch society, as well as the many extreme expressions of minority racism among predominantly Muslim immigrants. For a long time it has been politically correct to claim that such indifference is a sign of tolerance.

There are some signs of change. A majority of Dutchmen now think that the admission of large groups of immigrants was the greatest mistake ever made in the more than four hundred years of the country's history. The Dutch government has openly labelled many Moroccan and Antillean immigrants as belonging to problematic communities. A substantial percentage of the younger generation is suspected of criminal attitudes. It is due to the many years of indifference to such problems, as well as those caused by autochthonous Dutch, that this situation developed. The hate songs against the Jews were early signs of these problems, signs which the Dutch authorities preferred to ignore and which have now come home to roost.

ARTS & SCIENCE

Industry, Environment and Teaching Architects

According to many industry experts, contemporary building is perhaps the least environmentally conscious. It is often considered a rather inefficient industry which incurs multiple overruns of time and cost targets. The European Union's success or failure in reducing the emission of greenhouse gases depends largely on the building industry. Thus, over a period of a decade at most, the attitudes of this industry may have to change radically in order to become more environmentally-conscious, at least with regard to energy.

Environmentalist pressures are, however, likely to go beyond that. Once environmentalists focus their attention on one aspect of a specific sector of society, their continuous demands for change usually extend to a broader range of issues. Lowering energy consumption may be only the start of a long and growing list of pressures which will gradually affect all aspects of the building industry. Architects, as designers of new buildings and "definers of their material ingredients," will have to play a leading role in this metamorphosis.

Benchmarking

One can speculate about where ideological environmentalism will impact the building industry and architecture. To do this some information for the present can be gleaned by researching what has happened to business sectors targeted by focused environmentalist attacks in the past. Relevant findings can be translated into today's business and cultural reality. This methodology is commonly called benchmarking.

I am well aware that the values of those who create unique designs, i.e. architects, and those who duplicate products, i.e., industry, cannot possibly be the same. Nonetheless, there is a great deal to be learned from the strong pressures and experiences which other businesses have already undergone.

It is therefore worthwhile to assess how environmental pressure has changed industry's image and attitudes. In the 1960s, Western society saw industry as the top of the world. Industrial corporations provided employment to communities and wealth to the nations. This is expressed in the rather ironic saying, "What is good for General Motors is good for America." In the newspapers of the early 1960s, when many of you were students, long-forgotten company chairmen were highly admired figures.

Thirty or even twenty years ago, industrial waste could be emitted into the air. Waste could be buried in the ground or thrown into waterways. Noise pollution was not an issue. Quarries were run on a purely economic basis. Naked rocks standing out against the surrounding landscape were left as they were after the quarry was exhausted and the work was finished.

A Changing Image and Worldview

Over the years, industry's public image has changed. This in turn has altered industry's self-image and worldview. Part of this process was caused by the elimination of much of industry's managerial freedom.

The cement industry can no longer make holes in landscapes without restoring exhausted quarries, or at least parts of them. Providing employment to the many unemployed in Western Europe is now a top priority. It is no longer sufficient for industry to provide work for many people and pay their salaries. The cement industry can no longer emit dust from its plants in the direction of adjacent towns and villages, even if many of their inhabitants would be much poorer were the plants not in the vicinity.

The old worldview of industry which was the norm not so long ago—that society should accept it as it is—has become obsolete. Pressure groups are gradually stepping up their demands. In a city through which trucks carrying cement regularly pass, the authorities may first target the cement company. This may occur even if all data show that motorcycles make far more noise than cement trucks, and that the cement trucks do not in fact constitute the majority of the trucks passing through.

Looking Forward Further and Further

With this, we have not exhausted the environmental aspects of cement activities. For every important new project proposed, companies must themselves carry out detailed environmental impact assessments. Only then can the project be submitted to the authorities for evaluation. The project is laid open for comments and criticism by interest groups, concerned individuals, etc. This process of approval may take many years.

Sensible company executives are increasingly trying to look beyond to-day's environmental pressures to understand how ideological environmentalism may affect their businesses in the coming decades. This forces them to analyze in increasing detail what happens with their products at client facilities. This is called "product stewardship."

Thus, cement managers need to better understand how the ready-mix concrete industry uses the cement it buys. They also have to think more about the environmental problems of their clients and give them more guidance on how to use cement. This guidance may develop in many directions. In Greece, Heracles, the leading cement company has already offered saplings to some of its ready-mix concrete producing clients to plant and make their facilities esthetically more attractive.

Beyond the ready-mix concrete companies which are the cement industry's immediate clients, there is the building industry which ultimately determines how much cement is used and where. The way this industry uses concrete has a direct influence on the life-cycle environmental impact of cement.

As a result, the building industry's operations are increasingly becoming a major concern of cement-makers. Any discourse between the cement and building industries is incomplete without dialogue with architects—and often engineers as well—who prescribe what quantities of which materials go into individual buildings. Unfortunately, this discussion is still in the embryonic stage. Even its potentially multifaceted content has hardly been defined.

Understanding Each Other's Language

As environmental pressure continues to increase, understanding each stage in the cement chain—from beginning to end—becomes an imperative. Ultimately, this will require an integrated, ongoing discourse with all those involved in the lifecycle of cement.

This dialogue also requires understanding each other's language and concerns. Today the discourse within the cement industry is oriented very differently from the discourse used by architects. There is a gap in values between those who duplicate and those who create.

As an industrial strategist, I speculate about what the future may bring. I ask myself what it would mean for architecture if your clients were submitted to the same kind of environmental pressures and demands as basic industries. A further question is: What could you, yourselves, do? How can you integrate the preparation for what may happen in the future into the curriculum of your students? This is all the more problematic due to the explosion of knowledge required for future professional life, while the number of years of study remains the same.

Modern architecture reflects in its variety an expression of the intellectual fragmentation of our time. It seems logical that with all this fragmentation there must be major differences in the environmental friendliness of new buildings designed by individual architects especially insofar as energy efficiency is concerned. In the future, these differences will not go unnoticed. They are only partly dependent on the client's willingness to pay for environmentally-friendly architecture.

The Beginning

Once society's focus shifts to the building industry, a flood of environmental issues currently floating haphazardly in the media will become part of more consolidated demands. Rehabilitation of existing buildings and designing new ones with increased energy-efficiency would force builders—and thus architects and engineers—to pay far more attention to such issues as insulation and lighting. This is only the beginning of a series of possible environmental demands.

Contemporary architects have already been exposed to many environmental issues, though not always very systematically. There is much written about sustainable or even "green architecture," such as bio-climatic architecture. Anti-modern radicals have even mentioned the possibility of returning to the concept of "architecture without architects." Many of you may also have been confronted with the problems of modern and post-modern phenomena such as the spread of sick building syndrome.

Other environmental aspects which have been brought to your attention for several decades concern the materials used. Asbestos, which was quite common in new buildings a few decades ago, is now forbidden. PVC is not much liked. These are very basic examples from an environmental point of view.

In future, however, the architect will have to justify his choice of materials in much more detail and candor. How many architects know how their buildings—and the materials in them—will perform in ten or twenty years from now? And what indeed do you teach your students about how to make buildings as energy-efficient as possible? Under environmentalist pressure, the architect's freedom of choice in this field is likely to be reduced in the coming decades. Limiting one's degrees of freedom is even more painful for a creative person than for a mass producer.

There will certainly be much more pressure to use recycled materials. In Germany today, most building waste is already being recycled. In future, local materials will be preferred to imported ones. That is a pleasing thought for the cement industry which is mainly a local producer. Bringing marble to Western Europe from great distances involves the use of non-renewable fuels and may be frowned upon.

A More Sophisticated Future

Once environmentalist pressures increase, demands become more complex. There are already signs of a more sophisticated future. Life-cycle studies of materials and types of construction are being undertaken by many suppliers of the building industry, as well as independent institutions. Architects will soon be confronted with these issues. Can they know what they are doing environmentally without talking to those who make these materials? I doubt it.

There will be great diversity in the conclusions about which materials have the least impact on the environment. The architect will certainly have to familiarize himself with the considerations behind these differing conclusions. Many architects see themselves as new versions of Renaissance persons. But to succeed, the contemporary Renaissance person may have to have knowledge of many more disciplines than their Florentine predecessors had centuries ago. The contemporary Renaissance person will also have to familiarize him or herself with the concept of the life-cycle of materials as well as that of buildings.

Environmental indicators will also be extended to architecture and buildings. Some industries assess on the basis of a variety of measurements whether their operations are more eco-efficient than in previous years. What will happen if we ask the Calatravas and Frank Gehrys of tomorrow to prove to us that their newest buildings are more eco-efficient than their previous ones? A serious conflict is looming large on the horizon between limiting degrees of freedom on the one hand, and creativity and esthetics on the other.

Rebuilding the Eiffel Tower?

The environmental movement is very confused. Some sectors of the movement claim that everything in the past was better, although this is patently not always true. Are the major Gothic cathedrals environmentally-friendly? These are high, one-storey buildings, in which the tallest people praying are barely two meters. From a strictly environmental viewpoint, all that space above them and the materials used to build it are waste. The superfluous space must also be heated, a waste of non-renewable natural resources. If such a tall cathedral collapsed, should it be rebuilt? Today, people may say yes. In twenty years from now, it may be debatable.

As a mental exercise we may ask: What to do if the Eiffel Tower collapsed? Today we would say "It is a landmark of Paris and of course it has to be rebuilt." One architect told me in private that part of the myth of the Eiffel Tower is that it cannot fall, and thus, if it collapses, this myth goes down with it. Thus, the tower should not be rebuilt. In twenty years from now, we may also ask: Should we put all that steel in rebuilding a fallen structure which is fairly useless? The Eiffel Tower is simply a building with a view over the city and a restaurant. Can we not put the secondary steel made from the scrap of the collapsed tower to better use?

A similar view of Paris can be had from many existing high-rise buildings. A restaurant with a view over the city, can be put on the top-floor of one of those buildings. This would be more environmentally-friendly. So, if the Eiffel Tower collapsed, once the world is more environmentally-conscious, why should we even consider rebuilding it? If we are not careful, the environmentalist world view can rapidly lead society in the direction of ugly utilitarian buildings. Environmental technocracy might even bring back the concept of geometrical man where what is supposedly less harmful for the earth will become more important than what is pleasing for man.

Many issues can be seen in a different light when looking through the lens of this worldview. Should the Sagrada Familia in Barcelona not be finished rapidly and put to use? Today it is still a religious symbol. Soon this building, the construction of which started more than hundred years ago, may become the symbol of an extreme architectural waste of resources.

When looking at some recent museums, one wonders whether those architects who try to create memorials for themselves are not indeed major carriers of anti-environmental thought.

Futile and Ridiculous

You may consider some of my remarks ridiculous. Thirty years ago, if a speaker had told a gathering of cement industrialists that society would demand by law that there be no dust plumes over their factories, they would have thought that the speaker was hallucinating. Had he told them that, in some countries they would be forced to measure the impact of their plant's emissions kilometers away and that the public would have the right to know the result of these measurements, they would have believed that the speaker needed to be confined to a mental asylum. The more such a speaker would have described today's reality, the less industrial managers at the time would have believed him, and the greater a fool they would have considered him.

Today though, however ridiculous an environmental inquiry may seem, a good industrial manager evaluates it immediately. Queries from the public are addressed. In the environmental management systems that industry has voluntarily adopted, it has taken such responses upon itself. In doing so, a level of transparency has been reached which may well be followed by other sectors of society.

Unfortunately, those who taught industrial managers their profession decades ago did not envisage today's environmental problems, let alone their solutions. Thus, many industrial managers are still uneasy in analyzing environmental pressures and are uncertain how to respond. Industrialists often talk about being proactive; many more only react, often very hesitantly, to threats from the outside once they have become visible.

Defining Your Profession's Discourse

As teachers of the architects of the future, you can use the advantage of learning from the experience of others in order to prepare your students for possible demands on the profession in the decades to come. In doing so, you can define much of your profession's discourse with environmentalists and the direction it will take. Otherwise, chaotic pressures, of which there are already many warning signs, will be increasingly imposed on architects. The choice before you is either to prepare your students for what may come, or to send them out into the real world to be buffeted by the winds of change.

There is much to be gained from ongoing contacts between the disciplines interacting here today. This dialogue between architects and the cement industry must be an open one. It can take many directions. I am convinced, that it can be immensely fruitful for both of you.

For that reason, being outside both your professions, I have taken the liberty of drawing attention to the major changes concerning the building industry which require a better dialogue between the cement industry and architects. The management of Heracles, and its President, Ing. Giudici, have the great merit of having created a first opportunity for this connection.

This text is a modified version of a lecture at The Second Conference of the Heads of European Schools of Architecture, Chania, September 5, 1999. The author participated in the congress as a consultant to the Heracles company.

Can Contemporary Architects Remain Renaissance Persons?

A few days ago, I saw a poster in the Netherlands which said: "There is no need to plan. The future will happen anyhow even without planning." In light of this reflection of our time, where is university teaching going?

And a second question: Where is architecture going? Can the Libeskind of tomorrow acquire the skills of the Leonardo of yesterday? Can an architect in a complex and rapidly changing society be both a visionary artist and a solid engineer? Grappling with design alone is already difficult for the creative mind. Can one also continue to be competent in the technical aspects of construction and materials? Can visionary and technical skills still be combined in a single individual? Some observers claim that a negative answer indicates that the profession of architecture may disappear.

Two thousand years ago Vitruvius had few hesitations. He knew how materials should be manufactured: "Bricks should be made in spring or autumn, so that they may dry uniformly."[1] Today, one is frequently introduced to new materials and systems which characteristics are difficult to assess. A few weeks ago, a journal reported that a new pre-cast concrete hybrid frame had made it possible to build a 39-story building in San Francisco, the tallest concrete building ever erected in this earthquake-prone zone.[2]

Keeping up to date on new materials and construction methods is only one major challenge among many. Before discussing how to prepare architects for the future a broad analysis of social trends is necessary. Everywhere there is rapid change in technological and social arenas.

Making accurate forecasts is impossible. A few decades ago, an IBM study predicted that total world demand for computers would be six machines. A few years ago, other experts forecast that universities would disappear as students would turn to online internet courses where they could get all the education they needed . Although this is a threatening vision for those present here; it is unlikely to materialize. The earlier prediction of many experts that we would all work in paperless offices was wrong to a substantial extent.

Should we assume that it is better not to prepare for the future. Erroneous predictions can be more dangerous than waiting for destiny. To complicate matters further, one forecast, mentioned before, was not totally wrong. In many professions, including architecture, some functions of paper have indeed been superseded. *The International Herald Tribune* recently published how proud Frank Gehry was that he had designed the Experience Music Project in Seattle virtually, i.e. creating the model directly on the computer.[3]

The Future Is Already Here

In some fields, the future is already here. In a recent lecture, this year's Pritzker-prize winner, Rem Koolhaas, told American architecture students that in China 40-storey buildings are now computer-designed in one week. The message seemed simple: In the future, architects will have to work much faster. His underlying message might be interpreted as: You Americans are spending a few nice years at university and are sweating a long time over your projects. In the meantime, the outside world is changing rapidly. The skills you are taught may not even be adequate for what already exists by the time you graduate.

Koolhaas's observation also raises another question: How can architecture schools educate toward a professional life—of many decades' duration—if change occurs so quickly? The modification of architectural design methods is only a minor element in a rapidly moving social landscape. Society's mood changes swiftly with regard to many opinion issues, while the Internet has created a new economy, and El Nino has perhaps caused a new climate.

Key Characteristics of Future Society

Against this background, there are four main questions before us:

1   Can we speculate successfully about some major characteristics of the society in which students will have to make their careers well beyond the 2030s?
2   If the answer is positive, can university—and more in particular teachers of architecture—prepare them for at least part of the new challenges?
3   The remaining career span of architecture teachers is much shorter than that of students. To what extent do academics have the mental flexibility to change teaching methods? To what extent does a university prepare students for the important challenges of a changing society? These are relevant questions that I cannot answer for you.
4   And finally, can we suggest some instruments to prepare students for a changing society even though we cannot predict the future?

My perspective is that of an outsider. From the position of a business strategist, one can still predict some key developments even if there are no true prophets left. More importantly, future unknown challenges can be meaningfully confronted by many teaching professions. This depends on improved teaching instruments. Even if you strongly disagree with me, this presentation might still be of some help as it may provoke alternative ideas.

I intend to briefly address the interplay of four key characteristics of future society: 1) accelerating change 2) the fragmentation of ideas and trends, 3) the expansion of knowledge and 4) the increasing importance of communications. Analyzing the interaction between these may lead to some insights into the needs of architects in the future.

More characteristics of the future can be forecast. In last year's session devoted to the Heracles urban planning program, I argued that environmental pressures on architects will increase. In this context discussing with the European Cement Association (Cembureau) experts how to better understand the characteristics of building materials is very meaningful. It also seems evident that liberal professionals, including architects, will have to possess increasing managerial capabilities. Equally, they will have to shoulder more responsibilities and legal liability for their work. One can add other forecasts. Still the four general characteristics mentioned are more important for the future due to their broad nature.

Rapidly Accelerating Change

The first major characteristic of the future is that rapid change will accelerate further. One cannot predict the social, economic and intellectual conditions of society even ten years from now. The standard university answer to this is that students will require life-long learning. This is a good approach, but it is incomplete.

One pre-condition for meeting rapid, unpredictable change is to be mentally flexible. Two questions arise here: Can one teach students to be mentally flexible and what are the tools for this? What do I call "teaching tools"? A classic aid is the frequent repetition of a single message. Cato the Elder kept saying "And further, I am of the opinion that Carthage should be destroyed." This is usually interpreted as a political statement. Cato, however, used it mainly as an instrument for influencing people.

Instruments for Teaching Change

The teaching instruments I refer to are slightly more sophisticated. Each profession will have to develop them for their specific needs. As an example, let me suggest one instrument used in many diverse fields for other purposes. It complements the classical methods of teaching and partly meets the challenges of rapid changing society in which knowledge is exploding and each person is often confronted with issues he knows very little about.

The instrument proposed might be called the one-hour exercise. This is a modification of what happens in boardrooms of big corporations. When a new project is brought for approval company directors rarely have more than an hour to ask questions and develop an opinion. If they are experienced, they have the intuitive skills to obtain the essence of the proposal in that time and discover any weaknesses. Another variant of the same tool used in the business world is brainstorming. Managers sometimes use this technique to quickly raise aspects of a new issue under discussion.

The same goes for television documentaries. In one hour, documentaries have to provide a coherent understanding of a subject which the viewer may not be familiar with at all.

Consultancy, Academia, Politics

Potential clients usually give a consultany marketeer an hour to get one's message across. One has to be flexible enough to adapt one's message to the one goal needed: to convince your counterpart to receive you a second time.

One more example: two extremely successful university teachers among my friends, one a political scientist and the other a philosopher, use a similar method. When they approach a new subject, they put on paper, often in a very disorderly manner, all they know about a subject, thus getting a feeling for possible directions to investigate.

Now, while preparing the ground for the building of one teaching instrument, I have simultaneously introduced another: teaching the ability to recognize similar motifs in radically different fields. The examples mentioned come from the corporate board room, television documentaries, consultancy practice and academic study; they all use the same time management tool adapted to their specific purpose.

There are many other professions in which the same tool is frequently used. Politicians often have to make decisions at short notice on the basis of scant knowledge and whatever opinions they can rapidly collect.

The One-Hour Exercise

The one-hour exercise can be a valuable tool in academic teaching. It complements, rather than replaces, in-depth study of specific subjects over a long period. It teaches flexibility by training students to focus their minds rapidly on many diverse issues they may never have thought about. In doing so, they improve their mental flexibility. By putting the findings of many students together after the exercise, much greater collective insight can be gained in a short time.

How can the architecture teacher use this exercise for his students? As a layman in your field, I can only give some simple examples. Architecture teachers are in a much better position than I am to subsequently improve this tool.

One such exercise could be to ask to characterize in writing as many buildings as one can, preferably in a single word and to explain why that is correct. Some examples: Libeskind's Jewish Museum in Berlin, was visited in 1999 by 250,000 people before any exhibits were opened. In literature it has often been described by the single word "absence." Another example, also from Berlin, is less obvious: Foster's rebuilt Reichstag, where the public and the journalists look down upon the parliamentarians, is often defined as embodying "transparency" or more accurately: "the transparency of democracy." The name of the Colosseum speaks for itself.

How can the Guggenheim in Bilbao be characterized? Perhaps as "chaotic." And Utzon's original design for the Sydney Opera? "Unbuildable" might be the best. Why limit oneself to individual buildings? The same approach can be applied to Hyatt hotels by defining them as "atrium-centered."

Another one-hour exercise may deal with architecture as "social transformation." More original would be architecture as "image transformation." Which single buildings have not only become icons of a city but changed its image? Why have other, no less revolutionary buildings, not achieved this elsewhere? The typical nineteenth century case that comes to mind is the Eiffel Tower in Paris, high over the city.

Contemporary examples are the Opera House in Sydney, Gehry's Guggenheim Museum in Bilbao and—to a lesser extent—the museum that Mendini built in the Dutch provincial capital of Groningen.

An example of a revolutionary building which has not changed the image of a city could be Calatrava's Communication Tower in Barcelona. This still has a far greater impact than Steven Holl's Kiasma, the Museum of Contemporary Art in Helsinki. The strongest post-war example, however, of a construction which has changed the image of a city did not even require an architect. It wasn't revolutionary but reactionary: The Berlin Wall.

A good exercise could also be to discuss what the most important building in the world is and why. If my memory does not fail me, the nineteenth century critic John Ruskin thought that it was the Doge's palace in Venice. Yet another exercise: Which are the most suitable buildings no longer in existence to be reconstructed in virtual reality? And why these particular buildings?

Another very different topic for a one-hour exercise: Given the increasing divorce rate in the Western world, what should be the characteristics of a house that can be split in two so that future divorcees can either sell off one half, or live in the two halves of it? The subjects of the exercises are less important than their diversity. Their main goal is to teach students to quickly come up with a significant number of ideas.

Improving the Tool

One can improve this instrument by carrying out the exercise with students of different faculties. In this way, a multi-disciplinary perspective emerges. In real life we often analyze problems by talking to people from different professions. Two other important characteristics of future society have thus been introduced through the back door: the fragmentation of knowledge and the need for improved communication.

In other one-hour exercises, one may ask students to analyze some of the main dualisms in your profession, such as following tradition or radically breaking with it through innovation, globalism versus regionalism, universalism versus individualism and modernism versus post-modernism. A further topic was given last night by Prof. Hertzberger: identify buildings which have only insides, starting from the Epidaurus Theatre.

Yet another example of a one-hour exercise is: What can one learn from the effects of earthquakes? An effort in this direction has been made by the Middle East Technical University in Ankara in Prof. Teymur's recent book, *Learning from disasters*.

Prof. Teymur also told me about another potentially interesting subject for a one-hour exercise that he had once discussed with his students. In Catholic and Orthodox societies, miniature chapels are put alongside the road where traffic accidents have occurred. Can one design a non-Christian equivalent for other societies as roadside memorials for those who have died?

Other exercises could focus on more intellectual questions. For instance, architects are supposed to express in their works the spirit of their time. Nowadays, there are two main problems with this. The first one is that the "spirit of the times" changes fast. The second is that there are so many simultaneous trends that the one word which characterizes the contemporary is confusion. So, if architecture is a reflection of society, it must be confused.

Yet another exercise: Can architects capture the essence of a country's culture and give it form? "Yes," said the jury which awarded the Pritzker price in 1988 to the Brazilian Oscar Niemeyer. It wrote in its citation that "his building designs are the distillation of colors, light and sensual imagery of his native land."

Another variation of the one-hour exercise: During a lecture, one can ask students to write down as many questions concerning that talk as they can. It has always surprised me that so few students ask questions, while I know from experience that there is so much to ask. Asking questions is apparently a skill to be acquired.

Buildings with Memory

I picked up another idea for a one-hour exercise at last year's conference. How can buildings reflect their past? The opening lecture by Lebbeus Woods on teaching experimental architecture presented, among other things, a concept that damaged buildings in Sarajevo should be rebuilt carrying scars to memorialize the war.

Several conference participants told me afterwards that they found Prof. Woods' experimental drawings extremely far-fetched. In my opinion, that is what one should expect from experimental or anarchistic architecture. A few months later a more conventional modification of the same idea cropped up elsewhere. The architect of an Athens office building, damaged in last year's earthquake, suggested that when repaired, signs of the disaster should be left. Another variant of the same concept exists in the new Reichstag in Berlin. The architects have preserved the graffiti inside the building that was written by Russian soldiers after the war.

There is a much better and older example in Berlin: A late nineteenth century church, named after Emperor Wilhelm the First, was destroyed during the Second World War. The ruined tower was kept as a reminder of the destruction of the war and integrated in a new church building of the early 1960s.

Woods' basic idea was thus not so strange. It was even more than a thousand years old. Once again, the same motif appears several times in very diverse cloth.

The idea of putting a token memory of a past event in new buildings appears in ancient Jewish writings. The Talmud, written in the sixth century, says that every synagogue must have a small, unfinished part which memorizes the destruction of the Temple. If you visit the rebuilt synagogue in Chania, a few hundred meters from here, you can see that there is an unfinished quadrangle and next to it, written in Hebrew, "If I forget thee, Jerusalem, I shall forget my right hand." Could another exercise for students be to indicate different ways to include memory in buildings?

Doing More with Less

If students have gone through thirty or forty one-hour exercises in which they have rapidly confronted a great variety of subjects, they will think much more flexibly than before. An unknown future challenge is nothing but exercise forty-one or forty-two. To put it differently: serendipity can be taught; one learns to expect the unexpected.

Yet another lesson one learns from the one-hour exercise is that whatever impression or information one collects in life may be useful somewhere. As time is always limited, this helps us do more with less. As there is so much to know and time is limited, time management is crucial to avoid stress.

As teachers of architecture, you can invent much better exercises than me and build up a collection of them by exchanging ideas about them with your colleagues.

Fragmentation

The four characteristics of the future are all linked to each other. Rapid change is partly the result of the information explosion. As there is continually more to know, we need strategic access to knowledge. The information explosion is leading to the fragmentation of both knowledge and ideas. This characterizes post-modern society.

To succeed in life today, it is important to have in-depth knowledge in at least one field. Another requirement is to know how to access other fields one has no specific knowledge of. Vitruvius in his *Ten Books of Architecture* opened the first chapter with the following: "The architect should be equipped with knowledge of many branches of study and varied kinds of learning, for it is by his judgment that all work done by the other arts is put to test."[4]

The Renaissance person wanted to know all there was to know in many fields. But the art critic Bernard Berenson wrote rather scathingly of geniuses like Titian and Tintoretto: "The significance of the Venetian names is exhausted with their significance as painters. Not so with the Florentines. Forget that they were painters, they remain great sculptors; forget that they were sculptors, and still they remain architects, poets, and even men of science."[5] The Renaissance post-modernist in our days cannot know all there is under the sun. All he can do is to master diverse tools to access and interpret diverse sources of knowledge. Thereafter he may hope that he will understand more of the world than others.

For this reason, the ability to communicate is a fourth major characteristic for success in the world of the future. Good communications are crucial in order to cope with rapid accelerating change, a fragmented world and the explosion of knowledge. The communication issue has many diverse aspects. The first one is that we must know how to acquire specific information we need, for instance from the Internet.

A second aspect of the increasing importance of communications is that one has to learn to deal with many aspects in professional fields one knows little about. To obtain this information, establishing contacts and networking is needed. A real university has a great lasting advantage over an open one, a virtual one and certainly over the Internet.

Yet another aspect to confront the need for better communications is the development of better interpersonal skills. In 1995, Daniel Goleman wrote in his book *Emotional Intelligence*: "IQ offers little to explain the different destinies of people with roughly equal promises, schooling, and opportunity. When 95 Harvard students from the classes of the 1940s—were followed into middle age, the men with the highest ten scores in college were not particularly successful compared to their lower-scoring peers in terms of salary, productivity, or status in their field. Nor did they have the greatest life satisfaction, nor the most happiness with friendships, family, and romantic relationships."[6] One of Goleman's important conclusions was that emotional intelligence can be improved. If improved interpersonal relationships is a major factor for success in life, shouldn't universities teach it?

Competing with the Stars

The architect of the future will require much better communication skills to market his services. Computer-automated design is already helping to show clients how their future buildings could look, using different materials. The same goes for cost estimates. Architects need these tools as competition increases.

Globalization is already rife with respect to skyscrapers. When one sees part of a skyline, one has to be an expert to judge whether it is an American city or Hong Kong, or perhaps how Shanghai will look in a few years from now. One Israeli architect recently said: "This big object called a skyscraper wanders from place to place in the world and carries its own independent genes."[7]

A small group of elite architects is now receiving international assignments. Are we moving toward a world where star architects will also globalize—like leading accountancy firms and other liberal professions?

This trend is being promoted by cities themselves. Can a cutting-edge town do without a building by Libeskind, Pei, Foster, Piano, Rogers or Koolhaas? Berlin is perhaps the most characteristic example here. Will municipal councils compete to have the maximum number of Pritzker prize winners build within their boundaries? One critic put it nicely: "Nowadays, everybody wants his own 'Gehry' so that he can be as unique as everyone else."[8]

At the same time, other opportunities are opening up for gifted beginners. Internet technology is giving the new architect much improved marketing chances. A talented twenty-five-year-old student can put his architectural drawings on the Internet. His virtual buildings can potentially be seen by many more people than the real buildings of star architects who are physically confined to a single location.

The young architect's key problem is getting as many people as possible, particularly potential clients, to see his work. As this session is promoted by industry, perhaps there are also networking possibilities here: Can industry promote promising young architects cheaply by including their drawings in company web sites? At Heracles, this possibility is being evaluated.

An architect cannot build unless he has a contract. Should universities teach people what they need in life, including how to market their services?

In order to market better they need to improve their emotional intelligence. Perhaps interpersonal skills should be taught in university.

Networking

The world will continue to change rapidly. Internet opportunities for architects will diversify beyond our imagination. The information explosion will make it even more fragmented. There are other crucial aspects of communications. One of these is better networking.

The architect of the future must have a knowledge of his profession. Still much teaching time will be focused on design. But he, or she, can no longer live in ivory towers, and not only because ivory is an environmentally taboo building material. Better networking combined with improved communications technology, should provide easy access to people who know many more things. His contacts will also be able to interpret facts he cannot decipher himself.

To be successful, the architect has to know many people outside his own field. In this context, today's meeting with industry takes on even greater relevance. Last year, the Heracles Group started an extremely important mode of industry-architecture networking by sponsoring the second Chania Conference. Since then, the Heracles Urban Planning Program has also been exhibited at METU in Ankara and shall be exhibited from the end of October at the Technical University in Delft.

As a result of Cembureau sponsoring this year's session, a further step has been taken. The potential importance of this networking between architects and industry goes far beyond today's subject which is, in itself important: how building materials are taught and how they should be taught. It is in the contact between two poles of the same business sector that the seeds are being sown for better confronting a future we can only predict to a limited extent.

Lecture at The Third Conference of the Heads of European Schools of Architecture, Chania, September 3, 2000.

1   Vitruvius, *The Ten Books on Architecture*. Translated by Morris Hicky Morgan (New York: Dover, 1960) 43.

2   *Urban Land*, June 2000, 31.

3   *International Herald Tribune*, May 17, 2000.

4   Vitruvius, *The Ten Books on Architecture*, 5.

5   Bernard Berenson, *The Italian Painters of the Renaissance*. 3rd ed. (Oxford: Phaidon, 1980) 39.

6   Daniel Goleman, *Emotional Intelligence: Why It Can Matter More Than IQ* (New York: Bantam Books, 1995) 34.

7   Tzadik Elyakim, as quoted in *Haaretz*, June 29, 2000.

8   Esther Zandberg in ibid.

Jewish Environmental Policies from the World's Creation to Zionism

How does Judaism view an ideal relationship between humanity and the environment? To find an answer to this, we have only to open the first chapters of Bereshit (Genesis). In Paradise, Adam and Eve live in an environmental Utopia.

Let us investigate this in some detail. What pollution did man and animals create in the Garden of Eden? Or another question: What risks to the ecosystem did they represent? The answer seems to be: Almost none. Basic human needs like housing, transport and safety did not yet exist in Paradise. Not even clothing was required. Humanity used neither textiles nor other materials. There was no potential scarcity of resources. Man did not yet consume products or use tools. There were no production residues.

No artificial fertilizers or pesticides were required for plants to grow. Man and animals ate only vegetables. All that humanity used, which seems exclusively to have been food, was biodegradable and if there was post-consumer waste, it was probably metabolized into plants. There were no landfills. Animals did not require special protective measures, as they were not attacked by any other creatures. Biodiversity was thus maintained.

Most probably vegetarian, not-yet-violent man did not harm nature in any way, Nor did he have any other impact on the ecosystem. Application of environmental analytical tools reveals that a situation of perfect sustainability reigned in Paradise. It was also a very lush environment. There was no shortage of water with all the rivers that surrounded it.

There is much more we can understand about the environment from the first chapters of Genesis. For instance, despite the fact that food was readily available—humanity still had two tasks: to work the land and to guard it. Another thing we can learn from Genesis concerns biodiversity. Adam had to name all the animals. This is a way of identifying them and establishing their individual identity.

Secular Perplexity

From a modern, secular environmentalist perspective, there is only one perplexity concerning this environmental paradise. Why, through eating from a particular tree that God has forbidden, sustainable human society becomes unstable and humanity is chased from the environmental Utopia. What cannot be understood from the environmentalist viewpoint is fully clear from the Jewish one. Man cannot live well in his environment if he doesn't fulfill God's commandments.

A Utopian situation—very similar to that of Paradise—is forecast at the end of days, as described in the prophecies of Isaiah: "The wolf shall dwell with the lamb, the leopard lie down with the kid; the calf, the beast of prey, and the fatling together, with a little boy to herd them." and "The wolf and the lamb shall graze together, the lion shall eat straw like the ox, and the serpent's food shall be earth." There is also a prophecy that there will no longer be conflicts between man and animal. Thus, according to Judaism, the beginning of the world and its end are environmentally perfect.

A Very Bad Environment

So much for an ideal environment. If we want to know what—according to Jewish tradition—is a very bad environment, we have only to go a few chapters further to the story of Noah. The Flood is the greatest natural disaster mentioned in the Tanakh (Hebrew Bible). It is also an ecological disaster. The Torah (Five books of Mozes) gives a very clear reason for the Deluge. Humanity has sinned against God, so He destroys large parts of the eco-system in order to get rid of immoral people and animals. In the Jewish view, God uses

311

nature as an instrument of punishment. Large parts of the ecosystem are destroyed by the rising waters.

We can draw from this another important Jewish teaching. God has created nature and as such is its master. As God is above nature it can be a tool in his hand to punish people, to reward them or teach them a lesson. Many other environmentally relevant lessons can be learned from the story of Noah. Through his survival and that of his family the continuity of humanity is maintained. Seven pairs of certain types of animals also remain, protected in the Ark while of other species, only one pair is saved. Biodiversity is thus assured, despite the environmental catastrophe. From an environmental perspective of the story, it is very positive that Noah takes all species of animals into the Ark.

Again, however, there is in this Biblical story one aspect that the secular environmentalist cannot understand. Why would man's general immorality affect his relationship with nature to such an extent that it causes a destructive flood. This is a similar question to not understanding why man was thrown out of Paradise. From a secular environmental viewpoint, all that can be said about this part of the text is that a huge natural disaster has taken place. One can only guess the reason. Most people and animals are killed, some escape miraculously.

A Jewish View of a Secular Story

Let us now look at a contemporary scientific issue and look at it from a Jewish viewpoint. We then realize that a modern secular version of the story of the Flood is currently being promoted. This view says that humanity is sinning against nature. Heating and cooling buildings, industrial production, and driving cars all lead to the emission of greenhouse gases and to manmade global warming. In other words environmental studies are telling us that man is sinning against nature. Now nature is going to take its revenge. El Nino and the extreme weather it causes are only the first signs. They will be followed by the melting of the polar ice caps and increased flooding.

I have already given you a number of significant indications of the Jewish attitude toward the environment. The first is that environmental considerations feature prominently in the Tanakh. The second is that ancient religious motifs reappear as modern secular motifs. The third is that there are significant differences between the value judgements of Judaism with regard to the environment and the ideology of contemporary environmentalists.

I could fill my entire presentation here with the detailed development of all three of these conclusions. If I did so I would, however, be misleading you methodologically. The way I have started this presentation is not correct. Biblical stories can be interpreted in many ways. This is one of the great problems Christianity faces when it tries to build an environmental ethic based on the Bible and its classical sources.

Even though Judaism also has difficulty translating the religious/spiritual wealth of its past into confronting actual issues, its problem is of a different nature. One may be able to solve this more easily, even though it will take many years.

Judaism is based on halakha (Jewish law). I should thus not have started with stories from the Tanakh, but rather with analyzing halakha for environmental aspects. So keep in the back of your mind what I have said so far, and after this false start let me begin again.

A Halakhic Approach

Now I start my second attempt to discuss Judaism and environment. Can the Jewish attitude toward the environment be defined in one sentence using Jewish Law as a guide? Before I do so, I should clarify what environmental concern is about. The central worry is about human impact on the resources of the planet. Environmental thought is based on the assumption that most resources of the earth are finite. The more of these non-renewable resources we use, the worse our situation and that of our children may get.

The central aim of the environmental mainstream has been defined in a United Nations study laid out in a book called *Our Common Future*. It defines the idea of "sustainable development" as "development that meets the needs of the present without compromising the ability of future generations to meet their own needs."[1]

This one sentence embodies the basis on which the environmental mainstream thinks that a responsible "resource policy" should be developed. The next question should thus be: Can we define for Judaism also in one sentence how we should approach resource policies? In my view it is described in a verse in Psalms: "The heaven is Yours, the earth too; the world and all it holds—You established them."

Tenancy Versus Stewardship

If heaven and earth belong to God, and humanity lives on God's earth it must make a contract with the landlord to use it. This idea has been developed somewhat in the non-Jewish world. In English it is called "stewardship." This translates more or less as a mixture of *shomer* (custodian) and *apotropos* (guardian) in Hebrew. In Christian thought stewardship usually derives from Bereshit 2:15: "The Lord God took the man and placed him in the Garden of Eden, to till it and tend it."

But the non-Jewish world has had great difficulty in developing this concept of stewardship in much detail. If one investigates halakha then one understands that we are not so much dealing with *apotropsut* (guardianship) and *shmira* (custodianship) but much more with *arisut* (tenancy).

If we investigate man's right to use God's resources on Earth we will see that the contract of God with the Jews in general, and in particular concerning the Land of Israel, is extremely detailed. This contract can be looked at as a paradigm of the general relationship between humanity and the environment.

God's Ownership of the Land

What does halakha tell us about the Israelite and his attitude toward the land, the main resource of human sustenance? The one halakha which clearly mentions that God owns the land is that of the jubilee year. It is written explicitly in Vayikra (Leviticus) 25:23: ". . . the land must not be sold beyond reclaim, for the land is Mine; you are but strangers resident with Me." So God the landowner makes a contract with the Israelites, the tenants and the first clause of the contract tells us that this Divine resource, the Land, cannot be sold permanently. As the Jew cannot become a full owner, he cannot do with the Land whatever he wants.

What we might call the second clause of the contract of tenancy is that you are forbidden to work the land in certain years, the sabbatical and the jubilee year (*shemitta* and *yovel*). The third one is that you are forbidden to sew everything you want (*kilayim*). The fourth one is that you have to give tithes from the yield of the land to God the landlord and His representatives, or to others such as the poor.

The fifth clause is that you cannot just eat the produce of the land straightaway (*chadash*). First one must bring produce to the Temple, and only then is one allowed to eat from it. Similarly (the sixth clause), one is forbidden to eat the fruits of the tree before a certain year (*orla*). The seventh clause is that produce cannot be eaten at given times of the year: none at all during the fast days, and no leavened food (*chametz*) at Pesach. Eighth, one is forbidden to destroy fruit trees (*bal tashchit*). This concept has developed in the Jewish tradition far beyond that to any wanton destruction. Ninth, do not impose upon yourself ascetic conditions as far consumption is concerned which go beyond what is forbidden. The nazir (*nazirite*) is not viewed very positively. He has to bring a sacrifice at the end of his period of denial.

There are other stories in Tanakh which illustrate these same legal aspects; for instance, that of Cain's sacrifice. Why is this refused? God owns the land. And the Divine owner merits the donation of the best portions. The Midrash (ancient commentary on biblical texts) interprets his offering as "refuse."[2] It indicates that Cain resembles a bad serf who eats the first fruits and honors the king with the last ones.[3] We find a further back-up in the story of Divrei Hayamim (Chronicles) in which we are told that the land kept the sabbatical years that the Israelites did not keep. Similarly, the land will not yield its crop if the Jews do not fulfill the commandments of Jewish law in general.

To summarize what we have found out so far in reading the halakha: First, the Earth's resources belong to God. He makes them available to man on certain conditions. Second, there are many laws which regulate the Jews' relationship to the Land of Israel in which he is not the owner but a tenant. Third, the same principles of thought contained in the halakha can be found and are developed by Tanakh and Midrash.

Attitude Toward Animals

Animals are a second important resource for humanity. I am not saying that Judaism sees as the only task of animals to serve humanity. Yet it is one of their tasks. Animals serve humanity in several ways. The main ones are as sources of food, clothing, energy and as a means of transport. We can carry out the same type of analysis for the resource "animals" as we did for "land." We find that the halakhic approach is very similar. It does concern Kashrut (dietary laws), but not only that.

First, the Jew is forbidden to eat certain animals. The pig is the best known one, but many other animals are equally forbidden. Second, many of the animals which are allowed as food have to be slaughtered in a specific manner. Thirdly, particularly frowned upon is the consumption of *ever min hachai* (a limb from a living animal).

Fourth, certain parts of the animals are not allowed to be consumed, such as blood, fat and the *gid hanashe* (sciatic nerve).

Fifth, there are additional conditions upon collecting animals for food: you may not slaughter the ox on the same day as its young, nor take a mother bird along with its eggs. The dietary laws thus play a crucial role in resource policies.

There is a long discussion about whether vegetarianism is viewed positively or negatively in the Jewish tradition. Once again, the question is whether Jews should be more extreme than the conditions of tenancy of the earth that God has imposed upon them. Some halakhists frown upon vegetarians. This is similar to the story of the nazir, who went also beyond what was demanded by halakha.

Animals also fulfill another function. They are a source of energy and as such, there are conditions. There is the concept of kilayim which instructs that ox and asses should not work together. The second condition is that mixed breeding should not be practiced. A third is that animals have to rest on Shabbat. The latter also concerns another very basic function of animals for man: transport. Man is not allowed to ride animals on Shabbat.

Water

Another important resource of the earth is water. On the face of it, there are very few halakhic limitations on the use of water. The one halakha that comes to mind is that water cannot be consumed on fast days. However, the Tanakh story devotes much attention to water and how God makes it available to the Israelites in the Land of Israel.

Another aspect of this theme is that religious observance and God's role in maintaining the patterns of nature become interdependent. This is frequently stressed in Tanakh in the specific punishments threatened for the transgression of certain commandments.

For instance, obedience to the commandments will bring with it the rain which the land needs: "If you follow My laws and faithfully observe My commandments, I will grant your rains in their season, so that the earth shall yield its produce and the trees of the field their fruit. Your threshing shall overtake the vintage, and your vintage shall overtake the sowing; you shall eat your fill of bread and dwell securely in your land. I will grant peace in the land, and you shall lie down untroubled by anyone; I will give the land respite from vicious beasts, and no sword shall cross your land."[4] "You shall eat old grain long stored, and you shall have to clear out the old to make room for the new. I will establish My abode in your midst, and I will not spurn you. I will be ever present in your midst: I will be your God, and you shall be My people."[5]

The same message is repeated time and again in the Bible. God makes the sustainable functioning of nature explicitly dependent on the Israelites obeying His laws. If they behave as He wishes, He will "grant the rain for your land in season, the early rain and the late. You shall gather in your new grain and wine and oil—I will also provide grass in the fields for your cattle—and thus you shall eat your fill."[6]

Time

Halakha works rather similarly with respect to an issue which we usually do not consider a natural resource. This is due to the way we define nature. Time is also a God-given resource to humanity. Thus, God puts limitations on its use.

The central condition on the use of time is Shabbat. Every week, there is a specific time—one day, starting with sunset and ending when there are three stars in the sky—on which many things should not be done. Second, we should use this spare time to study. *Bitul zman* (destruction of time) is a concept which says that we should not waste time. In modern times, in English, there is one word for *bizbuz* (squander) and *psolet* (that what is discarded). We call them both "waste" in English.

What has been said so far shows that Jewish law indicates that man's use of the environment is subject to a detailed system of regulations which is developing. Some laws are from the Torah, while others have been instituted by rabbinical authorities.

Developing Law

An example of a law which has been instituted by rabbinical authorities, and which concerns land use, for instance, is the prohibition of behema daka. This is the prohibition against raising goats and sheep in the Land of Israel. This is a taqana, a later rabbinical enactment approved for the public interest. The reasoning behind this is one of basic sustenance. These animals eat the produce in the fields.[7] It was permitted, however, to raise them in the deserts of Israel and in Syria.[8]

The Talmud mentions that one is permitted to slaughter goats roaming freely in the marketplace and causing damage after one has warned the owner two or three times.[9] The Talmud also tells us that when the Jews lived in Babylon they also instituted the taqana of behema daka.

So far, I have laid the halakhic infrastructure. Now we come to the true problem of a contemporary Jewish environmental policy. Judaism has a large number of halakhot which have developed over the centuries and which deal with environmental problems. We might say that as modern problems are complex developments of ancient problems, the core has already been established.

Great Wealth of Environmental Sources

Maimonides' hilchot shkhenim (the laws of the neighbors) can be considered the first Jewish environmental codex. These laws do not deal so much with resource policies, but rather with another central issue in modern environmental concern: the prevention of nuisance and pollution. Probably if we had grouped all existing environmental halakhot at the beginning of the nineteenth century in one book, we would have had the most sophisticated environmental codex in the world.

In my contacts with the American editors of the Encyclopedia of Religion and Nature, I found confirmation that Judaism has the greatest wealth of environmental material in its classical sources. The editors knew what they were talking about because they obtained a total of 1,000 entries from all main religions.

Halakha—including what we would now call its environmental elements—developed over the centuries. In the sixteenth century, Rabbi Shlomo Cohen, the Maharschach, referred to the damage caused to the inhabitants of the town by the textile dyeing industry. He decided that the economic interests of a city, dependent on the textile industry for its livelihood, take precedence over the damage caused to neighbors in the vicinity. However, he comments that the owner of the business would do well to reduce the hindrance as much as possible.[10]

Rabbi Shimshon Morpurgo of Ancona issued a similar statement in the seventeenth century, writing that Jews are not allowed to establish damaging industries, and those which already exist in the city must be removed. He added, however, that because Jews were confined to special quarters, the community could not survive economically if such a removal were carried out.[11]

Contemporary Halakha

To some extent, environmental halakha has also developed further in our times. For example, Rabbi Eliezer Waldenberg, the Tsits Eliezer, states in a teshuva (a responsum), that no matter what the reason is for a person's fasting, his animals must be fed first in order to prevent their suffering.

Some halakhic attention has also been given to the contemporary question of animal experimentation. Rabbi Yechiel Ya'akov Weinberg, the Seride Esh, a prominent twentieth century rabbinical authority, permits this, stating that the elimination of human pain and suffering are more important than the prevention of pain in animals.

Rabbi Waldenberg also considers medical experimentation permissible, stressing at the same time, however, that efforts must be made to minimize the animals' pain.[12] In his view, medical or economic purposes override the prohibitions of both bal tashchit and tsa'ar ba'alei chaim (the suffering of animals). Other rabbinical authorities have discussed this subject and have reached varying conclusions.[13]

A number of years ago, the wearing of fur coats led a concerned Israeli to put a halakhic question to the late Rabbi Chayim David Halevi, who was at that time the Sephardi chief rabbi of Tel Aviv.[14] The person posing the question wrote that he had attended a concert in Tel Aviv where several women in the audience were wearing fur coats. Demonstrators outside the hall had staged a protest against the wearing of fur. The questioner was surprised by the respective stances taken in the argument. The mainly religious concert-goers had defended the practice, while the non-religious demonstrators had stressed tsa'ar ba'alei chaim.

For similar reasons, the late Israeli Chief Rabbi Ovadia Yosef stated that Jews should not attend bullfights. Some halakhic experts have also discussed vegetarianism, but there is considerable debate within Judaism as to whether this is desirable or not.

There are other examples of contemporary halakha. Yet if one wants to hear what Judaism says about the pollution of the water aquifer, the waste of water at home, and the road crossing the country, he will be disappointed. Does this mean, however, that Judaism has nothing to say about such issues? Not necessarily.

Confronting the Problem

The problem is that halakha has not developed. This has a combination of reasons. The first is that environmental concern as a serious matter of interest to the mainstream of Western society dates only from the early 1960s. The publication of Rachel Carson's, *Silent Spring*, is usually considered its beginning. We are thus talking about a post-modern movement which is only a few decades old.

A second reason is that environmental concern is among religious Jews often identified with the secular world. For some people, environmentalism has indeed become an alternative religion. The organized religious concern for the environment as a phenomenon of some significance dates mainly from the last ten years.

Third, Israel—where the main religious decision-makers live—has many more pressing problems on its agenda than concern for the environment.

Fourth, in order to receive decisions, one has to ask questions to rabbinical decisors. People who pose their questions to rabbinical decision-makers belong to specific circles. In those circles, very few questions are asked on environmental matters. Thus, few decision-makers provide answers on these issues. There are some who say that the people who might ask questions consider—probably sub-consciously—that environmental issues are in the public domain and not in the religious sphere.

In discussions on this subject, I have frequently heard that if you were to address environmental questions to rabbinical decision-makers, you would get rather inadequate answers because they don't understand what you're talking about. This, in particular, because the environment is such a complex issue that few people really understand it. This argument, in my opinion, can quite easily be refuted.

First, the few contemporary responsa that I have found seem quite reasonably structured. Second, as a new field of halakha develops rabbinical decision-makers who specialize in the field gradually increase in number. While leaning on experts, they develop an understanding and a method for developing such issues, based on their halakhic knowledge.

This can easily be proven with the example of the way in which medical halakha has developed. It did develop because there were doctors and religious people who, before undertaking or undergoing certain treatments, wanted to know what halakha had to say about them. As there were many such cases, there is now a significant corpus of medical halakha which has developed over the last twenty years. Some of the most prominent *poskim* (rabbinical decisors) are now involved in this field.

In order to progress toward a better understanding of what Judaism has to say about the environment we have to do two things simultaneously: one is that those who are religiously concerned should start to pose questions on environmental questions to rabbinical decision-makers.

What could such questions be? For instance, to what extent is it permissible for a municipality to plant trees and flowers which cause people allergies? It is not often realized that nature itself poses significant environmental problems. This question could be developed further. In the planting policy, should common allergies be taken into account, or should rarer allergies also be considered?

Another question could be whether there is any halakhic commitment to save water in a country like Israel, where there is a severe shortage. Is this a matter of halakha, or is it a matter of ethics? Or alternatively, is it a matter of public policy and social responsibility? Similarly, we may ask whether fluoridation of water has any halakhic aspects.

These are only a few examples. They can easily be expanded and the more people that ask questions, the more environmental halakha will develop and can, in twenty years, lead to a large corpus of environmental halakha.

Jewish Learning

To the best of my knowledge, there are very few places in Israel where, on a regular basis, people study Jewish sources which relate to the environment. If, for instance, we take the many Tanakh texts which refer to the environment and read them with the commentators and with the midrashim, we can get an idea of how Judaism views the environment.

My book, *The Jewish Environmental Tradition: A Sustainable World*, gives a lot of attention to what Judaism has to say about the themes which are part of the sustainability discourse. We consider issues such as dematerialization, biodiversity, geo-chemical cycling, recycling, inter-generational equity, the prevention of conspicuous consumption, resource policies, durability etc. as very contemporary. If one studies Tanakh and other Jewish sources, one finds that many of these issues have been addressed in various preliminary ways in our classical sources.

Unfortunately, in the United States, a different approach has developed among Jewish environmentalists. Many of these people are committed environmentalists, yet do not know much about Judaism. They feel that the movement must say the right things about the environment, just as in the 1960s it had to say the right things about the war in Vietnam. What one then gets are so-called "Jewish environmental opinions." These are modern environmentalists looking for a few Jewish texts which happen to support the movement's opinions. This approach has very little to do with Judaism.

Zionism and the Environment

Zionist policies toward the environment are a complex subject on which I have published a major essay in Hebrew. The founder of Zionism, Theodor

Herzl, had little interest in the environment. The Zionist movement wanted to build a state which of course meant development. One of Israel's leading poets, the late Nathan Alterman, wrote a poem which became a song in which it was said that "we would cover the land with concrete." Yet, at the same time, the Jewish National Fund became a symbol of reforestation of the land whose trees and nature had been severely damaged by the Turkish occupiers.

The kibbutz and the environment is yet another subject that merits attention. The kibbutzim wanted to have their industries and animals within their own perimeter. This meant that the stench of the cowshed often became an integral part of kibbutz life.

The religious kibbutzim, however, developed the land during the week, but on Shabbat they admired the nature around them. In a nutshell, this is a very diverse approach from the classic Jewish attitude toward the environment.

Jewish Environmental Studies

If one wants to further Jewish involvement in environmental issues one can start thinking about questions to put to rabbinical decision-makers and start study groups of Jewish environmental sources. Besides this first approach, however, there is a second, very different, approach to Judaism and the environment. The progress to be made in this field should be matched by progress in a second area: academic study of Judaism and the environment.

In an essay entitled *Jewish Environmental Studies. A New Field*, I have tried to set out what I consider to be the areas of interaction between Judaism and the environment which could be studied. I have defined eleven areas:

1   Jewish environmental history
2   The environment in the Hebrew Bible
3   The environment in later classical Jewish texts
4   Jewish environmental thought, with particular emphasis on the Jewish perspective on nature and elements of it
5   Jewish law and the environment
6   Jewish environmental ethics
7   Environmental-economic interaction

The greatness of Judaism has been exactly the opposite. We have moved away from the laws of nature to the laws of God. Above nature there is God, its Creator. God doesn't require resources; He is non-material. One is not allowed to use any resources to make a statue of Him. This is strictly forbidden. The great innovation of the God who appears to Abram is exactly the opposite of subjecting oneself to living in harmony with nature.

Summarizing my main conclusions: Judaism has a unique view on the environment. The core of this view is expressed in halakha, but the same ideas are developed in different ways in Tanakh, Mishnah, Talmud and Midrash. Second, with so many environmental references dispersed through Jewish sources, we need a number of actions to integrate this field and advance in it. This can be achieved, on one hand, by questions to and answers from rabbis, a greater number of Jews starting to study Jewish environmental sources; and, on the other hand, the development of Jewish environmental studies as a new academic field.

Lecture at Limmud UK, December 2013.

1   *The World Commission on Environment and Development: Our Common Future* (Oxford: Oxford University Press, 1987) xi.
2   Bereshit Rabba 22. (Theodor Albeck edition)
3   See also Yalkut Shimoni Bereshit 35.
4   Leviticus 26:3-6.
5   Leviticus 26:10-12.
6   Deuteronomy 11:14-15.
7   See Nachum Rakover, *Eihut haSviva* (Jerusalem: haMishpat haIvri, 1993) 42ff.
8   Bavli Bava Kama 7:7. See also Maimonides, Hilhot Niskei Mamon 5:2.
9   Bavli Bava Kama 23b. See also Maimonides, Hilhot Niskei Mamon 5:1.
10   Responsa Maharschach 2:98.

11   See Manfred Gerstenfeld, *Judaism, Environmentalism and the Environment* (Jeru-
     salem: The Jerusalem Institute for Israel Studies/Rubin Mass, 1998) 122.
12   Responsa Ziz Eliezer 14:68.
13   J. David Bleich, "Animal Experimentation" In: *Contemporary Halakhic Problems*,
     vol. 3 (New York: Ktav, 1989) 231–232.
14   Responsa Mayim Hayim, Tome Two, Tel Aviv 1995, 50.

www.ingramcontent.com/pod-product-compliance
Lightning Source LLC
Chambersburg PA
CBHW060246100426
42742CB00011B/1659